Folger Documents of
Tudor and Stuart Civilization, No. 20

Essays
Politic and Moral

Essays
Moral and Theological

Daniel Tuvill

Essays Politic and Moral

and

Essays Moral and

Theological

EDITED BY JOHN L. LIEVSAY

Published for
The Folger Shakespeare Library

The University Press of Virginia
Charlottesville

Preface

THE edition of Tuvill's *Essays* here published, begun years ago and long delayed for a tedious variety of reasons, has not been brought to its present state without the incurring of numerous obligations on the part of the editor. I am embarrassed that public acknowledgment should have had to wait so long but am not the less grateful to all who have helped along the way.

My especial thanks are extended to the Huntington, the Newberry, and the Folger Libraries for the awarding of research fellowships enabling me to make close study of the texts of Tuvill and of the supporting contemporary literature; to the Houghton Library of Harvard University for a gracious interlibrary loan of the 1631 *Vade Mecum* before I could obtain a copy of my own; and to the reference staffs of the University of Tennessee and Duke University, who have been most helpful in answering my frequent and vexing questions.

Acknowledgment is here also gratefully made to the Librarian of the Huntington Library, San Marino, California, for permission to print the manuscript marginalia in its copy of Tuvill's 1609 volume, formerly belonging to John Evelyn; to the Harvard University Press for permission to use in my Notes translations appearing in the Loeb Classical Library, published by that Press; and to the *Journal of English and Germanic Philology,* published by the University of Illinois Press, for permission to reprint in slightly modified form part of an article on Tuvill printed in that journal in 1948.

Many friends and colleagues have been helpful with advice and suggestions which I cannot here specify, but for which I am deeply thankful. For more extensive aid I should be remiss if I failed to offer special acknowledgment to certain individuals: to my old friend, the late Samuel C. Chew; to Kenneth Curry, of the Department of English, University of Tennessee; to my colleague William Willis, of the Department of Classical Studies, Duke University; and to the late Virginia LaMar and Miss Megan Lloyd, of the Folger Shakespeare Library. They are responsible for saving me from many an egregious blunder; for such as remain they can claim no responsibility.

J. L. L.

Duke University
July 20, 1970

Contents

Introduction

T HE writer whose essays are here reprinted for the first time since the seventeenth century remains something of an enigma for the would-be biographer. His earliest publications[1] were initialed simply "D. T."; later ones, on title pages or in prefatory matter, carried the name "Dan. Touteville." In the Pollard and Redgrave *Short-Title Catalogue* only three works are entered to him under "T., D." with cross reference to "Tuvil, D.," where there are, nevertheless, *four* works, all described as bearing the initials "D. T." A fifth work, as if by a different author, is listed under the entry "Toutevile, Daniel"; and a sixth, *Christian Purposes and Resolutions* (1622), is left unrecorded. From the available scattered references to him, it appears that his name was also spelled, variously, Tuvel[l], Tuvalle, Tewell, Tuffeild, Torvil, and even Tuvill—a confusion which the *Cambridge Bibliography of English Literature,* perhaps the most commonly consulted bibliographical guide, has done little to reduce by bestowing upon him a first name of *David.* Probably the most extravagant piece of name fantasy, however, is the attempt by a modern writer[2] to identify him with a tutor in the employ of the Harington family, a certain "Master Tovey" —especially since Master Tovey's first name was *John.* The writer's own practice of title-page punning on his name[3] is not of much help. But whatever the authentic form of his name, there is ample evidence that "D. T.," "Dan. Touteville," and the writer here called Daniel Tuvill are one and the same person.[4]

From such spare and scattered life records as are available to us, we learn that *this* Daniel Tuvill (and not another named John-David

[1] Including three prefatory poems appearing in later editions of Sir Thomas Overbury's *A Wife* (1614).

[2] See the article by "A. S.," *Notes and Queries,* 10th ser., V (Jan.–June, 1906), 462–63.

[3] The title page of *Christian Purposes and Resolutions,* for instance, quoting Rom. 7:18 reads: *"To will* is present with me" (my italics), the same pun reappearing at the end of the dedicatory epistle, sig. A4r. On the title page of *The Dove and the Serpent* (1614) appears the Latin motto, "Tuta velis; *Tutus eris."*

[4] Most of this evidence is conveniently gathered in my *Stefano Guazzo and the English Renaissance* (Chapel Hill, N.C., 1961), pp. 107–13, and in the Notes to the present volume.

Tovey-Torvil-Tuffeild) was the Cambridge student and, later, preacher-author with whose works we are concerned. From John and J. A. Venn [5] we learn that he was born in London; that he was admitted sizar [6] at the newly founded [7] Sidney Sussex College (Cambridge), September, 1598; [8] that he proceeded B.A. in 1600–1601, M.A. in 1607; that he was Vicar of St. Bartholomew-the-Less, London, 1620–31, and preacher of Sutton's Hospital, 1635; that he died September 13, 1660, [9] and was buried at St. Bartholomew-the-Less. From John Spencer [10] we learn additionally that he preached a sermon—presumably heard by Spencer—at Sutton's Hospital as early as 1631. And from the prefatory "To the Christian Reader," signed "Thine Anonym. Musophil," [11] in the 1629 edition of the *Essays*, [12] we learn that Tuvill was somehow connected (as a chaplain?) with the ill-starred British naval expedition to La Rochelle in 1627:

Not to derogate in anything from the worth of the author, know that this *Manual of Essays* was first composed by Mr. D. T. (a man whose pious endeavors in his pastoral charge hitherto, and his both zeal and courage for the poor afflicted members [i.e., the Huguenots] of Jesus Christ, hath of late [margin: "Before Rochel"] been sufficiently demonstrated).

The dedication of the *Essays Politic and Moral* (1608) to Lady Anne Harington and of the *Asylum Veneris* (1616) to Lady Alice Colville does not tell us much of Tuvill, though his dependency in some man-

[5] John and J. A. Venn, *Alumni Cantabrigienses,* Pt. I (Cambridge, 1922–27), IV, 280.

[6] The sizars were semicharity students with certain menial services to perform. Spenser, it will be remembered, was a sizar at Pembroke.

[7] See John Le Neve, *Fasti ecclesiae Anglicanae,* ed. T. Duffus Hardy (Oxford, 1854), III, 702–3: "May 20th, 1596, was the first stone laid of Sidney college in Cambridge, (the whole fabric whereof was finished three years after,) at the cost of the Lady Frances Sidney, countess of Sussex, daughter to Sir William, sister to Sir Henry, (lord-deputy of Ireland,) aunt to Sir Philip Sidney, and relict of Thomas Ratcliffe, the third earl of Sussex."

[8] Assuming, with the late William A. Jackson, *The Carl H. Pforzheimer Library* (New York, 1940), III, 1052, that he was about fourteen when he entered Sidney (1598), this would place Tuvill's birth *ca.* 1584. It should be noted that the first Master of Sidney was James Montague, to whom, upon his later becoming Bishop of Bath and Wells, Tuvill was to dedicate his *Essays Moral and Theological.*

[9] E. N. S. Thompson, *The Seventeenth-Century English Essay* (Iowa City, 1926), p. 44, is thus clearly wrong in his statement that Tuvill "died shortly before the appearance of *Vade Mecum* in 1629."

[10] Καινα και παλαια; *Things New and Old* (1658), No. 1482, p. 514.

[11] In my opinion, Tuvill himself.

[12] *Vade Mecum: A Manual of Essays Moral, Theological. Interwoven with Modern Observations, Historical, Political.* Later editions under this title were published in 1631, 1638. The principal additions are from the works of Bishop Joseph Hall, Sir Walter Raleigh, and Owen Feltham. See Appendix.

ner upon the important Montagues is clearly to be read in the dedication of three other works[13] to members of that family. Roger Mar-
beck's extravagant laudation of an unidentified "D. T." in his *Defense
of Tobacco* (1602)[14] seems to refer to an older man than Tuvill then
was.[15]

Since Tuvill was thus apparently willing to preserve at least a sem-
blance of anonymity, we may justifiably and perforce turn from the
man—or, rather, shadow of a man—to the works he left. Two of these,
reprinted here, are reserved for later discussion; the other four are now
given cursory notice.

Following his two early series of essays (1608, 1609), Tuvill's next
publication was a thin quarto, in 1614, entitled *The Dove and the
Serpent*. It is much of a piece with the politically oriented essays of
the earlier volumes and is, as I have elsewhere[16] attempted to show, a
deliberate expansion of a suggestion made by Sir Francis Bacon in his
Advancement of Learning. Bacon had observed that "the wisdom
touching negotiation or business hath not been hitherto collected into
writing";[17] and Tuvill, taking his cue from this and from Bacon's own
combination of "serpentine wisdom with the columbine innocency,"[18]
responds with "a large description of all such points and principles, as
tend either to conversation or negotiation."[19] The little volume com-
bines an Aristotelian discussion of the suasive arts best making for
that smooth social adjustment which the Renaissance called "civil conversation" with a Machiavellian opportunism of "policy." It contains, in
short, Tuvill's composite version of such "books of policy and civil
discourse, and other the like enablements unto service of estate"[20] as
Bacon felt to be lacking in the then state of effective learning. Except
that it has the greater unity of a continued (if dangerously bipronged)

---

[13] *Essays Moral and Theological* (1609) was dedicated to James Montague: *The
Dove and the Serpent* (1614) to Sir Henry Montague, then Recorder of the City of
London; and *Christian Purposes and Resolutions* (1622) to the same Henry, now
become Baron Kimbolton, Viscount Mandeville, etc., and soon thereafter to be created
first Earl of Manchester.

[14] Sig. D2r.

[15] This paragraph is substantially reprinted, with permission of the Editors, from my
article " 'D. T., Gent.,' Spenser, and the Defense of Women," *Journal of English and
Germanic Philology*, XLVII (Oct., 1948), 382–83.

[16] See "Tuvill's Advancement of Bacon's Learning," *Huntington Library Quarterly*,
IX (Nov., 1945), 11–31.

[17] *Advancement of Learning*, ed. W. A. Wright (5th ed.; Oxford, 1926), p. 219.

[18] *Ibid.*, p. 201; see also, in the *Meditationes sacrae* of Bacon's 1597 *Essays*, sig.
D1r, the meditation entitled "De Columbina innocentia, & Serpentina prudentia."

[19] *The Dove and the Serpent*, title page.

[20] *Advancement*, p. 79.

argument, in form and method *The Dove and the Serpent* does not greatly differ from the two sets of essays. The fifteen separate chapters are, in effect, fifteen isolable essays—and are so treated by E. N. S. Thompson in his discussion of the volume.[21] As with all of Tuvill's writings, there are present in this one a heavy draught of classical quotation and allusion and a marked repetition of phrase and idea from his own earlier publications. Chapter I, for instance, "Of Secrecy," will recall "Of Three Things Prejudicial to Secrecy," in *Essays Politic and Moral;* and Chapter III, "Of the Wisdom of Behavior in General," duplicates much of the essay "Of Civil Carriage and Conversation" in *Essays Moral and Theological.* The final chapters (X–XV), dealing with aspects of rhetoric, have much in common with the trio of essays opening *Essays Politic and Moral* to which Tuvill gives the inclusive title "Of Persuasion."

Two years later, in the midst of the Swetnam-aroused controversy over women, although perhaps not in direct answer to the "Woman-hater's" pamphlet, Tuvill published his *Asylum Veneris; or, A Sanctuary for Ladies* (1616).[22] Following the pattern established in the two sets of essays of generalization supported by copious citation of "cases," [23] Tuvill here presents a mild-tempered defense of the maligned sex. Within the framework of a "Proeme" and an "Epilogue," he devotes ten chapter-essays [24] to the following: "Of Women's Worth in General," "Of Their Beauty," "Of Their Chastity," "Of Their Outward Modesty," "Of Their Humility and Supposed Pride"; "Of Their Silence and Falsely Objected Talkativeness," "Of the Constancy of Their Affections," "Of Their Learning and Knowledge," "Of Their Wisdom and Discretion," "Of Their Valor and Courage." As with his other works, Tuvill's illustrations are drawn from the well-worn *exempla* of history and legend; his originality, such as it is, resides in the mildness of his tone and the sturdiness of his advocacy of an unpopular cause.

Something of the same sweetness of tone, but with a more distinctly religious inflection, appears in his *Christian Purposes and Resolutions* (1622). This is possibly the most original and personal of Tuvill's works; but even it is cast in the pattern of a currently popular literary

---

[21] Thompson, *The Seventeenth-Century Essay,* pp. 44–45.

[22] In *Stefano Guazzo and the English Renaissance,* p. 222, I have discussed the *Asylum Veneris* from this point of view, and, on pp. 383–86 of the article mentioned above in note 15, from the point of view of its Spenserian connections.

[23] Tuvill often follows that practice of triple illustration jestingly mentioned by Pliny (*Epistles,* II, xx) as a characteristic rhetorical device of his time.

[24] The point is recognized by Thompson, *The Seventeenth-Century English Essay,* p. 45.

genre, the "resolve."[25] Tuvill was always remarkably responsive to contemporary literary tastes and fashions. In this instance, what he was responding to was a loosely articulated variety of the literature of prose meditation, akin to the essay and generally "consisting of a short, reflective examination of some human characteristic, shortcoming, or general situation, followed by an even briefer conclusion in which the author sets forth a proposed manner of action introduced by the [reiterated] formula '*I will therefore* do so-and-so,' or an easily recognizable variant."[26] Of this type of essay-related writings, the principal exemplars preceding Tuvill's were Joseph Hall's *Meditations and Vows Divine and Moral* (1605); Anthony Stafford's *Meditations, and Resolutions, Moral, Divine, Political* (1612); Thomas Tuke's *New Essays, Meditations, and Vows* (1614); and Francis Rous's *Meditations of Instruction, of Exhortation, of Reproof* (1616). Among those published later than Tuvill's are the better-known *Resolves Divine, Moral, Political* (first "century," 1623?; second, 1628) of Owen Feltham and the *Spare Minutes; or Resolved Meditations* (1634) of Arthur Warwick. The "resolves" that Tuvill sets for himself are earnestly pious and socially commendable. It is *perhaps* his own authentic voice which we hear in the epistle "To the Reader":

I know I feel my own frailty and imperfection, and yet, trusting to the power and mercy of my God, I have set my rest to practice these published purposes and resolutions. It is my hope that my boldness will encourage others not to think the way hard, or the journey troublesome, being undertaken by so impotent a traveler. I have not in the prescribing of my intended course affected curiosity, but proceeded in a natural and free strain as the matter which then came into my mind did seem to lead me. I expect not, I desire not popular applause.[27]

If this is not simply an echo of Hall's similar protestation, it may be even as the good man says.

In *St. Paul's Threefold Cord* (1635), Tuvill's last publication, he is once again following a well-established pattern, this time that of the conduct manual. Specifically, the form the work takes is that of the handbooks dealing with domestic economy.[28] Various books of "offices," classic and patristic, lie behind Tuvill's work, but the contemporary treatises most nearly akin to it are perhaps Book III of Guazzo's *La civil conversazione* (Brescia, 1574; English tr., 1581) and

---

[25] See my analysis in "Daniel Tuvill's 'Resolves,'" *Studies in Philology*, XLVI (April, 1949), 196–203.

[26] *Ibid.*, p. 196.

[27] *Christian Purposes and Resolutions*, sigs. A5v–A6r.

[28] For a general discussion of this type, see Chilton L. Powell, *English Domestic Relations, 1487–1653* (New York, 1917).

the "economic" section of Bishop Joseph Hall's *Salomon's Divine Arts* (1609). The topics discussed in the three "tomes" into which Tuvill's pudgy duodecimo is divided are "The Wife's Duty," "The Husband's Duty" (Tome I); "The Children's Duty," "The Parent's Duty" (Tome II); "The Servant's Duty," and "The Master's Duty" (Tome III). The work is religious in tone throughout, although many secular authorities are quoted and the matters discussed are sometimes of an extremely earthy, practical nature. *St. Paul's Threefold Cord* is, in effect, a series of six sermons on domestic relations, each "Book" (or sermon) preceded by a scriptural text which is then expounded in semisystematic fashion. This sermonizing manner has much in common with the double series of Tuvill's *Essays*, to the examination of which we now turn.

As the reader will have before him the text of the *Essays*, together with full explanatory notes and a separate "foreword" to each essay, it seems unnecessary here to provide more than a few general observations.

Essays Politic and Moral, to give the work the modernized title adopted for the present edition, contains nine brief essays. Of these, the first three constitute a unit, entitled collectively in the original "Of Persuasion." In matter and form, although usually by-passed [29] by writers upon the subject, these essays are pertinent to any consideration of the place of rhetoric in Elizabethan and Jacobean society. The remaining six essays treat severally of other topics long the commonplaces of moralists and epistlers. The temper of this first collection is, on the whole, secular; that of the second collection, *Essays Moral and Theological*, leans rather to the religious.

A first glance at either set of essays will leave the reader with the impression that he has before him the work of a man deeply versed in the classics, for Latin and Greek dot the pages right and left. Familiar with the classics, one way or another—as with the Scriptures and the Fathers—Tuvill certainly was. But a closer study of the *Essays* will quickly reveal (as the Notes to the present edition amply show) that he often quotes his authorities from unacknowledged intermediaries. Like many another, and more notable, of his contemporaries, Tuvill was not at all squeamish about taking his good where he found it. And he no doubt justified his somewhat shady practice by pretending to himself that such pillaging was that function of art which in those days bore the label of "imitation." We must not think too badly of him (or of his fellows in the practice) if we should

---

[29] Not entirely: William G. Crane, *Wit and Rhetoric in the Renaissance* (New York, 1937), p. 151, in a single brief paragraph does notice this aspect of Tuvill's volume.

nowadays style his "imitation" plagiarism. Other times, other manners.
What does become clear from such a close scrutiny is that Tuvill
was a sincere admirer of the classical and Continental historians and
that he was a diligent reader of the contemporary publications, original
or translated, of his own countrymen. Among the former his favorites
are easily Tacitus, Livy, Sallust, and Suetonius; and to them may be
added the moralists, Plutarch, Seneca,[30] and the Roman satirists. Concerning the reading of history, in Chapter VIII of *The Dove and the
Serpent,* entitled "What Literature and Knowledge Is Required in a
Man," he lays down a piece of advice of which he was obviously himself a sedulous follower:

He must taste of all kind of literature in general but make the ancient
registers of former ages his mind's more ordinary food. . . . For by the
knowledge of things past we learn how to manage things present and how
to dispose of things that are to come. And indeed, he that is altogether
unacquainted with the state of those times, which were long before Time
had any estate in him, I esteem him no other than an infant, whose
discursive faculty never traveled beyond the arches of his cradle; for
though his body be aged, yet his wit is childish, as being wholly destitute
of experience and unexercised in the course of worldly affairs. And therefore Polybius did not rashly and without mature deliberation term this
historical kind of learning . . . the truest discipline, exercise, and institution by which men may be trained and brought up to civil actions. History
therefore, I mean both ancient and modern, must of necessity be one part,
and that not the least, of his study.[31]

As regards more modern historians, the *Essays* show a continued
draught upon Guicciardini (in Fenton's translation), Machiavelli, Bodin, and Comines. For writers in other fields, their chief indebtedness is
to Montaigne (in Florio's translation), Bacon (the *Advancement,* not
the *Essays*), Guazzo, Thomas Wright,[32] and Richard Hooker. To
these must be added, of course, the constant use of the Bible and the
rather casual introduction of brief *sententiae* from a few of the Fathers,
Tertullian and Augustine especially.

Essays Moral and Theological, containing twelve essays, continues
to draw upon the same sources. That it was a more popularly received
offering is witnessed by the fact that twenty years after its first publication it was reprinted and enlarged under a new title: *Vade Mecum:
A Manual of Essays Moral, Theological. Interwoven with Modern
Observations, Historical, Political* (1629). Under this title, and with

---

[30] In the dedicatory epistle to his *Christian Purposes and Resolutions,* sig. A2v, Tuvill
calls Seneca "the worthiest of the Stoics."

[31] Sigs. G4v–H1r.

[32] *The Passions of the Mind in General* (1601).

further additions and revisions, it was reprinted in 1631 and 1638.[33] Modern critics, too, seem to have preferred this volume. Thompson[34] says that it contains "the best of Tuvell's work"; and William A. Jackson,[35] though no admirer of either work, was *sure* that the *Vade Mecum* is Tuvill's and that the new title is more suited to the collection than was the original. Notwithstanding the machinery of anonymity with which the *Vade Mecum* was introduced to the reading public, it seems perfectly obvious, considering the repetition of Tuvillian themes and phrases and the incorporation of material from other of his works,[36] that the additions to it and to the successive reprints are the work of the author himself—especially since they all appeared during his lifetime.

The titles of the essays in *Essays Moral and Theological* are, with two exceptions ("Of Temptations," "Of Poverty"), reduplicative: "Of Learning *and* Knowledge," "Of Alms *and* Charitable Deeds," "Of Gifts *and* Benefits," "Of Reprehensions *and* Reproofs," and so on. This is in keeping with the general looseness of structure and imprecision of thought which characterize the whole collection. Obviously, Tuvill is still under the influence of the earlier essays of Montaigne: his desultory chattiness often needs a curb; his ideas often need to be drawn into a more logically coherent sequence. It is a pity that he could not have had the benefit of Bacon's tightly developed, concise essays (eds. 1612, 1625) to guide him in the composition of his own "two garrulously discursive and unpractical volumes."[37] His most usual technique is to "set his text" (after the manner of the sermon) and then to bring to its support a succession of detached illustrative anecdotes, dicta, proverbs, and assorted musings. At best he will divide his subject into heads and then pursue each as a separate topic, using the same unmortared pattern as with the undivided topics. If the whole lacks form and centrality, at least no one could accuse him of lacking *copia*. "I could add more," he says at the end of the final essay, "but the humor of essays is rather to glance at all things with a running conceit than to insist on any with a slow discourse."[38]

Aside from such evidence of popularity as the four editions of one set of *Essays* indicate, there have survived several other indications that Tuvill did not go unread in his own day. Barnabe Rich, for instance, in his *Honesty of This Age* (1614) made free of the *Essays*

---

[33] For the changes and additions, see Appendix.
[34] *The Seventeenth-Century English Essay*, p. 45.
[35] *The Carl H. Pforzheimer Library*, III, 1051.
[36] See evidence in Appendix and Notes.
[37] *Cambridge History of English Literature* (Cambridge, 1907–16), IV, 345.
[38] "Of Poverty," below, p. 142.

Moral and Theological;[39] Robert Chamberlain, in his *Nocturnal Lucubrations; or, Meditations Divine and Moral* (1638),[40] adapted a passage from the essay "Of Learning and Knowledge"; and John Spencer, in his *Things New and Old* (1658), quoted numerous brief passages from the *Essays,* sometimes with, and sometimes without, acknowledgment of his source. In the Huntington Library there is preserved a copy of *Essays Moral and Theological* once belonging to John Evelyn and containing manuscript marginalia[41] presumably by him; and the Folger Library preserves a manuscript (Folger MS V.a. 178; De Ricci 767.1) by Thomas Grocer, "A Banquet of Sweetmeats" (1657), containing numerous quotations from the 1638 edition of *Vade Mecum.* It is recorded also that among the printed books in Scipio Le Squyer's library in 1632 there was a copy of Tuvill's *Asylum Veneris* (entered under its half title, *A Sanctuary for Ladies*).[42] Tuvill was not, then, it would seem, a prophet quite without honor in his own country and time.

The copy texts for both series of essays are those in the Folger Library. The readings of these texts have been carefully compared with those of texts in the Huntington Library, the Newberry Library, and (for *Essays Politic and Moral*) of a copy in the possession of the editor. No extended or significant variations occur, but a few minor divergences are recorded in the Notes and Appendix. Except for an occasional turned letter or obvious misprint, silently corrected, foreign words, phrases, and quotations are left as Tuvill had them.

In accord with the editorial policy of the series in which they appear, Tuvill's *Essays* are here presented in a modernized text. Except for a few words no longer in common use or for a few verb forms and pronouns existing in the frozen forms rendered familiar through Shakespeare and the King James Version of the Bible, spelling has been made to conform to modern American usage. Obsolete words or words used in a sense differing from the usual modern meaning are glossed in notes at the foot of the page. No attention has been paid to the capitalization and italics of the originals.

Tuvill's punctuation and sentence structure offer such an inextricably interwoven tangle that nothing short of a Gordian solution has seemed

[39] See J. L. Lievsay, "A Word about Barnaby Rich," *Journal of English and Germanic Philology,* LV (July, 1956), 389–92.

[40] Pp. 72–73.

[41] Here reproduced, in the Notes, by permission of the Director of the Huntington Library.

[42] See F. Taylor, "The Books and Manuscripts of Scipio Le Squyer, Deputy Chamberlain of the Exchequer (1620–59)," *Bulletin of the John Rylands Library,* XXV (1941), 158.

possible. I have, accordingly, been quite arbitrary about the reshuffling of marks and the shortening or lengthening of his periods. Naturally, I have left the *order* of the words undisturbed; and where my regrouping of units may have changed the intended rhythm of the original, I can only hope that the change has made for easier reading and readier comprehension. Actually, I think that the modernization may have done Tuvill a double service. It has, for one thing, reduced to compassable shorter units sentences which originally sprawled at length. The result has been, to my ear at least, a considerable increase in crispness and firmness. At the same time, the recombination of his shortest "paragraphs" into longer and more logically related groupings has tended to reduce the visual impression of helter-skelter scrappiness produced by the occasional multiple paragraph indentions on a single page. Conversely, and especially in the *Essays Politic and Moral,* a dozen or so very long paragraphs have been divided, with a resulting gain in clarity and emphasis.

The following single *sentence,* reproduced without change from the original, will serve to illustrate in small the tangle of Tuvill's syntax and punctuation, which can be a maddening chaos when the paragraph runs on unbroken for two or three pages.

For, howsoeuer it may seeme, for the faciliting of treacherous, and disloyall practises, a necessarie *Axiome,* by force whereof, the lewd Conspirator being emboldned, dooth freely open himselfe, to such as hee is perswaded may be easily drawn to second his mischieuous attempts; knowing, that if his expectation should chaunce to faile him in any one, hee keepes himselfe notwithstanding out of the danger, and compasse of the law; whose *Equitie* pronounceth not the sentence of death against any man, without a iust, and lawfull conviction, which in this case (considering the many disordered passions, wherewith men are led to scãdalize each other) can not be had (witnesse those seuerall duells, and combats, which heere-to-fore both in this Kingdome, and diuers others, haue beene assign'd by Princes for the avoyding of such differences; the staine of infamie and dishonour, resting alwaies, how iustly often-times God knowes, with the partie vanquished, whither Plaintife, or Defendant): yet for the concealing of honest counsailes, it is very hurtful, and dangerous.[43]

Preserving Tuvill's words, the essential statement runs thus: "For howsoever it may seem for the facilit[at]ing of treacherous and disloyal practices a necessary axiom, . . . yet for the concealing of honest counsels it is very hurtful and dangerous"—29 words. The intruded qualifying matter, however, amounts to 137 words; and the tangle of parentheses and suspensions must somehow be resolved into readily

---

[43] Compare the modernization, below, p. 50.

comprehensible sense. Whether I have been successful in my attempts at such resolution, the reader must judge for himself. My aim has been, always, to arrive at an effective clarity without disturbing the word order of the original, and I have not scrupled to adopt any means that promised such an end.

A final word may be said about the Notes. If they appear fuller than the intrinsic worth of the *Essays* would seem to warrant, I can only say that I would gladly have made them even fuller had my ignorance permitted. Most of them are attempts to trace Tuvill's statements to their sources—not to their ultimate sources only, which would be of little significance for so crafty an "imitator" of the Ancients and would leave a false impression as to the true nature of his reading, but to those unmentioned intermediaries to whom he was so often indebted for his seeming "classical" learning. So little is Tuvill's originality, I am convinced, that hardly a sentence in his writings is the product of his own unaided thought. To discover these authentic sources, therefore, I have read widely among the books published in England in the decade preceding the publication of the *Essays,* and with some reward, as the Notes will demonstrate. Nevertheless, despite all my efforts to track them down, some dozens of obviously borrowed passages remain undocumented. The Notes represent what I have been able to find; for what is yet lacking, I crave the indulgence of the Benevolent Reader.

PART I

Essays Politic and Moral

Essays Politic and Moral

——

By D. T., Gent.

——

Printed
By H. L. for Matthew Lownes,
dwelling in Paul's Churchyard.
1608

To the Right Honorable and
Virtuous Lady,
the Lady Anne Harington

MADAM:

The desire I had to manifest my serviceable affection toward Your Honor in outward compliment hath, on such idle hours as remained free to me from your employments, begot this young and tender infant, whom I presumed, upon his birth (being yet an embryo in his father's brain), to devote and consecrate wholly to your honorable self as to the chief and final end of his being. His capacity is not of the weakest; and therefore, howsoever he may now seem altogether unfashioned, I make no doubt but, by conversing with Your Ladyship (whose bosom the hand of heaven hath so richly furnished with all exemplary virtues that, from among so many, Wisdom selected you to be the governess from whom the princely issue of a royal bed might receive instruction), his ruder ignorance may be reduced to a better form. Essays are the things he uttereth. His years deny him that length of breath which should enable him to hold out in a continued and long discourse. Myself have imparted unto him part of that beauty and perfection which art and nature hath bestowed on me. Such, therefore, as he is I present him to Your Honor's view; who, I hope, will afford him such worthy entertainment as may hold some even correspondency with his desires as well as his deserts. And so, in the humblest degree of service that either love or dutiful observance can imagine, I kiss your honorable hands, desirous of nothing more than always to be reputed,

Madam,

Your Honor's
most affectionate
servant,

D. T.

[I-III.] *Of Persuasion*

I.   [*Of Opinion*]

TO GROUND a persuasion of what nature soever in the hearts of a public audience, there are three things necessarily required: the one consists in the opinion had of the party persuading; the other,[a] in the affection of the parties to be persuaded; and the last, in the perspicuity and soundness of the reason itself by which he labors to persuade them. As concerning the first, it was thought by the magistrates of Sparta to be a matter of so great importance that when they perceived one of a loose and dissolute behavior ready to propound unto the people an advertisement,[b] the approbation whereof they knew would be no small enlargement to the good and quietness of their state and commonwealth, they did immediately command him silence (fearing, it should seem, lest his known manners might have prejudiced the excellency of the thing) and entreated one who for his grave and virtuous carriage was of some honor and reputation amongst them to take upon him the invention and to deliver it unto them as if it had proceeded merely from himself. And it hath been always the practice of wiser statesmen, for the better composing of exasperated minds, whether it were in the bloody factions of the greater or in the tumultuous broils of the meaner, to choose someone whose grave representation, accompanied with a remarkable, honest, and virtuous disposition, might, upon his very first approach, work an awful[c] respect toward his person and, withal, a reverent attention toward his words in the hearts and minds of such as should behold him. For there are not any so mutinous and turbulent assemblies, howsoever they may seem to consist of those active and working spirits *quibus quieta movere,* as Sallust said of some of his time, *magna merces videtur*—that think the very disturbance of things established a sufficient hire to set them on work—but will somewhat (though incensed passions arm them with never so desperate a resolution to effect their mischievous projects and designs) honor the sight and presence of such a one, especially when they think he is not interested in the cause or induced by any private obligation to seek the good of the one party with any hurt or disadvantage to the other,

---

[a] *Other:* second.   [b] *Advertisement:* proposal.   [c] *Awful:* awe-filled.

but that his love and affection doth equally border upon both and that the reducing of them to a peaceable agreement of their differences for the public good and welfare of the state is the chiefest and only mark he aims at. And this was excellently described by the poet when he said,

Magno in populo cum saepe coorta est
seditio, saevitque animis ignobile vulgus:
cumque faces, et saxa volant, furor arma ministrat:
tum pietate gravem, ac meritis, si forte virum quem
conspexere, silent: arrectisque auribus adstant.

And for this cause it hath been a custom among the Spaniards to make a choice of churchmen for the better managing of such businesses. Yea, they have been oftentimes employed by him in matters of treaty with an intent and purpose to lend a greater majesty to his negotiations and more feignedly to color his subtle fetches [d] and devices. As when for the assurance of his new-got conquest of Navarre, he sent two Cordeliers [e] into France to talk with the Queen about a peace, who, by reason of the credit their profession had gained them, returned homeward with no ill success. Whereas, if they be men of a differing fame that have the carrying of such affairs, their reasons, be they never so apparently good, do lightly serve to no better use than to sharpen and stir up the ill-affected humors of their crazy [f] minds the more, whereby in the end themselves become a subject for their distemperature [g] to work upon—especially when that small sparkle of understanding which is usually the portion of the vulgar is dimmed and obscured with any mist of prejudice or cloud of passionate affection. And the reason hereof is the shallow ignorance of a wavering and unsteady multitude, which, being for the most part led to judge of matters only by a sensitive apprehension [h] they have of them and not able of themselves to look further into the depth of things than the superficial bark will suffer the eye of their external sense to wind itself into them, do oftentimes by reason thereof grow jealous even of virtue itself (as the many exiles and ostracisms practiced in those democratical and popular states of elder times can sufficiently witness) and therefore are the more to be excused if they suspect the ends and purposes of such as are not known to them at all, or not known to them at least for any eminent good quality that is in them

[d] *Fetches:* schemes, ruses.
[e] *Cordeliers:* Franciscan (or Gray) friars.
[f] *Crazy:* unsteady, diseased.

[g] *Distemperature:* derangement, unbalanced condition.
[h] *Apprehension:* impression, understanding.

but rather for the contrary, it being an axiom approved of most men
that *malus, ubi bonum se simulat, tunc est pessimus.* So that howsoever good wine let [1] not to be good by being poured out of an earthen
vessel, yet to present a wholesome medicine to a weaker stomach in
an unhandsome box is to the grieved patient ofttimes a cause of
distaste and, by consequence, may fall out to be a means of utter
refusal.

For indeed τὸ καλὸν οὐ καλὸν, ὅταν μὴ καλῶς γίνηται, good things lose the
grace of their goodness when in good and convenient manner they be
not performed; and so, likewise, when by good and convenient persons they be not propounded (Ecclus. 20:19). *Invisum semel principem,* saith Tacitus, *seu bene, seu male facta premunt.* A prince, after
he hath once incurred the hatred and ill opinion of his subjects and
by some one particular bad action or other alienated and estranged
their affections from him, shall find the glory of whatsoever enterprise he shall undertake to be blasted even in the very blossom by
some sinister [3] and scandalous interpretation; neither will the lawfulness or goodness of his intention be a sufficient plea to prevent it from
being burdensome unto him. For the illustration whereof I need
produce no other instance than that of Vitellius, who, as Tacitus
reports, after his entrance into Rome, *omnem infimae plebis rumorem
affectabat,* endeavored all he could to mark and fashion out his actions by the square and rule of popular approbation, doing many
things which, had they proceeded from a virtuous ground, would
have been received as pleasing and acceptable; but in him, *memoria
vitae prioris, indecora et vilia accipiebantur,* by the memory of his
forespent life they were of most men accounted as dishonorable and
base.

Tiberius, when Spanish adulation would have erected a temple to
the perpetual honor of his name, did most earnestly oppose himself
against their determination, even in open Senate. *Ego me P.C.,* saith
he, *mortalem esse, et hominum officia fungi satisque habere, si
locum principem impleam, et vos testor, et meminisse posteros volo:
qui satis, superque memoriae meae tribuent, ut majoribus meis
dignum, rerum vestrarum providum, constantem in periculis, offen-
sionum pro utilitate publica non pavidum credant: haec mihi in
animis vestris templa, hae pulcherrimae effigies, et mansurae:* that I
am mortal and that I undergo the offices of human frailty and that it
sufficeth me if I can perform the place whereunto I am called, I take
you to witness, O chosen Senators; and I would posterity should be
mindful of it, who shall sufficiently honor my remembrance when

---

[1] *Let:* cease.   [3] *Sinister:* wrenched, distorted.

they are persuaded that I am worthy my ancestors, provident in your affairs, constant in dangers, and careless of offenses where question is of the public good. These shall be to me those honorable temples and those excellent statues which, once grounded in your minds, shall remain forever. Whereof one saith, they were *praeclara verba, sed non pro Tiberio:* they were excellent words had they been uttered by an excellent man, but proceeding from him they served but to aggravate and make worse the foreconceived suspicion they had of his dissembling carriage.

So likewise, *legi a se militem, non emi,* said Galba. Whereof Tacitus speaking saith it was *vox pro Repub[lica] honesta, sed ipsi anceps,* an honest and well-beseeming voice in regard of the commonwealth but doubtful in respect of himself, *nec enim ad hanc formam caetera erant,* for the rest of his life was not agreeable hereunto. And hence it is that the Oracle of Heaven, speaking by the mouth of Timothy, warneth everyone that calleth upon the name of Christ to depart from iniquity: ἀποστήτω ἀπὸ ἀδικίας πᾶς ὁ ὀνομάζων τὸ ὄνομα τοῦ κυρίου. *Non est enim,* saith Theophylact, *speciosa laus in ore peccatoris.* And this is the reason why Christ himself, in Mark 1:25, rebuked the unclean spirit and commanded him to hold his peace even then when he proclaimed Him to be τὸν ἅγιον τοῦ θεοῦ, the holy one of God; and why Paul likewise, being vexed with the praises and commendations of the Pythonist who, following him and his company, continually cried out, οὗτοι οἱ ἄνθρωποι δοῦλοι τοῦ θεοῦ τοῦ ὑψίστου εἰσίν, "these men are the servants of the most high God," οἵτινες καταγγέλλουσιν ἡμῖν ὁδὸν σωτηρίας, "who make known unto us the way of salvation," commanded the spirit to come forth of her, *quasi nolens sanctus ab immundo ore commendari.*

Neither was it without reason that a grave and wise philosopher of former times suspected the uprightness of his own carriage when he heard himself commended by one whose life and conversation was of a differing strain. How then can those impious, those irreligious and pharisaical Levites of this corrupted and depraved age free themselves from those aspersions and imputations which, even by the least discerning judgments (such is the palpableness of their irregular enormities), may be justly cast upon them? For that notwithstanding the Spirit of Truth and Knowledge[k] hath ennobled them so far as to entitle them the salt of the earth (wherewith whatsoever is not seasoned is fatuous[l] and unsavory) and graced them with so high a vocation as is the dispensation of His heavenly mysteries, they run themselves

---

[k] *Spirit of Truth and Knowledge:* Christ.

[l] *Fatuous:* flat, insipid (L., *fatuus*).

breathless in a course of life which is altogether disproportionable to the grounds and principles of virtue, derogating [m] thereby not a little from the excellency and majesty of His celestial and eternal Word. For whence is it that profane atheism hath taken such a sure footing in the hearts of ignorant and simple men, who, for the most part, being unable to judge or conceive of universalities suffer themselves (as I said before) to be wholly guided by their external sense, but only from the boundless dissolutions [n] of some churchmen who practice not themselves that which they propound to others?

Wherefore I cannot choose but commend his policy who having converted a Jew, a friend of his, to Christianity and perceiving him presently [o] after desirous for his better satisfaction to go to Rome labored by all means to dissuade him from it, fearing lest the corrupt and disordered manners of the clergy there might have wrought in him some dislike of the religion and so by consequence have moved him to turn Jew again. So that whosoever would effectually work upon the minds of men with advantage to himself, he must not only say well but do well also. *Facta mea, non dicta vos milites sequi volo, nec disciplinam modo, sed exemplum etiam a me petere, qui hac dextra mihi tres consulatus, summamque laudem peperi*, said Valerius Corvinus to his soldiers when they were to march against the Samnites. The very air and echo of which words, according to the apprehension myself have of them, was sufficient to have breathed a warlike motion and resolution into the very steel wherewith their hands were armed and made the palest-livered wretch amongst them suddenly turn conqueror.

Wherefore he that thinks much the words of his mouth should be neglected, he must so carry himself that his deeds may be always ready to give authority and countenance to his words; yea, there must not be anything in him or about him but what may work a wondrous admiration of him in the hearer's eye and a zealous imitation of him in his heart. Finally, he must have in him those three tongues whereof the Scripture maketh mention, and which are found in every well-disposed natural [p] man. The first is the tongue of the heart: *Qui loquitur veritatem in corde suo* (Psalm 15:2). The other is the tongue of the mouth: *Qui non egit dolum in lingua sua* (v. 3). The third and last is the tongue of our works, whereof Christ saith, τὰ ἔργα ἃ ἐγὼ ποιῶ, ταῦτα μαρτυρεῖ περὶ ἐμοῦ, *opera quae ego facio, testimonium perhibent de me;* and whereat St. John the Baptist aimed when, after the Jews had sent their deputies to inquire of him what he was, his answer

[m] *Derogating:* harmfully depreciating.

[n] *Dissolutions:* irregularities, dissoluteness.

[o] *Presently:* immediately, very shortly.

[p] *Natural:* sinful, unconverted.

to them first was altogether negative, to wit, that he was not Christ, that he was not Elias, that he was not a prophet; till, constrained by their importunacy to tell them positively what he was, he said unto them, ἐγὼ φωνὴ βοῶντος ἐν τῇ ἐρήμῳ: "I am the voice of him that crieth in the desert"—showing thereby that his whole course of life was but a tongue, the particular actions whereof were so many several voices which with a silent rhetoric did most apparently make known the soundness and sincereness of that infallible truth which he was sent to teach. So that, without the help and assistance of this last, all the exhortations, persuasions, encouragements, and instructions that can possibly be produced by any man, be they never so good, can little or nothing prevail.

And therefore was it that God himself, being about to send Isaias abroad to preach, He did first of all to purify his lips touch them with a coal from the altar; and that to encourage Jeremie He said unto him, *antequam exires de vulvam, sanctificavi te. Spiritu principali confirma me Deus,* "establish me, O God," saith the kingly prophet, "by thy free spirit," and then, *docebo iniquos vias tuas,* "I will instruct the wicked in thy ways," *et impii convertentur ad te,* "and sinners shall be converted unto thee." Wherefore, *ἰατρέ θεράπευον σεαυτόν,* thou that takest upon thee to reform the manners of others, redress thine own that thou mayst free both thyself and that which thou utterest from the traducements⁴ and detractions of a vulgar ignorance and that it may not be said of thee, *Clodius accusat moechos, Catilina Cethegum.* For then shalt thou be able to graft a persuasion of whatsoever thou shalt deliver in the minds of thy auditors.

It is an excellent harmony, and I know not if unparalleled by that concent⁷ of spheres, to see the words of men accompanied with their thoughts and followed by their deeds; and besides, there is a natural inclination in all men to learn the theory of such as they know to have been excellent in the practic.⁸ Hannibal will but scorn the philosopher that takes upon him in his presence to discourse of war; and Cleomenes will account that orator but a chattering swallow that shall presume (he being by) to describe the office and duty of a general. The like happens to those depraved and exulcerated minds

qui de virtute locuti
clunem agitant.

---

⁴ *Traducements:* misrepresentations.

⁷ *Concent:* harmonious agreement.

⁸ *Practic:* execution, practical application.

For who can with patience endure to hear Vitellius preach against intemperancy, or Gracchus complain of seditious and mutinous assemblies? *Manus, quae sordes abluit, munda esse debet*, saith St. Gregory; and therefore

Quis coelum terris non misceat, et mare coelo,
si fur displiceat Verri, aut homicida Miloni?

Wherefore let every man (as St. Paul saith) so run that he may obtain, so fight that he may not beat the air; but, as in other things, so likewise in this be the followers of his example: ὑποπιάζω μου τὸ σῶμα, etc. I beat down my body and bring it into subjection, lest after I have preached to others myself should be reproved.

It is said of Vespasian that, being himself *antiquo cultu, victuque,* he was to the Romans *praecipuus adstricti moris author,* even when riot and excess were the only stewards that attended them in public and private meetings. *Obsequium enim inde in principem, et aemulandi amor validior quam poena ex legibus, et metus,* saith Tacitus.

And hence it came that Theodoric, king of the Goths, writ unto the Roman Senate in this manner: *Facilius est errare naturam, quam dissimilem sui princeps possit rem[publicam] formare,* than that a prince should frame a commonwealth unlike unto nature to err, *Facilius est errare naturam, quam dissimilem sui princeps possit rem[publicam] formare,* than that a prince should frame a commonwealth unlike unto himself, so much available¹ with inferiors is the force of an example in any person of authority. But if I may lawfully and without offense oppose my weakness against majesty, I will briefly show him that his opinion doth in some sort merit contradiction. For Sulla, being a disordered liver, made his citizens reformed; and Lysander, on the contrary, polluted his with vices wherewith himself was no way blemished.

¹ *Available:* persuasive.

A SECOND THING to help and further persuasion is affection, which, being once thoroughly wrought and settled in the hearts and minds of a multitude (and that specially through a good opinion conceived of the party persuading), is sufficient of itself, though the matter which is propounded be never so weak and the reasons that should usher it never so lame, to make an easy and speedy passage for it through all the oppositions and contradictions of any deeper discerning spirit whatsoever. Witness Pisistratus, who, being brought (according to his own appointment) in a chariot to the market place and there having in the sight of all men charged others with those wounds which his own hands had wrought, Solon could come and tell him that he did not rightly counterfeit[a] the person of Ulysses; for the Ithacan's intent was only to beguile his foes, whereas what he did was to deceive his friends. But he could not prevent him, for all this, from being followed by the people, so great a commiseration toward himself and so wrathful an indignation toward his enemies had the view of those self-made hurts effected in the hearts of the vulgar; who, not discovering the depth of his designs (nor yet considering with themselves that the desire of sovereignty and rule is so great in the minds of ambitious men that they will not stick to purchase it at the highest rate the heavens can hold it at), gave sentence in his behalf according to the apprehension they had of that bloody object which was before their eyes.

And the reason hereof is not far from hand. For passions are certain internal acts and operations of our soul, which, being joined and linked in a most inviolable and long-continued league of friendship with the sensitive power and faculty thereof, do conspire together like dis-obedient and rebellious subjects to shake off the yoke of reason and exempt themselves from her command and controlment, that they may still exercise those disordered motions in this contract world[b] of our frail and human bodies which during her weaker nonage they were accustomed to do. And for the better effecting hereof they do

[a] *Counterfeit:* imitate.   [b] *Contract world:* little, or narrow, world (microcosm).

first of all, through the help of a corrupt imagination, set upon the wit and afterward upon the will; which, harboring in itself two diverse inclinations—the one to follow reason as her sovereign, the other to content the senses as her friends—is easily brought (being by them corrupted and bribed with pleasure) entirely to love the one and utterly to leave and forsake the other; or, at least, like a careless magistrate (who, for the avoiding of some particular men's displeasure, neglects the good and profit of the commonweal), to omit that care which as governess of the soul she is bound in duty to have over it, loathing to see the quietness of her own estate interrupted by the divided factions and tumultuous partialities of inferior ministers, especially when she perceives the soul to be partaker likewise of those benefits wherewith herself is feed [e] and undermined by the passions. So that when our hearts are once possessed with any vehement affection, the wit on the one side labors to find out reasons presently that may countenance and grace it, and the imagination on the other side, like a deceitful counselor seeking to blind the eyes of the judge, represents them to the understanding in a most intensive manner and with more show and appearance than they are indeed. Neither can the soul (which, by reason of her limited influence, cannot possibly at one and the same instant impart sufficient activity to two differing operations) exactly then consider the soundness of such arguments as might stay the violence of her course in following the affections but like a weaker prince suffers herself, for quietness' sake, to be led away by the suggestions of such her followers.

And hence it was that a certain orator, with no small advantage to himself, as often as he was to plead would most earnestly entreat the judges that he might be first heard, but specially when himself distrusted the soundness of his cause. For he knew full well that when he had ended, their minds would be so busied in examining the weight and firmness of his reasons that they could not possibly give any diligent attention to the allegations of his adversary. Wherefore, whosoever perceiveth those proofs and inducements that should maintain his cause to be wanting, let him settle himself to work upon the affections of such as are to further it. For if he gain never so little footing here he need not despair of anything.

It was a saying of a prince of Sparta that for a man to keep himself strictly to the rule of justice in matters which concerned his friends was but a color [d] wherewith such as were unwilling to do for them were content to shadow their inhumanity; and therefore, writing to Idrien, prince of Caria, for the deliverance of a certain friend of his,

[e] *Feed:* hired, bribed.   [d] *Color:* pretense.

"If Nicias," saith he, "have not offended, deliver him; if he have offended, deliver him for my sake. But howsoever the matter go, deliver him."

Brutus and Cassius contending one against the other for the urban praetorship, Caesar, having heard their allegations, said unto his friends: "It is true that the reasons which are alleged by Cassius are most just; but Brutus nevertheless must be preferred." So Brutus had the first place and Cassius the second.

Out of which examples we may easily discern that reason may give out precepts which passion will not stick to countermand. For reason teacheth us that it is a point of civility to continue always steadfast and faithful to our friends—but with this caution, μέχρι τοῦ βωμοῦ, not beyond the altar; that is, no further than the rules of piety and equity will give us leave, which blinder passion doth not a whit regard. And this Agesilaus knew full well when, being constrained one day to unlodge ° somewhat in haste and to leave a certain sick friend of his who, as he was ready to depart, besought him that he would not abandon and forsake him, "Oh," quoth he, returning back, "how difficult a thing is it to love and to be wise, and both at once!" Besides, it is the nature and property of passions even to make those things make with them which (were not the eye of our understanding dimmed and obscured with such misty humors as distill from them) would otherwise peradventure prove to be as rubs and lets ᶠ which would turn the bias of men's consent a clean contrary way from our desires. And therefore they are not much amiss compared to a green glass, which makes everything seem of the same color that is seen through it. That forealleged Spartan, being very much importuned by his wife to make her brother Lysander his admiral for the seas, considered with himself that he had many nobles of far more years and greater experience than he and that to invest him, being but a youth, with a charge so far surmounting his sufficiency was to hazard at one cast the flourishing estate of his whole kingdom. But in the end, after many long suspensions and irresolute determinations, the vehement affection which he bore his queen commanded him to throw the dice and to abide the chance.

It is said of Agrippina that she did so work upon the love which Claudius bore her that, *nondum uxor potentia uxoria utebatur,* being as yet but only affianced unto him, she took upon her the state and power of an empress. But afterward, when she was thoroughly assured of her marriage and that her thoughts had got a stronger wing to

---

° *Unlodge:* break camp, retreat.

ᶠ *Rubs and lets:* obstacles and hindrances.

soar withal, then did she dare to motion a match between Octavia, Caesar's [g] daughter, and Domitius; which (because her father had betrothed her to Silanus not long before) could not be brought to pass without impiety, but that did nothing discourage her. For *nihil arduum videbatur,* saith Tacitus, *in animo principis, cui non judicium, non odium inerat, nisi indita, et jussa:* no difficulty could hinder her from obtaining anything at the hands of a prince that had neither life nor soul but what was breathed into him by her and hers.

And hence it was that Vitellius, veiling his servile flatteries under the name of Censor, was emboldened to fasten upon Silanus, laboring by forged accusations to obscure his merit and procure his overthrow, which shortly after he effected, Caesar being (as our author saith), *accipiendis adversum generum suspicionibus caritate filiae promptior,* somewhat prone to entertain suspicions against his son-in-law by reason of the charitable affection which he bore his daughter. And indeed the malignant aspect [h] of any person in authority toward his inferior is thought a sufficient warrant for every man to wrong him. And this is the reason that in the courts of princes few or none, after they once begin to slide, can recover their footing and keep themselves from falling finally. For those court parasites that have their eyes continually fixed upon the sky of their sovereign's inclination and make the sundry revolutions of his affections the only heaven of their contemplation do labor, upon the least distaste [i] that is offered, to procure an utter dislike that so they may come to be sharers in those offices and places of dignity which, while they were gracious in the sight of their master, were appropriated to none but them—verifying hereby that excellent saying of the Greeks, δρυὸς πεσούσης πᾶς ἀνὴρ ξυλεύεται: when the tree begins to fall everyone hastens to gather sticks.

Wherefore, let no man fear to be overbold in this case but rest undoubtedly assured that where reason cannot prevail affection will. And therefore it is not without cause that such as aspire to a crown and scepter do first of all (considering their want of right that should authorize and make lawful such a claim) endeavor (as the only means to wind themselves into the hearts of the people) to seem religious and virtuous; as Pepin did, who, striving to put the house of Merovée [j] from the throne of France and to appropriate it wholly to him and his, did most infinitely honor and most affectionately embrace such as had any charge or office in the Church, knowing well that those which have rule over the conscience are of great authority and estimation

---

[g] *Caesar's:* the emperor's.

[h] *Aspect:* attitude. The term is drawn from the technical jargon of astrology.

[i] *Distaste:* cause of offense.

[j] *Merovée:* the Merovingians.

among the rest. Secondly, they do labor to perform all offices of love that may serve to shadow forth in some apparent manner a desire in them to further the public good of the state and commonweal. And thus did Absalom when to everyone that came toward him he put out his hand and took him and kissed him, wishing withal that he were once made judge in the land, that such as had any suits or controversies might come to him that he might do them justice. And thus likewise did those ancient Roman captains who poured out the wealthy treasures of whole kingdoms in excessive donatives and prodigalities toward their soldiers, and that with no better intent than to make sure such hopes and expectations as ambition long before had nourished in their breasts by the so-won aid and assistance of their military and warlike legions.

For indeed these two actions are the only harbingers[k] that must lodge persuasion in the bosom of a multitude. And therefore have they always been put in practice by the chief patron of wicked policies, Satan, the common and professed enemy of mankind. For, as concerning the first, the Scripture doth assure us that he doth oftentimes, the better to deceive, transform himself into the glorious similitude of an angel of light. And hence was it that, not without good advice and judgment of the painter, in some ancient impressions of the Testament he was pictured out in the religious garment of a monk; not to signify that the life and conversation of such monastical persons was diabolical, but to show that, this being the habit[1] of holiness and piety, there was not a more easy and certain way for him to surprise the conscience of well-meaning men than it. And as concerning the second, experience hath taught us that all he aims at is to work an impression in our weaker minds that whatsoever he seeketh to induce us to is for the good and benefit of mankind; and therefore, in his very first assault, wherein was successively included the utter ruin and overthrow of us all, he told our first parents that God's forbidding them to eat of the tree of good and evil proceeded not from any other ground than from an envious fear He had of that happiness and prosperity which was like to redound to them thereby. And, withal, having considered with himself that all things in the world are said in some sort to seek the highest and to covet more or less the participation of God himself, but especially man (whom he knew did foster in his breast these three desires: the one, to live always, as God is eternal; the other, to rule all, as God is lord over all; the third, to know all, as God is wise above all), he came like a cunning rhetorician, whom practice and long experience hath taught how to advantage himself by working upon the known

[k] *Harbingers:* advance agents.   [1] *Habit:* garb.

inclinations and affections of his auditory, and lays before them a full and perfect satisfaction in every one. For, saith he, if once ye but taste of this forbidden fruit, *nequaquam moriemini,* ye shall never die (here was a continued being); *sed eritis sicut Dii,* but ye shall be like gods (here was an absolute command); *scientes bonum et malum,* understanding both good and evil; and herein was comprehended a universal and boundless knowledge.

Wherefore, he that can handle men aright in their affections and knows at what times, in what manner, and by what means they may best be stirred up may rest assured that, before his mind be thoroughly known, he is already master of what his heart desireth.

III. *Of the Force of Reason*

T HE third and last means to ground belief in the minds of men is, out of probable conjectures, to gather sufficient reasons by force whereof we may demonstrate the thing which we propound to be either actually or at least apparently necessary and convenient and no ways repugnant to the rules and principles of justice or honesty. And these are so much available that, where there is neither opinion nor affection (but rather an obstinate and self-willed resolution in the hearer to put back all persuasions), they will enforce him, notwithstanding, to alter his so-decreed determination and to give credit and approbation to what he hears. Witness Caesar, who, when he understood that Cicero had taken upon him to defend Ligarius, whom the unhappiness of the times had accused to have borne arms against him, and having not heard him of a long time before, "What will it now annoy us," said he (by way of jesting) to certain of his friends, "if we go and listen awhile to Cicero? For as for Ligarius, he is by me already irrevocably condemned." But the pregnant reasons and forcible allegations of the orator did so wonderfully move him that before he departed, mauger [a] that prejudicate [b] opinion wherewith he came, he was constrained to absolve him.

And for a further confirmation hereof I will produce that memorable apothegm of Thucydides, who, when Archidamus demanded of him which was the better wrestler of him or Pericles, his answer was that when he had cast him he had so excellent a tongue to deny it that he made the standers-by believe he was not soiled [c] and persuaded them the contrary of what their eyes had seen.

So that here we may discover an incongruity committed by Marcus Brutus in the managing of state affairs when, not considering the force of eloquence but presuming upon the good opinion his citizens had of him and the great affection they bore toward him, he permitted Antony to perform the exequies of Caesar in such solemn manner as he would himself. For by this means the hearts of such as were so

---

[a] *Mauger:* despite (Fr., *malgré*).
[b] *Prejudicate:* prejudiced.

[c] *Soiled:* disadvantaged, beaten.

desperately bent and inclined to embrace his faction that they would not at the first so much as lend an ear—no, not upon his entreaties—to the speeches of the other, upon the hearing of his funeral oration were on a sudden violently carried a clean contrary way. Such is the force of these rhetorical enthymemes and inductions, especially when they be seconded by a lively and decent [d] action. To which Demosthenes did attribute so much that, in defining an oration, he said the first and principal part thereof was action; the second, the same; and the third, no other. For in an orator there is both an eloquence of speech and a decency of action necessarily required. He must not only *ornate dicere, sed etiam concinne agere.* The one consists in the fitness of his words and the soundness of his reasons, the other in the variation of his voice and the qualifications of his gestures. So that when I consider in how eminent a degree these two things did appear in Cicero, I cannot so much admire (as otherwise I should) that notable speech of his when, being vehemently displeased with Munatius (whom once his eloquence had patronized in a most dangerous cause) for that he did eagerly follow the extremity of law against a certain friend of his, he could not refrain from telling him that it was not long of [e] his innocency that he was last absolved but of the dust which he had cast into the eyes of his judges, which hindered them from discerning aright the quality of his misdeed.

Aeschines, after his banishment being arrived at Rhodes, in an oration composed for the purpose, laid open to the people the cause of his exile; who, wondering thereupon at the Athenians that had banished him so undeservedly, "Oh," quoth he, "ye did not hear the forcible reasons by which Demosthenes countermanded mine," ascribing wholly the cause of his misfortune to the eloquence of his adversary. Wherefore he did not greatly err that compared rhetoric in an ill cause to a dangerous weapon in a madman's hand. It is an instrument which was at first invented for the easier managing of an unruly populace, and which is never employed in his right kind but in the weak and crazy languishment of estates. [f] And indeed if we do well consider, we shall find that it hath most flourished where quietness of government hath been most impoverished, as in those commonwealths where either the people, or the ignorant, or all, have borne all the sway; as, namely, that of Athens, of Rhodes, of Rome, where all things did continually labor of a dangerous epilepsy. For in better-established governments, as those of Sparta and of Crete, it was never had in any

---

[d] *Decent:* appropriate.
[e] *Long of:* because of.

[f] *Estates:* commonwealths.

great account or estimation. Nay, they would have whipped him out of their dominions that should have made profession of such a lying and deceitful art.

But it is not my purpose for the abuse of anything to condemn the use of it. I will only hereupon advertise him that goeth about by reasons to induce persuasion to imitate herein the practice of wise physicians, who apply the same medicines to the same maladies but with particular respect and consideration of the constitution of the patient. For the learned and the ignorant are not to be handled both alike. Popular allegations they prize not, and deeper demonstrations these pierce not. Wherefore, he must labor to find out a mean^g by which he may deliver deep reasons perspicuously and plausible persuasions sharply, that by the plainness of the one and the acuteness of the other he may yield a full and perfect satisfaction to them both. And for the better performance hereof I will refer him to a diligent survey of such topical heads and commonplaces^h as are by orators accounted to be the arsenals and storehouses of persuasive provision, from whence, as need requires, they draw those solid amplificationsⁱ which lend a majestical and glorious luster to their reasons; for, being nakedly delivered, the motion they produce is either weak or none at all. So that, where there is neither opinion nor affection to purchase credit, we must seriously endeavor to find out reasons and inductions that may serve the turn and know that it will be no small furtherance to our intention if, either by the representation of any visible object or by some preceding extraordinary action that carrieth engraven in the very front^j of it the honored characters of love and loyalty, we can strengthen our own persuasion and work an alteration in the hearers' passion.

An example of the former we have in Cato, who, perceiving that the Rom[ans] did neglect and contemn the forces of the Carthaginians because they were somewhat remote and far distant from them (whereupon some inconvenience might happily^k have redounded to the commonwealth), showed them presently green figs which at that instant were brought from thence; whereby they conceived that the country was not so far as they imagined, for otherwise the figs would have been dried or corrupted, and thereupon altered their opinion and became more respective. Of the latter, in Sejanus, who, having very prodigally ventured his own safety for the preserving of Caesar's—and

^g *Mean:* compromised method.
^h *Topical heads and commonplaces:* tabulated commonplaces.
ⁱ *Amplifications:* rhetorical ornamentations.
^j *Front:* forehead (L., *frons*).
^k *Happily:* haply, perchance.

that in a most dangerous and disastrous accident,[1] where sad destruction seemed to have enlarged her throat for the speedier devouring of them—got this advantage thereby that, as Tacitus saith, *quanquam exitiosa suaderet, ut non sui anxius, cum fide audiebatur;* when his so doing, peradventure, was grounded upon no better consideration than the minority of his ambitious purposes.

But, for a final conclusion of this discourse, let Delphidius assure himself that if reasons and arguments be altogether wanting it will little avail him to accuse Numerius and afterward, feeling himself sorely travailed[m] for want of proofs and witnesses to convince him, to cry out in the vehemency of his distempered passion, *Ecquis erit nocens, florentissime Caesar, si negare sufficiet?* Will any man be found guilty when to deny the fault may be sufficient to absolve him? For Julian, out of the serener calmness of his more settled judgment, will presently reply, *Ecquis erit innocens, si accusare sufficiet?* Will any man be found guiltless when to accuse him may be sufficient to condemn him?

---

[1] *Accident:* event, happening.   [m] *Travailed:* troubled, pressed.

IV. Of Praises

THE LOVE of praise, though it be a vice, yet because that by means of it far greater vices are suppressed, hath always (of the better sort of judgments) been honored and respected as a virtue. The contempt whereof was made an argument to convince Tiberius of contemning likewise those heroical and princely actions whereby men are led, through many difficult and dangerous passages, in a most eager and violent pursuit thereof. *Contemptu famae contemni virtutes,* saith Tacitus. *Optimi n quique mortalium altissima cupiunt.*

And indeed if we but cast an eye a little on the Romans, we shall find that the only thing which made men think that some extraordinary genius did continually wait and attend upon all their attempts, raising the valor of every particular and individual person amongst them to a far higher pitch than human weakness was ever thought possible to attain unto, was only an unsatiable desire to leave behind them a prosperous remembrance of their name, from the effecting whereof not death itself (had he never so fearfully disguised his countenance) could ever have deterred them. Witness that undaunted Curtius, who, when the Oracle had commanded someone to be cast headlong into that open pit, which seemed to threaten ruin and desolation to them all, as an atonement that might allay the incensed fury of the gods toward the people, armed himself presently and with such a fearless and constant resolution hied him to the place as if upon his very first approach he had intended to triumph over death and give destruction the overthrow. So Brutus, when for the good and preservation of his country (against the liberty whereof his sons, as men wholly possessed with dislike and discontentment at things present, did underhand oppose themselves) he was to be not only a spectator but an actor likewise in their tragic fall, could not choose but feel himself sorely shaken with the furious and violent encounters of divided passions, popular applause distracting him on the one side and fatherly affection on the other. But this, in the end (like too weak an enemy to confront so great an adversary), was constrained to forsake the field and to resign the honor and glory of the victory to us. *Vicit amor patriae, laudisque immensa cupido.*

But, not to stand upon particulars, the whole nation in general was so transported with this appetite of praise that all other irregularities whatsoever did, as it were, lie buried in this one. Wherefore I think there is no readier way to breed a willingness in the minds of unriper youth whereby to make them seriously addicted to embrace the harsher rudiments of virtue (that afterward they may attain to a more essential knowledge in the managing and performance of honorable employments) than to inflame their tender bosoms with a desire of commendation, which is, in every generous and ingenious disposition, the only spur to any virtuous action. *Compertum ego habeo,* said Catiline to his soldiers, *verba virtutem non addere, neque ex ignavo strenuum, neque fortem ex timido exercitum oratione imperatoris fieri.* No, no (saith he), *quem neque gloria, neque pericula excitant, nequicquam hortere.* By virtue of which words he did inspire them with such a valiant resolution that after the unfortunate event ᵃ of war had bereft them of their general it was wonderful to see the invincible courage which had spread itself through every particular branch of his whole army. For, as Sallust writes, *quem quisque vivus pugnando locum ceperat, eum amissa anima corpore tegebat:* look what ᵇ place everyone had taken to fight in whilst he was alive, the same did he cover with his body after he was dead; leaving behind them an example whereupon posterity might ground the memorable saying of that worthy martialist Gonsalvo, who, when his captains advised him (by reason of the weakness of his forces) to turn back to Capua, did utterly repel their counsel as prejudicial to the honor and reputation of a soldier, telling them if the true spirit of magnanimity had harbored in their bosoms they would have desired rather to have had their graves digged presently a foot further than, by retiring, to have prolonged their lives a hundred years.

The forealleged historian, speaking of the ancient flourishing estate of Rome before such time as the dissolute excess and effeminate niceness of corrupter age had (like a canker) eaten into the very marrow of her and through a vicious inbred habit and disposition altered the sweet complexion of her countenance, ranks this desire of praise amongst the chiefest causes of her transcendent happiness. Her children, saith he, were *laudis avidi,* full of thrift in husbanding their honor, but *pecuniae liberales,* very prodigal in spending of their wealth; *gloriae maximum certamen inter ipsos erat:* glory was the only subject of all their differences and contentions. *Sic se quisque hostem ferire, murum ascendere, conspici, dum tale facinus faceret, properabat*—which I cannot think proceeded so much from vanity as from a desire to publish and make known their sufficiency, that after-

---

ᵃ *Event:* outcome.   ᵇ *Look what:* whatever.

ward, for the good of their country, they might be called to offices of a higher nature.

A certain Laconian,[c] at the feast of Olympic games, being offered a great sum of money not to present himself to combat, would by no means be persuaded to accept it. And in the end, being demanded of one what the praise which with such labor and sweat he had purchased could avail him, his answer was, in smiling manner, that he should fight for it in battle before the king. *Eo labor, et periculum a plerisque impenditur, unde honos, et emolumentum speratur,* saith Livy. And indeed, if we suffer our senses to be guided a little by observation, we shall easily perceive that in those camps where praise and honor have been joined patent[d] with exercise for the training up of youth in arms, there hath not been a private soldier but, when occasion hath brought him on the scene to bide some trial of his proficiency, hath been thought worthy by reason of his martial carriage and aspect to have the leading and conducting of an army. Witness the Ottomans, who, by taking notice of every extraordinary action performed by the least and meanest in their troops, have so inflamed the courage of their Mussulmans that now the sounding of a trumpet amongst them is but to foretell the erecting of a trophy[e] and the striking up of a drum is as a passing bell to give warning of the approaching ruin and subversion of a kingdom.

And by this means have they marched like triumphant conquerors over the bellies of the most victorious nations, making, as they pass along, the wretched carcasses of slaughtered Christians litter for their ambitious and aspiring pride to trample on. Poverty, with them, is not made an argument of baseness and pusillanimity, nor thought a let or impediment to hinder desert from any place of eminency. It is no principle in their philosophy to measure virtue by the ell of fortune or to respect her the less for having been trained up in a homely cottage. No, the greatest among them will think it no detraction from their reputation to come, when or wheresoever the star of merit shall appear within the compass of their hemisphere, and offer presents of great value to her dear-dear infants—lay they in a manger. And herein may their practice serve like a severer censor to condemn us of high treason against her glorious and imperial majesty; and, summoning the blood into our faces, make us ashamed of our erroneous and senseless folly, *qui omnia prae divitiis humana spernimus, nec honori magno locum, nec virtuti putamus esse, nisi effusae affluant opes,* that judge of her greatness by outward circumstances, thinking it a thing

---

[c] *Laconian:* Spartan.
[d] *Joined patent:* incorporated by agreement.

[e] *Trophy:* a monument commemorating a military victory (Fr., *trophée*).

impossible that such a puissant and mighty princess should abase herself so far as to vouchsafe to lodge within the enclosure of a smoky roof or vail [f] her glory under the threadbare habit of a miserable and wretched want. But for all this, the goodness of such proceedings makes me not so far delighted with those barbarous and hellish infidels as that I should erect a tabernacle with an intent to dwell in a continual meditation of their virtuous disposition in this kind; and therefore I will now pass them over and come to other considerations of more weight and moment in this discourse.

The first whereof is, *whom* we praise; the second, *to whom;* the third, *for what;* the fourth and last, is the end *why.* In the first, men are very likely to err by too easily granting out their commendatory letters, making them the escort and guide to bring a man, upon some future hopes, into the love and favor of a third. Herein, therefore, ought everyone to be very circumspect; for if the merit of the party do not in some sort answer the relation that is made of him, it is always so much out of the writer's reputation.

> *Qualem commendes, etiam, atque etiam aspice; ne mox*
> *incutiant aliena tibi peccata pudorem.*

Polyperchon, having entertained [g] a fellow for the report Xenocrates gave of him, and finding afterward by his actions that he did no way deserve it, writ to him that thenceforward he should be more diligent in examining the worth and value of a man before he did commend him. But because the hearts of men are to Him only known who is the searcher of all hearts (and who alone could testify of Nathanael with such certainty as He did that he was an Israelite in whom there was no guile) and that [h] the rules of piety command us to conceive of their inward disposition by their outward conversation (that is, by conjectures of charity and not by demonstrations of knowledge), our judgments may be easily mistaken in them: *Fallimur, et quondam non dignum tradimus.* And therefore the verse following may serve here for a precept: *Quem sua culpa premet, deceptus omitte tueri.* For he that takes upon him the patronage of any man in this case, he makes himself an accessory to the crime.

But for the better avoiding of all these inconveniences it is good in matters of this nature to make use of that restraint of Plato, who, writing to Dionysius the Tyrant in behalf of Helicon the Cyzicenian, and fearing lest he should attribute too much to his words, limited his belief with this caution, that what he writ, he writ περὶ ἀνθρώπου

---

[f] *Vail:* abase.   [h] *That:* for that, because.
[g] *Entertained:* employed.

ζῴου φύσει εὐμεταβόλου, of a creature who by nature was the very object of change. And indeed man is a tree, the fruit whereof is never ripe but in the latter season: his nature cannot easily be discerned while it is in green; we must see the flower and the fruit of it. His first actions lightly [1] never issue forth but shadowed with the beauteous mask of formal dissimulation; and such a one enters into the popedom, as a common rumor did report of Boniface, like a fox that reigns in it like a lion and goes out of it like a dog. *Il dì loda la sera,* saith the Italian: it is the evening must commend the day, and the life of man must be censured [J] by his end.

There are some which now resolve with themselves to put on the gravity of Cato but presently show themselves in public appareled with the dissolute lightness of Vatinius. One while Curius is not austere enough for them, Fabricius not poor enough, Tubero not sparing and thrifty enough; yet by and by they will not stick to provoke Licinius with their riches, Apicius with their riots, Maecenas with their dainties. So great and difficult a thing is it *unum hominem agere,* to measure out this earthly course of ours with one and the same pace. No, there are few in this corrupted age that are not somewhat tainted with the humor [k] of that fantastical musician, who, as the poet writes of him,

> *saepe velut qui*
> *currebat fugiens hostem: saepe velut qui*
> *Junonis sacra ferret: habebat saepe ducentos,*
> *saepe decem servos; modo, reges, atque tetrarchas,*
> *omnia magna loquens: modo, sit mihi mensa tripes, et*
> *concha salis puri, et toga, quae defendere frigus*
> *quamvis crassa queat*

when, notwithstanding this his outward profession of frugality,

> *decies centena dedisses*
> *huic parco, paucis contento, quinque diebus*
> *nil erat in loculis: noctes vigilabat ad ipsum*
> *mane: diem totum stertebat: nil fuit unquam*
> *sic impar sibi.*

Yea, there is not one of whom that may be truly said which the Spirit of all Truth observed to be true in Elkanah, Samuel's father, who, for that he suffered not himself to be carried away with any such humorous [1] fluctuation but remained continually firm upon his

---

[1] *Lightly:* almost, virtually.
[J] *Censured:* judged.
[k] *Humor:* disposition.

[1] *Humorous:* temperamental, constitutional.

square ^m and unshaken, was said to be *unus vir,* one and the self-same man always, what sinister accidents soever did befall him. And therefore let not him that is careful of his credit launch too far out into the praises of any man, but keep near unto the shore and on the lee side of such unfortunate events as may anyways endanger it; let him not be too forward in superlatives, but so commend good men as he may still reserve a caveat for their errors.

The second consideration that we are to have in matters of praises is *to whom.* Many men—what by reason of the weakness of their judgments somewhat tainted with self-conceit or the greatness of their spirits not principled, peradventure, with such sound instructions as they ought to be—are so tender and jealous of their own reputation that whatsoever they hear attributed to the worth and merit of another is presently taken by them as derogated from their own. And hence it is that to commend a man for any special virtue or eminency that is in him, either to his superior or his equal, is to make him oftentimes suspected of the one, envied of the other, and himself that doth it hated of both.

Solyman the Great, having heard the acclamations and cries of joy which by a general consent of the whole camp were given to Mustafa his son at his return from Persia, grew so enraged thereat that after he had most savagely strangled him in his inner chamber he caused his dead body to be cast out to the view of his whole army, proclaiming withal that as there was but one God in heaven, so there was but one Sultan upon earth. Nor was the massacre of this his warlike son the period of his fury. He likewise exercised this his inhuman and beastly cruelty upon Sultan Gobé, his second son, for bewailing only the fatal and untimely miscarriage of his brother, and upon Sultan Mehemet, his third, because he fled for fear, construing these their actions by no better rules than his own disordinate and criminal affections to be most sensible reprovers of that his barbarous and unnatural inhumanity. So little could he brook a sharer with himself in the glory of his so great an empire.

But (alas!) he is not the only man that hath been subject to the command of such irregular and confused passions. Many have deserved to be paralleled with him in the like kind. For howsoever they made not so open a profession of tyranny as he, but, like cunning painters, could so shadow their malicious proceedings as that they never came abroad in their own likeness but appareled with the outward habit of law and justice, yet can they not be altogether freed from the deep-wounding stroke of such deserved imputations.

^m *Firm upon his square:* true to fundamental principles.

I could instance the truth of this assertion upon many, but for brevity sake I purpose to omit them and come to Tiberius, who, understanding that the Senate was minded to grace the remembrance of his mother with fresh additions of honorable titles, endeavors by wise pretexts to alter their so-decreed determination, tells them they must observe a moderation in granting any special preeminences or prerogatives to women; himself would express the like temperancy in qualifying those that should be attributed to him. But whatsoever he pretended in words, it is manifest that this his outwardly professed modesty proceeded from no better ground than from an envious distaste he had of her advancement. And therefore, as Tacitus reports, he would not so much as assign her one lictor, *muliebre fastigium in diminutionem sui accipiens,* thinking with himself that unless he topped the spreading branches of her glory they could not choose but fall out to be very hurtful and prejudicial, by their overshadowing greatness, to the prosperous and flourishing uprising of his own. Alexander will at no hand admit of any more than one only sun; and whosoever shall presume to parallel his achievements (were it with the valorous attempts of his father) shall hardly free himself from being made the tragic subject of his incensed fury.

Princes cannot brook that either their virtues or their fortunes should admit comparison. As they have the start of all men in the one, so love they not to be outstripped by any in the other. Such as are beneath them in estate and bound by reason of their birth to acknowledge as inferior homagers a dependency upon their greatness must in their presence esteem of themselves, how qualified soever, but even as bare and naked ciphers. Themselves alone will be thought the numbers that give a substantial existence to the being of them all. Dionysius, because he could not equal Philoxenus in poetry nor Plato in discourse, condemned the one to the galleys and sent the other to be sold for a slave in the island of Aegina. And hence was it that Brisson, running a match with Alexander, was willing (instructed, peradventure, by the like examples) somewhat to conceal and obscure his own ability in the course, knowing (as it is indeed) that as to be permitted to contend in anything with a prince is glorious, so to do it with that obstinacy as not to give over without victory is very dangerous. Favorinus, therefore, the philosopher, had reason when his friends upbraided him for yielding himself vanquished by Hadrian the Emperor in a controversy which was betwixt them about the interpretation of a word, to fashion them this reply: "What!" said he, "would you that I should seem to be more learned than he who is commander over thirty legions?" Augustus writ verses against Asinius Pollio. "And I," saith Pollio, "hold my peace." It is no wisdom for a man to show himself a scribe against him who, if he once be ne'er so little moved, can easily proscribe. And from this consideration grew that witty saying of Carneades, that the children of princes never learned anything so well as the managing of horses. For in all other exercises they took in hand every man was content to disableⁿ himself to hearten them; but a horse, that was neither courtier nor flatterer, threw the heir apparent of a kingdom with as little respect as he would the son of a cobbler. Wherefore every man, as well for his own security as his friend's safety, must be very nice° in commenting upon his worthiness in the hearing of any sovereign authority.

Regibus, saith Sallust, *boni, quam mali suspectiores sunt; semperque his aliena virtus formidolosa est:* the goodness of a subject gives princes oftentimes occasion to suspect, and his virtue doth but furnish them with matter of fear. Yea, the like respect must not be altogether neglected in relating it, though but before their equals and such as in the nearest degrees of consanguinity may seem allied unto him; for oftentimes there is danger even in those. For proof whereof I will produce one only accident which not long since happened between two brethren of Ferrara. The one was the Cardinal Hippolitus da Este,^p who fell extremely in love with a near kinswoman of his own. And perceiving that she with no less affection doted likewise on Don Giulio, his natural brother, whom very often even unto him out of the vehemency of her passion she would commend for the best-deserving gentleman that Italy then afforded, extolling among many other extraordinary parts^q wherewith nature had sufficiently enriched him both in body and mind the beauty and fairness of his eyes, which, she protested to the Cardinal, were the principal and chief solicitors of her affections toward him; hereat he grew presently so much enraged that, having waited his time and opportunity, one day as Giulio was ahunting most inhumanly he deprived him of them both, glutting the violence of his beastly fury with the ruinous defacing of those parts which were the main disturbers of his hopes. A tragedy^r fit to be recorded, as well in regard of the person by whom it was acted as in regard of the thing that occasioned the action. Which may serve us likewise for a precedent whereon to ground this caution: that it is not good to commend any man so as that the hearer may think himself any kind of way disabled thereby. And therefore it will not be amiss for wiser men so to

ⁿ *Disable:* belittle.
^o *Nice:* discriminating.
^p *Hippolitus da Este:* Ippolito I d'Este (1479–1520).

^q *Parts:* gifts.
^r *Tragedy:* bloody action.

qualify the approbation of their friends' deserts as that they may not seem, either by their inward passion or their outward words, to insinuate an impossibility to the standers-by of ever matching their so-eminent perfections or to upbraid them with a defective want of such good parts as they confidently give out to be so excellent in them; for this is but to expose himself to danger and his friend to envy.

L. Quinctius, surnamed Cincinnatus, when he took upon him to plead for his son Caeso (who, by carrying himself as a professed enemy to popular * proceedings, had incurred the hatred and dis-pleasure of the tribunes and thereby so endangered his life as that nothing was left him but the very bare chance of the dice to save it), knew that to allege his worthiness and known deserving, as other [of] his friends had done, was not the way to secure him from their malice but a means, rather, to set an edge upon that envious dislike which so apparently threatened his utter overthrow. And therefore, directed (as it were) by a better-discerning wisdom than the rest, he chooseth out a path for the safety of his son directly contrary to that which they had trod; omits the recital of his merits, as things not fitting to be seen of a distempered ᵗ sight; acknowledgeth a fault; and in that regard with great instancy desires the people, in humble and sub-missive terms, to bear with the weakness of his years and not to urge the forfeiture of his unadvised error.

And indeed it is far better sometimes to confess ourselves tainted with such imputations as, being undeservedly cast upon us, cannot greatly blemish our reputation than, by standing obstinately upon terms of innocency, to contend with greatness; who would willingly enough, perhaps, in colder blood admit a reconcilement, so it might not seem to proceed from any diversity or alteration of opinion in themselves.

The third consideration is *for what. Non omnis fert omnia tellus:* every ground is not fit for every seed. No more is every man for every action. The powerful hand of irreprovable Wisdom hath divided our sufficiency into little portions, so that he who is excellent in the lead-ing of a company may haply prove unsufficient in the guiding and conducting of an army—which Saturninus did not stick to instance on himself when those which were his equals in the wars were minded to invest him with that absolute command. Wherefore, whosoever he be that out of desert, as it were, shall seem to challenge a special approbation of his own dexterity beyond all men in the right per-formance of all things, he doth but manifest his overweening weak-

---

* *Popular:* originating among the peo-   ᵗ *Distempered:* unsettled, disturbed.
ple.

ness in presumptuous arrogancy; and whate'er he be that shall yield to him herein, his unworthy baseness in servile flattery.

The heathen thought it a thing impossible that any one deity should be of a power so infinite as to be able of itself to sway the rule and government of this whole universe. And therefore did they seek out gods of an inferior nature, on whom (as upon ministering spirits) Jupiter, the Superior of the covent,[u] might in some sort unburden himself of so great a care, allotting to every one of them, according to their several endowments, a special charge.

And herehence[v] it came that one was surnamed Enyalios; another, Mantoos; a third, Kerdoos; and that Venus had her sovereignty allotted her in nuptial chambers rather than in martial tents, as being a thing altogether undecent that one of her composition should any way intermeddle with arms.

But that we may descend again a little lower to creatures of our own mold, do we not plainly see that in the dispensation of spiritual gifts there is so great a difference and variety that he who hath the spirit of wisdom may want the utterance of knowledge, he that hath faith may be altogether destitute of the power to work miracles, and he that is endued with divers tongues may be thoroughly unfurnished of the means to interpret them? The reason whereof is delivered by the mouth of Truth in the 12 of the first to the Corinthians to be only this, viz., that there might be amongst us a necessary use one of another and that, like so many several[w] members, we might serve for the comforting and building up of one and the same body. Moses, howsoever he excelled in all the learning of the Egyptians, yet because himself was not an Aaron that could utter things nor a Jethro that could order them in such manner as was requisite, he was fain to crave the assistance of the one and willingly follow the directions of the other. There is the like diversity in the distribution of such gifts as are usually termed natural, so that he who is swiftest in running is not always the nimblest in wrestling. *Castor gaudet equis; ovo prognatus eodem, pugnis.* Every man hath his special talent given him from above and ought, therefore, to endeavor as much as in him lies to beautify and adorn that Sparta which is befallen him. For whosoever shall attempt further, he shall but manifest his weakness and reap deserved laughter for his recompense.

Antony, angling one day in the presence of Cleopatra, grew dis-

---

[u] *Covent:* a coven or conventicle of witches (probably here with a play on the word *convent,* of which it is an early form).

[v] *Herehence:* from this fact.

[w] *Several:* separate.

content because he caught not anything; but she, perceiving it, willed him (in smiling manner) to lay by the line as fitter for the Egyptians to handle than for him, whose hands were better taught how to subdue whole countries and conquer kingdoms than how to manage so mean an instrument.

Hence is it that to give out confidently of any man, and without exception, that he is skillful in many things is but secretly to insinuate that he is eminent in none. Man's judgment and capacity is bounded with very strict limits. And it is a proverb no less true than ancient that he which grips ˣ at most doth always lightly fasten upon least. Wherefore, whate'er he be that desires to advantage his friend by any commendations, let him instance his speeches always on particulars; besides, let him have regard to the quality of his person. Philip, hearing his son Alexander sing wonderful well at a certain banquet whereunto himself was invited, did not stick to upbraid him with his excellency therein, asking him if he were not ashamed to be so skillful in a faculty which was so far below him: thinking, it should seem, that the following of such things as were no less full of vanity than void of profit might argue a neglect of honorable enterprises and so fall out to be prejudicial to his then growing reputation rather than otherwise.

And indeed praises are no way graceful unless they be presented with the troupe and in the train of such as are proper to us. It is a kind of scorn and indignity to prize a man by such abilities as hold not some decent correspondency with his rank, as, likewise, by such as ought not to be the chief and principal in him. And this Demosthenes knew full well; who, having always been a professed enemy of the foresaid Philip, king of Macedon, and hearing that Aeschines and Philocrates highly commended him for that he was well spoken, fair of countenance, and could with ease swallow down the largest cups, did not stick to retort ʸ their speeches back to his disgrace, telling them that none of all those qualities were any way beseeming the person of a prince. For the one was rather the property of an advocate, the other of a woman, and the third of a sponge. So that praises, unless they be somewhat suitable to the estate and condition of the party whom we praise, they may prove to be burdensome unto him rather than otherwise; and, therefore, due consideration must be had of those things for which we go about to commend such as we affect before we do apply them, though of themselves and without extrinsical relation they be never so laudable. For that which

---

ˣ *Grips:* snatches.   ʸ *Retort:* twist, (re)turn.

is a beauty in one face, the right proportion of lineaments well considered, may be a blemish in another.

The fourth and last consideration is the end *why*. Men's actions cannot well be construed by a better rule than by the scope whereat they aim. The first appearances of things are very dangerous and deceitful; and, therefore, out of them it is impossible to extract a settled judgment of their sequel. The end alone is that which must intitule them by the attribute of good or evil. Wherefore, howsoever we are bound to give our neighbors' proceedings a charitable interpretation, yet in those things which may somewhat nearly concern ourselves, and wherein we discover not the drift of their designs, a wise distrust and slowness of belief is not prohibited. They are the sinews of wisdom; and whosoever is so nice and scrupulous as to refuse the benefit of them in this case is no way to be pitied if at length he reap the fruit of his superstitious folly.

Many there are that have honey in their mouths but wormwood in their hearts and, like unto our oarsmen, look one way and row another; which Alfonso, king of Naples, very wisely discovered in a certain gentleman that was a follower of his court. For having one day (with no better intent than to make the smoother passage for his calumnious detractions) exceedingly commended unto him the worth and good deserving of one whom he hated even unto death, "Surely," said the King to those that were about him, "this fellow goes about to lay some snare wherein to entrap his enemy." And herein was he nothing deceived; for shortly after (when, by reason of his former commendations, he thought his speeches might pass without suspicion either of envy or malice) he came unto him with a contrary note. Wherefore, it behooves every man to stand warily upon his guard — as well for other men's good as for his own. *Fronti nulla fides.* Harpies have virgins' faces but vultures' talents;[z] and the hyena, though it look like a friend, devours like a foe. This world is a theater, wherein nothing is represented unto us but in a personated[a] fashion. Look into Epeus's horse and, whatsoever the outside promise, you shall find in the bowels of it the destruction of Troy. It may well argue a generous spirit but, withal, a want of judgment in any man that on the sudden shall repose much trust and confidence in a reconciled friendship. The lion is a lion, though he shrink up his claws; and there be many who, notwithstanding they pretend a sincereness of love and affection in all their doings, want not a will to conceive a mischief if they had

---

[z] *Talents:* talons.

[a] *Personated:* disguised, under the mask of a persona.

means and opportunity to effect it. Tacitus, making a brief recapitulation of those causes which brought Agricola into disgrace with Domitian, among others, ranks these kind of persons as the chief. *Causa periculi,* saith he, *non crimen ullum, aut querela laesi cuiusquam: sed gloria viri; ac pessimum inimicorum genus, laudantes:* that which endangered him was not any crime in himself or complaint in others but the greatness of his worth and—the most dangerous kind of enemies—those that commended him. And indeed, in the courts of tyrants (where, as Tacitus reports, *honores pro crimine,* honorable achievements are accounted capital offenses, *et ob virtutes certissimum exitium,* and virtue is rewarded but with sure destruction) there needeth nothing to procure the downfall of a hated enemy but a cunning applauding of his once-suspected merits. *Sinistra illic erga eminentes interpretatio; nec minus periculum ex magna fama, quam ex mala.* It is the nature of those inhuman cannibals to grow jealous of such abilities as are reported to be so excellent in others and whereof they find so great a want and defect in themselves. Their own vicious disposition makes them apt and prone enough to interpret the nature and quality of men's desires by the greatness of their deserts.

Hence it was that Tigellinus, a man renowned under the government of Nero for devilish practices, that he might with the more ease and less suspicion effect the overthrow both of Plautus and Sulla, began (as our historian saith) *metum principis rimari,* to search the fears and jealousies of his sovereign. Which, after he had once found out, he did so cunningly work upon them that, with commending unto him their nobility together with their sufficiency, he brought him shortly after to be the bloody actor of that unhappy tragedy whereof himself had been the accursed author. But princes are not always to be burdened with the disastrous events of such proceedings. They do but as weaker patients, who, by the counsel and advice of their physician, do swallow oftentimes a deadly poison instead of a wholesome drug, themselves being altogether unable to discover the deceit when art and skill hath cunningly disguised it. In fenny regions, saith Varro, there are certain creatures bred of quantity so small that no eye can possibly discern them, which, being drawn with the very air through the nostrils into the brain and through the mouth into the body, are afterward the cause of many dangerous diseases. Thus in the head of an Italian, as Holerius writes, was engendered a scorpion—and that by his often smelling to the herb basil. For even so likewise may those little atomies [b] be snuffed up with the air. No marvel, then, if with the praises of an ill-affected mind there steal into the ears of princes

---

[b] *Atomies:* small particles, possibly microbes.

that which may poison and corrupt their judgment, moving their fancies to a causeless jealousy of the party praised.

All men are prone to believe those things that carry any show with them of securing either themselves or their estates, as likewise to distrust the contrary. And howsoever a Caesar or a Guisard,[e] who never understood the meaning of that word *fear*, out of the height of their undaunted courage might in a careless manner seem to neglect the true relations of intended treacheries, or (scorning, as it were, a strict inquiry) confront them only with an invincible spirit and say, *On n'oseroit*, they dare not attempt it; yet, where wisdom is used as an ingredient to qualify that which exceeds in either, they may be taken as sovereign preservatives, and that without fear of prejudice to a generous and virtuous mind.

But that we may not lose ourselves in things extravagant, let us draw somewhat nearer to our home. There are another kind of cunning underminers, who, when they see their adversaries or such as they affect[d] not advanced to any place of dignity the discharge whereof requires an extraordinary sufficiency, will not let,[e] as often as occasion is given, highly to commend their worth; but if we observe them, it is never lightly but with disabling them in the main. Thus hath subtlety been oftentimes the supplanter of true desert and crafty ignorance the deposer and dispossessor of an able virtue. Thus was Taurion wrought out of the government of Peloponnesus by Apelles, whilst he persuaded the King that he should do well to employ such worthy men as he about his person. Which consideration served but as a color to shadow his sinister[f] aims, for his direct and principal end was to invest a creature of his own with that charge and dignity. Wherefore it behooveth princes not to give too much credit to the informations that are given them, by others, of such as they employ in any charges of importance; but, for their own safety—and theirs— to have a certain experimental knowledge, of themselves.

The fencer sometimes cunningly takes his aim at the foot when his intent is to reach the head; and many men, by blaming the servant, have sought the overthrow of the master. Francis Sforza, being very desirous to remove both Troilus and Peter Brunorus, two leaders of no small account, from the service of Alfonso, king of Naples, framed a letter in the end whereof he willed that without delay they should put in execution the consultations that had passed betwixt them; which he conveyed in such manner as it fell into the hands of the King, who, understanding the contents, sent them thereupon as

[e] *Guisard:* the Duke of Guise (or a follower).
[d] *Affect:* favor, have affection for.
[e] *Let:* hesitate.
[f] *Sinister:* hurtful.

prisoners into Catalonia and by that means deprived himself of the benefit and use of two experienced commanders and gave his enemy that contentment which he looked for.

I could instance the truth of this assertion on many more examples, but I am called away by another kind of sinister praisers who are not absolutely led with any malicious intent to offend others but only with a desire to benefit themselves; and these are usually termed flatterers. Their end is altogether different from the former; and howsoever they prove to be no less hurtful than any of the rest, yet is it but by accident and as the ivy corrupts the wall which it embraceth. But because they are easily discerned by purer judgments and such as are not tainted with any humorous self-conceit, I will here leave both them and this discourse.

V.   Of Pains and Industry

THERE is no better mark of a true generous [a] disposition than to attempt those things which are hard to be achieved. The easiness of doing worketh oftentimes, in some, an utter distaste of what is to be done. *Ingrata quae tuta*—virtue admits not facility for her companion; the path she treads, it must be rough and thorny. No accidents have power to make her turn her back. Labor and pains are the only food wherewith she fats herself. The threats of tyrants, tortures, and torturers are so far from dismaying her that they serve rather to breathe a second life into her.

> *Duris ut ilex tonsa bipennibus*
> *nigrae feraci frondis in Algido,*
> *per damna, per caedes, ab ipso*
> *ducit opes, animumque ferro.*

> Like a topped elm, whom harder ax bereaves
> In Algid's fruitful soil of his black leaves,
> Through loss, through slaughter, and excessive pain,
> Even from her wounds she gathers strength again.

It is no part of hers to go creeping into a hollow cave or be beholding to a massy tomb for freeing her from the strokes of an incensed fortune. She breaks not off her intended purposes, neither doth she alter her propounded courses, whatsoever storm or tempest is like to happen.

> *Si fractus illabatur orbis,*
> *impavidam ferient ruinae.*

> Though the wide world, being broke, should chance to fall,
> Her may the ruins hurt, but not appall.

No, 't is in vulgar and adulterate spirits that the soul of motion is wholly derived from the likelihood of action. *Avida est periculi virtus:* true noble dispositions cannot relish any enterprise further than it is seasoned with difficulties and dangers. Edward III of England, understanding on what nice terms the life of the Black Prince, his son, did stand when at the town of Crécy (by reason of the great advantage the French had of him, both in multitude of men

[a] *Generous:* virtuously noble.

and commodiousness of place) he was in all men's judgments accounted but as matter out of whose ruins his enemies might frame unto themselves a glorious victory, and fearing lest by sending fresh supplies he might hap to derogate from his transcending reputation, returns him no better comfort than this short answer could afford him: that "either he must win the field or lose his life; himself would remain a witness of his valor, ready to second what he had begun when need required." This unexpected message, in so great a necessity, from a father, was so far from dismaying him as that it rather added vigor to his strength. So that, considering with himself if he overcame his glory would be the more, if he were overcome it could not be much less, he hastens to the field, gives the onset, and ennobles both the day and place by the fall of thirty thousand of his adversaries, fifteen hundred of them being earls, barons, and gentlemen of note; which, like a dangerous fever, did so shake every particular member of the realm of France as that long time after it lay bedrid of that overthrow.

And indeed the despair of conquering—yea, and sometimes the fear of being conquered—hath to many armies been the only means by which they have obtained what they little sought for. Witness the first just [b] battle which the Romans fought against Hannibal under the conduct of Sempronius the Consul, in which a troop of well-nigh ten thousand footmen were seized on the sudden with such an affright that, not seeing which way else they might make passage for their fainting baseness, they cast themselves athwart one of the thickest ranks of their opposites, which they pierced with a wonderful fury, to the great amazement and discomfiture of the Carthaginians. But (alas!) 't was but a shameful and dishonorable flight, bought at the same price they might have done a glorious and renowned victory.

Julius Caesar made known unto the world the singular proof of his valor when, being with his cohorts to pass the River Rubicon, which was the utmost bound and limit of his province, and having weighed with himself the danger that attended so high an enterprise (whereas peace and safety offered to kiss his feet upon the alteration of his proceedings), he sets up his rest,[e] throws the dice, and in a desperate resolution cries, "Have at all!"—intending (it should seem), rather than he would miss the purchase [d] of his aims, to polish and fashion out his then roughhewn fortune with the edge of his subduing sword and to make way for his ambitious hopes, through fields of

---

[b] *Just:* regular.

[e] *Sets up his rest:* takes his position.

[d] *Purchase:* attainment.

iron and streams of blood, to that imperial dignity wherewith in the end he saw himself most honorably possessed.

That virtue is but weak and ill deserves the grace and credit of so high a style (being of itself unable to give life to any heroical design) that cannot with a fixed countenance outstare the threatening eye of danger and make day for them through all opposed discouragements whatsoever. Pelopidas, being advertised that Alexander came against him with a far greater army than his, was nothing moved therewith but answered presently, "So much the better; we shall subdue the more." The Lacedaemonians were never wont to ask, πόσοι εἰσί, "How many are our enemies?" but ποῦ εἰσι, "Where be they?"—knowing their valor to be of so sound and strong a temper as could not any way be daunted with advantages. And this same warlike humor, which was naturally bred in them, hath upon urgent necessity been found in many.

It is an error, therefore, and an oversight which in a skillful commander merits no excuse, to deprive his enemies of all means and opportunity of flight, enforcing them to exercise the strength of their hands when their own baseness would willingly, perhaps, have embraced any occasion that might have put in use the swiftness of their heels. It was Scipio's opinion, *viam hostibus, qua fugiant, muniendam.* For indeed there is nothing so hard to be withstood as armed fear. Those of Gaunt, perceiving Lewis, earl of Flanders, unwilling at all hands to receive them again into his favor unless with halters about their necks they would ask pardon of him for their past offense, assembled themselves together to the number of five thousand, went and confronted his army of forty thousand, overcame it, and freed themselves wholly from that despotical kind of government to which before (upon indifferent terms) they offered to submit both themselves and theirs.

The Earl of Foix, who (in less than three months, showing himself a captain when he was scarce a soldier) had with such valor and celerity ennobled his name by so many victories obtained in Italy against the Spaniards, in the year 1512 was slain by a troop of their infantry whilst he strove to perfect his victory, being not able to endure that, all the rest being scattered and discomfited, it alone should depart the field as triumphant and with her ranks unbroken and unsevered.

It is not good, therefore, for any man to presume too much upon his fortune. *Vitrea est: tunc cum splendet, frangitur.* And, as the French proverb doth testify, *Par trop presser l'anguille, on la perd:* He that grips an eel too hard is in danger to lose it. Many have had the victory snatched, as it were, out of their jaws and themselves become the dishonorable prize of whom they had erst ° most honorably surprised, for not making a golden bridge for the retiring forces of their enemy to pass over. So great a power hath necessity to rouse up the drowsy courages of men and to inflame their paler livers with a resolution to sell their lives at as high a rate as possibly they can rather than offer themselves gratis and, unrevenged, to be like sheep slaughtered by the fury of their adversary. *Una salus victis, nullam sperare salutem.* What greater motives or encouragements could have been used to support the weakness of a yielding army than those which Vectius applied to his soldiers when he perceived them to faint under the furious encounter of the Romans? "What!" saith he, "Are you desirous to see your houses, your wives, your parents, and your children? Follow me. There are no walls nor ramparts to interrupt your passage. Arms only are opposed to arms. Your valor doth altogether equal theirs; but now necessity gives you the upper hand of them." And, indeed, where have we seen greater valiancy than in those desperate troops that, like Catiline's seditious followers, *divitias, decus, gloriam, libertatem, atque patriam, in dextris portarunt,* carried their wealth, their honor, their freedom, and their country in their hands? Witness those several inundations of warlike legions which the populous fruitfulness of Scythia and the rest of those colder climates in former times have afforded; who, wanting place to inhabit in at home, have sought abroad and by virtue of their swords entitled themselves in most of the chiefest parts of Christendom, disseizing ᶠ the right owners and making themselves frank tenants ᵍ of their kingdoms and possessions, both in law and deed.

The proof hereof we may see in the Longobards, who, being driven by want to forsake their native soil (which was an island in the Almain Sea ʰ called Scandinavia), entered into Italy, made themselves absolute lords of Gallia Cisalpina, and styled it afterward in remembrance of their so-won conquest by the name of Lombardy; as likewise in the Huns and Garians, who, under the ensigns of that victorious and so-renowned Attila, their king, after his expulsion out of the territories of France, possessed themselves with the whole country of Pannonia and, by a compound name, called it Hungaria. And that we may draw a little nearer to our own home, the Normans (a people gathered together not only from Denmark but from Suedland ¹ and other septentrional countries there adjoining) took

° *Erst:* at first.
ᶠ *Disseizing:* ousting.
ᵍ *Frank tenants:* freeholders.

ʰ *Almain Sea:* German Sea. It is not clear whether the North Sea or the Baltic is intended.
¹ *Suedland:* Sweden.

such sure footing in Neustria (by them now Normandy) during the time that Charles, surnamed the Gross, commanded it that he was fain—considering he could not do otherwise—to grant it them, conditionally they would acknowledge themselves ever after liege homagers for it to the crown of France.

Virtue is never in her proper element but when death and danger seem to have hemmed her in on every side; she scorns the prize whose purchase requires not the use of all her nerves. *Imperia dura tolle, quid virtus erit?* saith the Tragic. *Inveniet viam, aut faciet:* wheresoever she become,[1] she will either find a way or make one. No calamity is of power sufficient to bring her under. This majesty alone knows what it is to suffer check; it can neither be elevated nor dejected. Her greatness, like the highest heavens, is always firm and without clouds. Are you desirous to see her? You shall find her in the temple, in the market, in the court; you shall find her standing at a breach or scaling of a wall, her garments dusty, her countenance all tanned, and her hands as hard as iron. Wherefore, whosoever is possessed with her, let him prepare himself for dangerous assaults.

The gladiator thinks it a disgrace to see himself composed[k] with one either in strength or skill inferior to himself, knowing (as it is indeed) the victory cannot be glorious which is not dangerous. *Bellum cum captivis, et foeminis, gerere non possum: Armatus sit oportet, quem oderim,* said Alexander. And at the games of Olympus he would not run unless he might have kings for his competitors in the pursuit of the victory.

Paulus Aemilius, by reason of the base and fearful speeches that issued out of the mouth of Perseus after his captivity, thought himself nothing honored by the overthrow of so faint and cowardly a foe.

> *In tauros ruunt Lybici leones:*
> *non sunt papilionibus molesti.*
>
> Against stout bulls the Lybian lions hie:
> And ne'er molest the weaker butterfly.

The like doth Fortune. *Fortissimos sibi pares quaerit,* she looks out the strongest for her antagonists; the rest she passeth over with disdain.

> *Transit tutos Fortuna sinus:*
> *medioque rates quaerit in alto,*
> *quarum feriunt suppara nubes.*

Wherefore, whosoever he be whose happiness was never shaken with any rough encounter may rest assured that she sees nothing in him

[1] *Become:* come.   [k] *Composed:* matched.

able to sustain it, so that he need never fear her. His own baseness doth sufficiently secure him.

Servantur magnis isti cervicibus ungues;
nec gaudet tenui sanguine tanta sitis.

She seeks a Mutius when she is armed with fire and glories in his virtue that (like Fabricius) can show himself an Atlas against her under the heavy burden of poverty, or that can with Rutilius confront her in the force of banishment, or with Regulus outstare her in the horrible aspect[1] of hellbred tortures. Give her a Socrates for her adversary, that can swallow poison with as unchanged a countenance as he would a delightful potion; or a Cato, that dares challenge the field of Death and hold him at hard play with his own weapons, and then she is pleased. An easy-yielding spirit she esteems a subject too unworthy for her ambition to work upon. Wherefore, whosoever shall at all times have been so pampered with prosperity as that he never felt the heavy hand of affliction, let him not glory in the mildness of his stars, attributing that peaceable and calm tranquillity to the goodness of God toward him; for this were but to flatter himself in an erroneous opinion. Let him rather take notice of his own defects and be assured that he is altogether destitute of that heroical and generous heat that should enable him to make head against adversity, and is therefore purposely passed over. Had he been a Samson, many thousand Philistines should have bent the force of their malicious minds against him; or had he been a David, a lion should have been sent to try him and a giant to provoke him.

Did the all-seeing Eye of Heaven discern but the least spark of virtue in any, He would not suffer it to lie buried under the embers of a secure and uncontrolled estate; some stormy accident or other should have served for wind to kindle it and make it blaze forth to the sight of the whole world. Had not Rutilius been wronged, his innocency had ne'er been known. *Illustrat fortuna aliquos, dum vexat:* cross[m] accidents are oftentimes the publishers of a concealed virtue. Zeno knew himself fitter for a philosopher than a merchant; yet, seeing the life he led was both pleasant and profitable, he was loath to give it over to embrace the other; but, having understood that the ships he had at sea (being very richly laden and upon return) were cast away, he did then acknowledge a superior providence and out of a careless[n] apprehension (it should seem) of so great a loss tells Fortune "she did well to range him to the gown and to the study of philosophy." *Languet per inertiam saginata virtus:* the edge of

---

[1] *Aspect:* looking-on.

[m] *Cross:* adverse.

[n] *Careless:* unperturbed.

industry is clean abated by the force of pleasure and security. It is never busied but when some urgent inconvenience doth find it work.

After that° man had forfeited those fair possessions in which his Lord and Maker (out of the abundance of His fatherly love) had placed him and was enforced thereby, with his posterity, to shift for himself in so vast and desolate a wilderness as the world was then, how quickly sundry arts mechanical, which otherwise perhaps had ne'er been heard of, were found out, who can be ignorant? *Want* was their mother, howsoever *Plenty* afterward fell out to be their nurse. Yea, the like may be likewise seen in creatures of an inferior nature; and hence is that of the satirist:

> *Quis expedivit psittaco suum* χαῖρε,
> *picasque docuit nostra verba conari?*

> Where did the parrot learn "Good morrow, Sir" to cry,
> Or who the chattering pies did teach our words to prove
> and try?

The reason whereof is by himself set down in the verses following:

> *Magister artis, ingenique largitor,*
> *venter, negatas artifex sequi voces.*

> That which doth art impart and wit bestow,
> The belly, skilled voices denied to know.

"This was it that brought them to it," saith he. But there are many other respects sufficient of themselves, without the aid of this, to work the like effect in man; as hope of gain, fear of danger, and suchlike. Yet there be many of so effeminate and soft a disposition that they are ready to swoon at the very first alarm of any sinister and disastrous accident and, whereas they should employ themselves in seeking to redress what they cannot avoid, stand gazing one at another in the greatest dangers, expecting aid from the immortal gods but not remembering that (as the Grecian proverb saith) they must σὺν Ἀθηνᾷ καὶ χεῖρα κινεῖν, add their own industry to the invocation of divine assistance and not be followers of that rustic in the apologue who, when his cart was laid fast up in the mire, stood still and looked upon it, desiring Hercules by his celestial power to help him out with it; who, being present, bade him put his own hand to the wheel, prick forward his oxen, and so call upon God. For, as Cato said in his answer to Julius Caesar, *non votis, nec suppliciis muliebribus, deorum auxilia parantur:* God's help is not gotten only by wishes, prayers, and womanish supplications. It is by watching, by laboring,

---

° *After that:* after.

and taking good advice that matters gain a prosperous and true success. *Ubi socordiae, atque ignaviae te tradideris, nequicquam Deos implores: irati, infestique sunt:* if thou give thyself over to sluggishness and sloth, in vain dost thou call upon Him; He is displeased and offended with thee. The clay, unless it be thoroughly wrought, cannot possibly receive the form or fashion of a pot. Ceres, when she showed Triptolemus the use of corn, she gave him this aviso [p] withal: Ἄν μὴ καθαρῆς, καὶ ἀλέσῃς, οὐ μὴ φάγῃς, unless thou cleanse and grind it thou canst never eat it—insinuating (as it were) thereby that no man could possibly attain anything to the purchase whereof he added not his own industry.

Charles the Emperor bore for an impresa [q] the sign Capricorn, the constellation under which he was born, and the word [r] that gave it life was *Fidem fati virtute sequemur,* our virtue shall pursue that which our fate hath promised, a motto fitting the person of so noble and victorious a prince. For in every action it is God that gives the matter; but we are they that must second Him in the giving of it form. He doth nothing that concerns us without us, no, not so much as save us. *Dii laboribus omnia vendunt.* Without pains and industry nothing can be got; and with it, most things may: *et labor ingenium miseris dedit.*

Demosthenes had many imperfections which in an orator were much unseemly. To redress them, therefore (saith Valerius), *praeliatus est contra rerum naturam,* he made open war against nature and went his way at length with triumphant conquest, having by the obstinacy of his own mind mastered the malignity of hers. Whereupon it was rumored that his mother had brought forth one Demosthenes and industry another. Wherefore, though it be somewhat troublesome to take pains, yet once learn of a Mimic, *Feras quod laedit, ut quod prodest, perferas.* Bear that which doth a little displease thee, that thou mayest bear away that which will much profit thee. *Fortiter malum qui patitur,* saith the Comic, *post potitur bonum:* sour accidents are seasoned with sweet events, and stormy tempests are often followed with quiet calms. And this was, though obscurely, yet most elegantly set out by Homer in that herb moly, to which he attributes a black root and a white flower: signifying the troublesomeness of labor by the one, by which that tranquillity of mind is obtained which is the reward of an absolute virtue, expressed in the other.

---

[p] *Aviso:* instruction, warning.   [r] *Word: mot,* motto, inscription.
[q] *Impresa:* device, badge.

VI. *Cautions in Friendship*

IT WAS not without reason that Anacharsis, when he slept, was always wont to hold his right hand on his mouth and his left hand on his natural parts, as if one had needed a far stronger restraint than the other. For there are many men of such a temper that they can with greater patience endure to carry burning coals in their breasts than secrets; and hence is it that those things, oftentimes, which are whispered in the ear are presently after published * in the market.

There are few that can say, and say truly, as that Grecian of former times did, who, being told that his breath did smell, answered that it was by reason of the many secrets which had a long time lain rotting and putrifying within him. Nay, many are never quiet till they have unburdened their bosoms of what they go with—and that, oftentimes, without any respect or choice—upon the first they haply encounter, though the matter concern either themselves or their friends never so nearly; but (alas!) in the end they reap the fruit of their unadvised folly. It is an ancient saying, but very true,

> The good or ill hap in all a man's life,
> Is the good or ill choice of a friend or a wife.

Wherein the clearest and best-discerning judgments may easily be deceived. Many have honey in their mouths but a razor at their girdles; and few do use to carry a map of their minds engraven in their foreheads. *Multis simulationum involucris,* saith the Orator, *tegitur, et quasi velis quibusdam obtenditur uniuscuiusque natura. Frons, oculi, vultus persaepe mentiuntur; oratio saepissime.* Dissimulation hath set her foot upon the throat of simplicity; and howsoever it be good, yet is it dangerous to measure others by our own innocency. The Marquis of Pescara was wont (as Guicciardini reports) to draw men into dangerous practices and afterward, by his duplicity and double-dealing, to discover them himself, making other men's offenses the first step to his own greatness.

"It was not mine enemy," saith the kingly prophet, "that disgraced me, for then I could have borne it. Neither did he that hated me

* *Published:* openly revealed.

extol[b] himself against me, for then would I have hid me from him; but thou, a man whom I prized as dearly as myself, my guide and my familiar,[c] who[d] sweetened our secrets by imparting them together and went in each other's company to the house of the Lord."

As who should say, " 'T was not my open enemy nor my known adversary that wronged me, but he whose friendship I esteemed, not only for worldly respects but likewise for the zealous and religious affection which he seemed to nourish in his bowels toward the house of the Lord—'t was he, 't was he that deceived me." Hence was it that Antigonus, in his prayers, was wont to desire the gods they would defend him against his friends. And being demanded why not rather against his enemies, "From them," saith he, "that openly profess hostility I can easily beware; but from those that veil a wrinkled heart under a smiling countenance I stand in need of divine protection." And indeed fearful distrust secures us from the malice of the one, but fearless confidence betrays us to the treacheries of the other. Who but our Saviour Christ could have discovered the secret practices of Judas, considering how forward he was to kiss Him and likewise to perform all other ceremonious offices of love that were required?

Ave[e] is uttered oftentimes by some who, if their tongues should not belie their hearts, *cave*[f] would sound truest in their mouths. Joab takes Amasa by the beard to kiss him, when he intends to kill him; and indeed, as the poet witnesseth, *Tuta, frequensque via est, per amici fallere nomen.* It is a safe and common way, by friendship to deceive. And Socrates thereupon exclaimeth, φίλοι, οὐδεὶς φίλος: friends, there is not any man a friend; meaning such a one as the Comic speaketh of, *cui tuam rem cum credideris, sine omni cura dormias,* to whom, when thou hast committed any business that concerns thyself, thou needst not interrupt thy own sleep with careful[g] thinking on it. Some such there are, but not in every soil. They must be sought for amongst liberal arts, amongst honest and virtuous offices, amongst painful and industrious exercises; thy sumptuous entertainment affords them not.

Quae inter pocula contrahitur amicitia, saith Seneca, *vitrea est, et fragilis:* cup friendship is of too brittle and glassy a substance to continue long.

> *Hunc quem coena tibi, quem mensa paravit amicum,*
> *esse putas fidae pectus amicitiae?*
> *Aprum amat, et mullos, et sumen, et ostrea, non te;*
> *tam bene si coenem, noster amicus eris.*

---

[b] *Extol:* lit., raise up.

[c] *Familiar:* intimate, bosom companion.

[d] *Who:* (we) who.

[e] *Ave:* L., hail.

[f] *Cave:* L., beware.

[g] *Careful:* concerned, full of care.

Whom plenteous meals and tables make thy friend,
Think'st thou his love can have a trusty end?
He likes thy dainty cates,[h] he likes not thee:
Make me such cheer, and thou my friend shalt be.

These are like the swallow, that changeth her habitation with the
season and when comfort faileth her in one place repaireth presently
to another. And such a one was Crotto's mouse: for, while he was in
prosperity, it fed continually with him; but his house being set on
fire, it fled immediately from him. Whereupon he took occasion to
frame this distich, not so much to denote the ungratefulness of so
imperfect and base a creature as the mutability and fleeting disposition
of trencher amity: [i]

> *Vixisti mecum, Fortuna matre; noverca,*
>   *me fugis: at poteras aequa, et iniqua pati.*

> Thou wast content to live with me while Fortune was a mother;
> When she a cruel stepdame grew, thou left'st me for another.
> But if so thou a creature vile and thankless hadst not been,
> Thou wouldst not have denied to share the trouble I was in.

He therefore (saith Seneca) doth mainly [j] err, *qui amicum in atrio
quaerit, in convivio probat,* that seeks a friend in the court and, without further trial, confirms him in the cup. It is a preposterous order
first to trust and afterward to judge; a methodical proceeding would
require an inverted course. We are to deliberate of all things with our
friend—but first, of our friend himself. There is no man so simple
but, before he intend to make use of a new vessel, trieth by the
infusion of water whether it be well bound and fit to contain more
precious liquor, or no. Alcibiades conveyed the image of a man into
the darkest part of his house; and, thither having brought his friends,
one by one, told them he had slain a man and withal desired that by
their aid and counsel he might be so assisted as that the murder might
be concealed. All of them deny to be partakers with him in so great a
fact.[k] Only Callias willingly condescends to satisfy his demands by
doing him the best offices which in that case he possibly could, being
as yet altogether ignorant of the verity of the thing. Whereupon he
made no difficulty to embrace him ever after as his bosom friend and
confidently to impart unto him the utmost and inmost of his secrets;
yet, in those things by which his life might become questionable, he
would not trust his mother for fear she might mistake the black bean
for the white. Wherefore, every man ought to be somewhat nice and

[h] *Cates:* foods.
[i] *Trencher amity:* parasitic friendship.
[j] *Mainly:* strongly, greatly.

[k] *Fact:* deed (generally) or crime (as here).

scrupulous in this kind and not impart anything that may import[1] either himself or his friend but with sufficient caution. For, as the Italian proverb witnesseth,

Servo d'altrui si fà,
Chi dice il suo secreto a chi no'l sà.

He makes himself a servile wretch to others evermore,
That tells his secrets unto such as knew them not before.

Unity never passeth his bounds but remaineth in itself always one and is therefore called Monas; but the binary number is indefinite and the beginning of divorce because, in doubling the unity, it turns into plurality.

A word, whilst it remains in him that first knew it, is secret; but when it comes to another, it begins to have the name of a common report. And howsoever the Florentine be of opinion that with *one* anything may be spoken, because the affirmation of the one, in case of detection, is no more available than the negation of the other—provided, always, he have not suffered himself to be led by the persuasions of any (as Plautinus was by Saturninus the Tribune) to commit any part of his mind to writing, whereby his own hand afterward may be made the only means to convince[m] him—yet would I willingly give no assent unto him. For howsoever it may seem for the faciliting[n] of treacherous and disloyal practices a necessary axiom, by force whereof the lewd[o] conspirator being emboldened doth freely open himself to such as he is persuaded may be easily drawn to second his mischievous attempts, knowing that if his expectation should chance to fail him in anyone he keeps himself, notwithstanding, out of the danger and compass of the law, whose equity pronounceth not the sentence of death against any man without a just and lawful conviction—which in this case, considering the many disordered passions wherewith men are led to scandalize each other, cannot be had (witness those several duels and combats which heretofore, both in this kingdom and divers others, have been assigned by princes for the avoiding of such differences, the stain of infamy and dishonor resting always—how justly, oftentimes, God knows!—with the party vanquished, whether plaintiff or defendant)—yet for the concealing of honest counsels it is very hurtful and dangerous. I call honest counsels such as concern the public good of my prince or the private good of my friend; which, indeed, is so far forth to be accounted good as it stands with the good, or at least not against the good, of my supreme

[1] *Import:* gravely concern, be important to.
[m] *Convince:* convict.
[n] *Faciliting:* rendering easy.
[o] *Lewd:* base, ignorant.

sovereign, to whom, by a threefold law (to wit, divine, natural, and civil) I am bound to purchase[p] with my best endeavors all the good and safety that I can. I owe all faith and loyalty to both; and am, as a friend, to satisfy with all alacrity the desires of the one, so far forth as they impugn not the allegiance which, as a subject, I am to render to the other.

But as I would not willingly nourish a serpent in my bosom which in the end should devour me, so on the other side I would not be too strict and rigorous a censurer of his designs, lest by my rash and scandalous delations[q] I brand both myself and him with an opprobrious mark of everlasting ignominy, and that that of the satirist may not be truly said of me, *Stoicus occidit Baream delator amicum.*

Histories abound with examples of this kind; but the powerful hand of heaven hath frustrated the ambitious hopes of their effected villainy and, whereas they expected honor and promotion, hath justly requited them with never-dying shame and utter confusion. But because a tragical catastrophe[r] to a friendly discourse[s] might seem (peradventure) somewhat ominous, I will stretch the thread of my subject to a further length.

There are some that fashion themselves to nothing more than how to become speculative[t] into another, to the end to know how to work him, or wind him, or govern him; but this proceedeth from a heart that is double and cloven and not entire and ingenuous. And as in friendship it argues a great defect and want of integrity, so likewise toward some persons, a defect of duty; and such as please themselves in these barbarous speculations are to be no better accounted than the very gangrenes and cankerworms of human society.

Scire volunt secreta domus, atque inde timeri.

They seek the secrets of our house to know,
That thence in us some fear of them might grow.

And indeed if they chance to come where dissolution is the steward of a disordered family, their hopes fly right to their sinister aim; they gin[u] to be beloved, but (alas!) that love is but the spurious and adulterate issue of a conscious and guilty fear:

Carus erit Verri, qui Verrem tempore quo vult
accusare potest.

To him no kindness Verres will refuse
That, when he please, can Verres' life accuse.

[p] *Purchase:* secure.
[q] *Delations:* accusations, tale-bearing.
[r] *Tragical catastrophe:* unpleasant ending.
[s] *Friendly discourse:* discourse on friendship.
[t] *Speculative:* curiously inquisitive.
[u] *Gin:* begin.

Hence was it that Tigellinus (as our historian witnesseth), to add the better strength to his transcending fortune, endeavored as much as in him lay, *principem sibi societate scelerum obstringere,* to endear the prince unto himself by making him a partner in his villainies; which, according to his brutish expectation, he cunningly accomplished. But those that, like Agesilaus (who, in traveling, took up his lodging always in the temples, to the intent that men and gods might see into his actions) or like Julius Drusus, who, when certain masons had offered him for three thousand crowns so to contrive his house as that his neighbors should no longer enjoy that open prospect into it which they had, "I will give you," saith he, "six thousand, and frame it so that they may look into it on every side"—those, I say, that like these men do all things *tanquam spectet aliquis,* as if they had a Cato in their bosom that did continually behold them, cannot easily be touched or tainted with the noisome corruption of such dangerous and hurtful flies. Nor, likewise, those that shall but diligently observe the difference between a star and a meteor, a true friend and a false: The one is curious and inquisitive to learn more than he should; the other is afraid to know more than he would, following therein the example of Philippides, who, when Lysimachus demanded of him what of so many things that were his he should communicate unto him, "Whatsoever it shall please you, sir," answered he, πλὴν τῶν ἀπορρήτων, "so it be not of your secrets"—distrusting (it should seem) his own imperfection for the concealing them, or knowing (as it is indeed) *arduum nimis esse meruisse principis secretum, ubi si quid cognoscitur, prodi vel ab alio formidatur.* A prying eye, a listening ear, and a prating tongue are all birds of one wing and by reason thereof seldomtimes found separated one from another.

For the better avoiding, therefore, of such dangerous inconveniences as the commerce and society of such intemperate persons might haply bring with it, it would not be much amiss secretly to examine what his carriage hath been toward others, his associates in former times; and thereafter, as we find it, to frame a settled resolution in ourselves: if faulty, absolutely to avoid him; if otherwise, confidently to embrace him. For to distrust without a cause is very dangerous: I do but teach another to deceive by fearing overmuch myself to be deceived. This was it which did annihilate the practices[v] of peace between Charles V and Francis, king of France, in the year 1528. For having (in a manner) accorded all their differences, the question only was, which of them both did best deserve to be trusted. Caesar[w] gave

---

[v] *Practices:* tentatives, negotiations.   [w] *Caesar:* the emperor.

out he might not safely trust him that had once deceived him; whereunto the orators of France did wittily reply that the more he did
pretend himself to have been deceived by the King their master, the
more might the King their master imagine he should be deceived by
him.

Hence was it that Otho, after the overthrow of Galba, having
delivered Celsus *per speciem vinculorum,* under the color of severer
punishment, from the fury of his followers *non quasi ignosceret,* not
by way of pardon (for he would not seem to tax him of any crime)
but lest being an enemy, *metum reconciliationis adhiberet,* the sincereness of his reconcilement might any way prove questionable, he
ranked him presently amongst his dearest friends and made him,
withal, a special commander in his afterwars, in which he behaved
himself as loyally as ever he had done in the employments of his
formerly deposed sovereign. Upon the good event of which example
Louis XII did peradventure ground that memorable answer wherewith he nipped the bloody instigations of those parasites that, after he
was come unto the crown by the decease of Charles VIII, did animate
him to vengeance against Louis de La Trémoille, who, during the
reign of that aforesaid prince had in the battle of Saint Aubin overthrown his army and taken him. "It is not fit," said he, "a King of
France should marry ˣ the quarrels of a Duke of Orléans. If he served
faithfully the King his master against me, who then was but Duke of
Orléans, it is not to be feared but he will do the like for me hence-
forward, who now am King of France." But where we find a defect
of loyalty in any toward others, it is not safe to hazard ourselves upon
the hope of their amendment toward us:

> *vetabo, qui Cereris sacrum*
> *vulgarit arcanae, sub iisdem*
> *Sit trabibus, fragilemque mecum*
> *solvat faselum.*

It is true that many are content to take the benefit and advantage of
a treacherous subject against his master in cases of hostility but never
love to put him in trust with anything that concerns themselves; or,
if they do, it is with more than Juno's jealousy or Argus' observation.

Charles V, during the difference between the Imperials ʸ and the
French, was willing to make what use he could of the disloyal service
of the Duke of Bourbon against his lord and master, Francis I; but
howsoever he loved his actions, he never liked his person. His in-
fidelity had purchased him the hatred and dislike of all men. For after

ˣ *Marry:* assume, take as his own.   ʸ *Imperials:* followers of the emperor
(Charles V).

his arrival to the emperor's court, Caesar, having entertained him with all the friendly demonstrations that were possible, sent afterward to desire the house of one of his nobles for to lodge him in; who answered the messenger, with a Castilian courage, that he could not but satisfy His Majesty's demand. "But let him know," said he, "that Bourbon shall no sooner be gone out of it but I will burn it as being infected with his infamy and thereby made unfit for men of honor to inhabit in."

Virtue and vice are utter opposites; and howsoever many several accidents and occasions may bring them to some complemental interview, yet is it altogether impossible to establish a true and perfect league of amity betwixt them. There can be no true fellowship between light and darkness, between Christ and Belial, St. Michael and the Serpent. Where there is a difference, therefore, in religion, there is always lightly a discordancy in affection. And hence hath risen that deadly hatred between the pagan and the Christian and, among Christians, between Catholic and Protestant, the Protestant and the Puritan, the Puritan and others, whilst everyone contends to justify the soundness and sincereness of his own. But the Lord of heaven, the Unity of Trinity, unite their hearts and minds together in the bonds of charity and grant that the Church may not always speak in a confounded dialect to the distraction of weaker ignorance, who is not able (among so many divided cries) to distinguish the voice of her lawful Shepherd. The Church of Sardis gives out that she alone doth live, and that of Laodicea that she alone doth see, that she alone is clothed; whereas the Holy One of Holy Ones pronounceth of the one that she is dead, and of the other that she is both blind and naked.

But that I may not seem to gather sweetness from every flower, wandering too far from my propounded course, there can be lightly no great affection between those that are of one profession, whether it be liberal * or mechanical.ª *Figulus figulo* saith the proverb. There can be nothing but envy and emulation between those that run at one and the same goal, whatsoever (whether gain or honor) be the proclaimed prize of their contention. The one seeketh continually to supplant the other for his own advantage.

> *Hectora Priamidem animosum, atque inter Achillem*
> *ira fuit capitalis, ut ultima divideret mors:*
> *non aliam ob causam, nisi quod virtus in utroque*
> *summa fuit.*

So likewise where there is a disproportion either in means or minds,

---

* *Liberal:* pertaining to the humanities.   ª *Mechanical:* pertaining to technics.

there can be no other friendship than that microphily ᵇ which Plato had with Dionysius the Tyrant. *Quid enim communicabit olla ad cacabum?* Wherein can the earthen pipkin benefit the brazen pot? Which considered, the emperor had reason, when word was brought him that a certain cardinal of the court of Rome who beforetimes had much affected him was advanced newly to the popedom, to say that of a trusty friend, being a cardinal, he would become a deadly enemy, being a pope. And indeed he did prognosticate aright; for it fell out according to his expectation. Wherefore, if thou wouldst not be deceived, τὸν κατὰ σαυτὸν ἔλα, take one whose greatness may not overawe thee; and so, when thou standest in need of his assistance, thou shalt not fear that comfortless reply which Abraham gave to Dives in his torments: *Nimis magnus est hiatus inter te, et nos,* there is too great a distance between us and thee.

Last of all, there can be no safe or settled conversation ᶜ with him who, as the poet saith,

> *absentem rodit amicum:*
> *aut non defendit alio culpante: solutos*
> *qui captat risus hominum, famamque dicacis:*
> *fingere qui non visa potest: commissa tacere*
> *qui nequit.*

Gnaws, like a cur, upon his absent friend,
Or from detraction doth him not defend;
Affects profused laughter at a feast,
And would be famous for some biting jest;
Can feign the things which he did never see,
But not conceal ought that he knows from thee.

Hic niger est, he carries hay in his horn; and therefore *hunc tu Romane caveto,* avoid his company if thou respect thine own safety.

ᵇ *Microphily:* friendship of a lesser man with a greater (i.e., of higher rank).

ᶜ *Conversation:* social living.

VII. Of Three Things Prejudicial to Secrecy

H E THAT hath made his bosom *tanquam secretorum aerarium,*
as it were, the storehouse or exchequer of his friend's secrets,
must diligently take heed of three things, not suffering himself in any
case to be vanquished by any of them: and these are wine, women,
and anger.

As for the first, Momus, having taken a general survey of those
infinite deceits which continually were bred and fostered in the heart
of man, did most impiously tax his maker and creator of indiscretion,
in that he made not some window open into his bosom by which the
visual beams of our external sense, not meeting with an impenetrable
object, might easily discover what was done within. But we that know
the works of God to be every way so absolute that, as the poet saith,

> *non ullum carpere Livor*
> *possit opus Domini,*

will with Plutarch answer him that we need not the profane invention
of his fantastical imagination to make known unto us the darker
minds and meanings one of another. "Wine," saith he, "doth in a most
abundant manner disclose our inward thoughts and unbare us of that
disguised and personated habit* under which we are accustomed to
march." The wiser sort of princes, therefore, according to that verse
of Horace, are reported

> *multis urgere culullis,*
> *et torquere mero, quem perspexisse laborant,*
> *an sit amicitia dignus.*

And indeed the nature and disposition of man doth never lightly
(as a certain author wittily affirms) open and discover itself at full but
either in *oculis, loculis,* or *poculis.*

One of the chiefest causes of the overthrow of Claudius was a word
which unadvisedly slipped from him in his drunkenness: to wit,
ut conjugum flagitia ferret, dein puniret, that for a while he would
bear with the intemperancies of his wife, but in the end he would
severely punish them; which Agrippina fearing as fatal to herself went
presently about, for the better preventing of her own end, to hasten

---

* *Personated habit:* assumed costume.

his. And indeed *il vino non ha timone:* wine, saith the Italian, hath no stern. Wherefore, he that tastes of it beyond the cup of pleasure puts himself in exceeding great danger of suffering shipwreck, considering how many are the envious rocks and unsatiable quicksands that desire nothing more than to split such vessels in sunder, that they may see what merchandise the inward bulk contains. Yea, it hath been the practice of sundry nations (and that in the persons of ambassadors) under a pretense of drinking healths to their sovereign, first to drown their wisdom in their Grecian cups, that afterward they might draw from them that which by means of it was before kept secret to themselves. And surely few, or none, have ever failed in this their enterprise unless it were by overhastily striving to effect that which they so earnestly desired; it having then befallen them as it did to Aesop's woman who gave her hen more meat to make her lay more eggs—but it fell out otherwise: for, through extreme fatness, she surceased *ᵇ* from laying any. And no marvel the danger should be so eminent. For wit is not then any longer their pilot, nor the light of reason the pole *ᶜ* by which their actions should be conducted to their wonted haven. Judgment and discretion are both away, which, like two firm anchors, should secure them in the greatest tempests from the merciless and furious violence both of wind and wave.

Quid non ebrietas designat, saith the poet, *operta recludit.* And indeed, that which is in the heart of the sober is in the tongue of the drunkard. How many can with right apply that answer of Bias to themselves? Who, being carped at for his silence in a certain banquet by a fellow whose wit had been always trainbearer to his tongue, answered only this: that silence in wine was no argument or sign of folly—to show that his taciturnity proceeded not from any defect, as he had falsely and foolishly surmised. Surely there are few that are possessed with so great and marvelous a moderation and that have so absolute and powerful a command over themselves as this. Wherefore, let him that is wise keep himself from being overtaken with the envenomed cups of this enchanting and sense-bereaving Circe—unless he make light account of ruinating both himself and others.

The second thing are women: who, with an artificial *ᵈ* disposing of those several beauties wherewith nature (desirous, as it were, to stall forth *ᵉ* her treasures) hath prodigally adorned them, have made the spoils of the greatest conquerors trophies of their victories and led in triumph the hearts and minds of the wisest, and that in such manner as he that hath once suffered himself to be captivated by the powerful attraction of their starry looks thinks nothing to be done amiss that

---

ᵇ Surceased: left off.
ᶜ Pole: polestar.

ᵈ Artificial: artful.
ᵉ Stall forth: exhibit.

is done to purchase of them even the least favorable aspect that may be; deeming, in his fond conceit, that liberty is nowhere to be found but in the enclosure of his mistress' arms. And because he thinks his tongue too weak an instrument to express the strength and vigor of his affection toward her, he makes his heart ascend up into his eyes, through which, as through transparent glasses, he discovers [f] unto her (yet still thinks he discovers not enough) the very secret bedchamber of his most retired [g] cogitations; not remembering (silly wretch as he is) that such kind of creatures have oftentimes been made the instruments to effect the downfall and confusion of many, nor yet weighing with himself the weakness and imbecility [h] of the sex, which, as it harbors in itself a certain curious desire to know all things, so is it accompanied with a kind of careless respect to conceal any.

They are for the most part ἀγγεῖα σάθρα, leaking vessels, and like that comic servant,[i] *plenae rimarum, huc atque illuc effluentes.* And therefore hath the Spirit of the Highest (the better to express the nature and property of such a one) allotted her in the sacred volumes of His divinest oracles the name of Nachabah, from the word *Nacab,* which signifies *perforare,*[j] showing us (as 't were) that she is no fitter a vessel than either a sieve or a colander to have that infused into her the loss whereof we anything regard. A Roman lady was very importunate with her husband to know of him what secret matter had that day been handled in the Senate, with great oaths and protestations never to reveal it. He, desirous to try her, made use of his invention: told her that the priests had seen a lark flying in the air, κράνος ἔχοντα χρυσοῦν, καὶ δόρυ, having a golden helmet and a lance, and how they had consulted together to know whether this prodigy might portend either good or evil to the commonwealth. Scarce had she heard it but presently she disclosed it to one of her maids, the maid to another of her fellows; so that the report was spread and known throughout the whole palace before he came thither himself.

But all of them are not made in the same mold; there is, sometimes, *plus virtutis in stola, quam in armis.* Nero, after the detection of Piso's conspiracy, remembering that Epicharis was likewise of the faction, commanded she should presently be set upon the rack,[k] imagining (saith Tacitus) *muliebre corpus impar dolori,* that being a woman she would never be able to overcome the pain. But all the tortures that either he or his could possibly devise were not sufficient to draw from

---

[f] *Discovers:* uncovers, reveals.
[g] *Retired:* inmost, hidden.
[h] *Imbecility:* innocent helplessness.
[i] *Comic servant:* servant in a comedy.

[j] *Perforare:* L., to pierce.
[k] *The rack:* an instrument of torture by stretching.

her the least confession of anything that was then objected against her. The first day's question she so utterly contemned that the very chair in which they conveyed her from the place did seem as a chariot whereon she rid[1] triumphing over the barbarous assaults of their inhuman cruelty. The morrow following, being brought thither again to play her masterprize[m] with impious tyranny, her courage (after many rough encounters) remained so unshaken that wrath itself grew mad to see the strokes of an obstinate and unrelenting fury fall so in vain upon the softer temper of a woman and thereupon did add new vigor to the hands of her tormentors; which she perceiving took a scarf from about her neck and with it (to manifest their weakness in her fall) knits up within her bosom the knowledge she had of the fact, together with that little remainder of spirit whereof by force and violence they labored to deprive her. *Clariore exemplo* (saith our historian) *in tanta necessitate alienos, ac prope ignotos, protegendo, cum viri, Senatores, et equites Romani, intacti tormentis, clarissima quaeque suorum pignorum proderent.*

Former ages have likewise produced a Portia and a Leaena, the remembrance of whose virtue shall remain forever as an exemplary precedent to all posterity. For after her two lovers, Armodius and Aristogiton, having failed in the execution of their enterprise, had been put to death, she was brought to the torture to be made to declare what other complices[n] there were of the conspiracy; but she continued so constant that she never detected[o] anyone. In remembrance of which fact the Athenians caused a lion of brass to be erected, which had no tongue, and placed it at the entrance of a castle, showing her invincible courage by the generosity[p] of the beast and her perseverance in secrecy in that they made it without a tongue.

Sed non omne mare generosae est fertile testae. Every soil abounds not with golden ore, nor every channel with precious pearls; wherefore, it behooves a man to be very circumspect and wary in opening himself to any of them till sufficient trial shall have manifested the soundness of their disposition. But (alas!) *quid deceat, non videt ullus amans.* "Awake, Samson! The Philistines are upon thee," so often repeated, was a sufficient aviso of intended treachery had not the eye of reason, with the ravishing sound of Delilah's voice (as was Argus with the delightful tunes of Mercury's pipe), been lulled asleep in the lap of heedless sensuality. He must needs tell her (so far had the force of her enticing tongue prevailed with him) wherein it was

---

[1] *Rid:* rode.
[m] *Masterprize:* masterpiece.
[n] *Complices:* accomplices.

[o] *Detected:* revealed, betrayed.
[p] *Generosity:* nobility, worthiness.

that his strength consisted, though the hazard of his life, by revealing it, were never so eminent.[q]

Antony cannot choose but yield himself a prisoner in the height of his conquest to the imperious looks of Cleopatra, though the shameful eclipse of his glory be the sequel of his folly. Curius, to make himself gracious in the eyes of his Fulvia, will (whosoever saith nay) disclose unto her the secret plots and practices of Catiline, though himself have as deep a hand in them as he. The Prior of Capua can no sooner purpose anything against the state of the Venetians but his lovesick soldier will presently give notice of it to his courtesan and she to the Senate.

It is the nature of high-aspiring spirits always to affect that company where they may be most eminent, and therefore usually they make choice of women to frequent withal, imagining that whatsoever they do or say will be esteemed and wondered at by them. Whereupon, to make their admiration more extreme, they will not let to acquaint them even with their highest thoughts, and then the opinion that they are beloved begets a fearless confidence of secrecy, whereby whatsoever they intend to do shall be disclosed unto them. They must of necessity, now and then, out of the humor of their jollities give vent unto the smoke of their ambition, and then out comes that which racks nor tortures could ever have revealed. Yea, these are the creatures their wisdoms deem most fit to impart their high-built purposes unto, who, either for love or want of wit, will willingly (they think) conceal whatever they hear.

But (alas!) woeful experience hath taught many that they leveled, in so conceiting of[r] them, at a wrong mark. Wherefore, let us with David make a covenant with our eyes and, like Alexander, not vouchsafe so much as to glance a look upon the daughters of Darius, lest we be made the spoil of their beauty. For indeed the pregnant force of wisdom is hardly to be presumed upon in this case. *Nescio quid latentis veneni,* saith an ancient Father, *habet caro foeminea, ut prudentiores citius corrumpat.* And hence proceeded that pleasant motto of the Grecian courtesan in derision of those bearded Stoics, *Qui curios simulant, et Bacchanalia vivunt,* that in public places seem to be as grave as Saturn, but in private corners are as waggish as Jupiter. "I know not, I," said she, "what books, what wisdom, what philosophy; but sure I am such manner of men knock at my gates as oft as any other." They are angels in complexion, but if they be not the like in condition let him esteem of them no better than of whited sepulchers; for all this while they be but *semipulchrae.*[s] They have

---

[q] *Eminent:* possibly intended to read *imminent.*

[r] *Conceiting of:* holding opinion of.

[s] *Semipulchrae:* "half-fair," with a pun on *sepulchers.*

a face to beguile the eye and an eye to bewitch the heart; yea, there is not any one thing in them or about them but is (though a silent, yet a forcible) solicitor of man's will.

The Creator of all things did frame her exquisitely beautiful to please man, and the Devil made use of her perfection to deceive him. They have caused many to fall down wounded, and the strong men are all slain by them (Prov. 7:26). Their lips drop as an honeycomb, and their mouth is more soft than oil; but the end of them is bitter as wormwood and sharp as a two-edged sword. Their feet go down to death, and their steps take hold on hell. Yea, God himself (the searcher of all hearts and who alone intuitively knows all things) hath even from heaven assured us by that mirror of true wisdom, Solomon, that the precious life of man is the only thing which, like bloodthirsty tigers, they most eagerly hunt for (Prov. 6:26); and therefore not without just cause did he add to their style,[t] in regard of their proceedings, the attribute of *strange* (Prov. 5:3).

The Hebrew word *zonah* signifies not only *meretrix* but, withal, *caupona* and *arma;*[u] from whence we may gather the craft and subtlety of her practices, as she is *meretrix* in effecting the downfall and overthrow of such as are earnest and devoted followers of her sect. First she is *caupona,* and then *arma.* First she feeds and satisfies their desire with the daintiest dishes that possibly she can, giving them the best entertainment that an affected countenance and gesture can afford; but when they once draw near the lees, then begin they to be *minus grati,* less welcome unto her—and that for no other reason *quam quod inopia minus largire possunt,* than that poverty hath cut the wings of their former bounty. Then are her sweet words converted into sharp swords, so that look whatsoever she knows by thee or hath at any time known from thee that she thinks may procure thy overthrow shall now be revealed. She is become *arma;* she is become a weapon to destroy thee.

I speak not, all this while, of such as heaven hath allotted men for companions to beguile the tediousness of this their earthly pilgrimage, linking them together in love and unity by the bond of an honorable and lawful hymen;[v] though even in those, considering them as one and the selfsame body, it is not always requisite that the left hand should know what the right hand doth. Sejanus had no better means to work the tragic overthrow of Drusus, who like a dangerous rub hindered the smoother running of his ambitious thoughts, than by assaulting her whose bosom he had made (as 't were) the cabinet of his inmost purposes. For after he had tried many things, *promptissi-*

[t] *Style:* title, designation.   [v] *Hymen:* marriage.
[u] *Meretrix, caupona, arma:* prostitute, tavern, weapon.

mum visum, saith Tacitus, *ad uxorem eius Liviam convertere,* the readiest way he found was to set upon his wife; wherein he sped so well that, *corrupta illa, secreta eius prodebantur,* from her he had intelligence of all his secrets. The night itself could not secure him, for even then did she observe his upsitting and his downlying, leaving not so much as his sighs unregistered: *vigilias, somnos, suspiria patefecit,* she betrayed him wholly to his enemy. It was Aesop's lesson, therefore: Commit no secrets to the concealment of a woman. Which the poet secondeth in this manner:

> *Crede ratem ventis; animum ne crede puellis:*
> *namque est foeminea tutior unda fide.*

Octavius Caesar found a want of this principle in his friend Maecenas, who, being somewhat more uxorious than was meet and one who (as Seneca said of him in his *Epistles*) having but one wife was married yet a thousand times, revealed to his Terentia a secret that Caesar had imparted to him concerning the detection of Muraena's conspiracy, by which means it was suddenly vented ^w and became of no importance. And Augustus imputed this echolike disposition of reiterating whatsoever is heard to Fulvius, as the true symptom of a distempered and unsettled judgment. For, having disclosed unto him the grief which he conceived concerning the succession of his Livia's children in the empire for want of issue of his own, Fulvius went and related it to his wife, and she again to Livia, who sharply reprehended the Emperor her husband for it; whereupon, the morrow after, coming to salute him with *Salvus sis, Caesar,* he was requited with *Sanus sis, Fulvi.*

But lest I seem an uncivil and snarling satirist in taxing without exception a sex in general, I will add in praise of some particulars ^x that saying of Menander: ταμιεῖον ἀρετῆς, γενναία γυνή, *penu virtutis, generosa mulier.* And though neither Cato nor Euripides were so fortunate as ever to be partakers of so great a happiness, which indeed incited them to fasten those undeserved imputations upon them that they did, yet Rubius Celer is able to avouch it against the strongest opposer of them all; who, as himself commanded to be engraven upon his monument, "lived with Caia Ennia his wife 43 years, 8 months —and that, *sine querela,*" without any difference, complaint, or jar.

The third and last thing which is to be refrained is anger. Sejanus heartened Drusus against his brother Nero and made him an instrument to hinder him from succeeding Tiberius in the empire, yet in such manner as he did not forget to lay the groundwork likewise of

---

^w *Vented:* revealed, made public.   ^x *Particulars:* individuals.

his future overthrow; but he did not seem to hasten it at all, *gnarus* (saith Tacitus) *praeferocem et insidiis magis opportunum,* knowing, as experience teacheth, that the fiercest courage doth always lie most open to treacherous attempts. Fabius, therefore, notwithstanding the provocations of his enemies and the exprobrations [y] of his friends (who, not sounding aright the depth of his proceedings, challenged him, by reason of his protractions and delays, of a base and servile cowardice), would never be diverted from that course which in his own reason and judgment he thought surest and fittest to recreate the ill-affected forces of the empire; and indeed, *si tantum ausus esset, quantum ira suadebat,* it had utterly been subverted. For anger is prone to rashness and, so it endanger others, cares not for securing itself. Wherefore it were not amiss for any man to imitate those ancient champions whose policy, like to Fabius, was only to ward the blows of their adverse parties [z] till such time as they perceived their strength in assaulting to be well-nigh spent, never using [a] to strike themselves when wrath persuaded them, but when occasion.

The wakeful eye of reason must continually keep sentinel over his passions, and settled patience must be the fort that must protect him from the furious battery of all incensing and blood-disturbing speeches whatsoever. They are charms of a cunning charmer, against which if (like the wiser adder) he stop not his ear, his utter ruin cannot choose but instantly follow. For they are used either to avert him from some course he hath already undertaken (which, in the end, being thoroughly followed would prove prejudicial to them, as by the fore-alleged example of Fabius may be easily discerned) or to urge him thereby to manifest some part of his most inward and private thoughts; whereof the poet, being nothing ignorant, doth most elegantly call passions *tortures,* whereby men are urged and enforced to confess their secrets: *et vino tortus, et ira.*

Tiberius, who (as Tacitus reports) *nullam aeque ex virtutibus suis, quam dissimulationem diligebat,* feeling himself stung with a sharp invective of Agrippina concerning the accusation of Claudia Pulchra, her cousin-german, [b] came a step forth of his dissimulation when he said, "You are hurt because you do not reign." Of which our historian saith: *Audita haec raram occulti pectoris vocem elicuere, correptamque Graeco versu admonuit, [non] ideo laedi, quia non regnaret.* And Catiline, *qui ad omnia dissimulanda paratus,* did likewise err in this. For had he prosecuted his first design (which was, with an outward and forced appearance of true humility, expressed by the liveliest

---

[y] *Exprobrations:* accusations, reproaches.

[z] *Adverse parties:* adversaries.

[a] *Using:* being accustomed.

[b] *Cousin-german:* first cousin.

characters he could, both in his gesture, countenance, and words, to dash the accusations of his adversaries and to insinuate himself into the love and favor of the Senate), he might peradventure, having freed himself by this means from all sinister conceit ° of theirs, easily have effected his purpose. But when he heard those odious titles of enemy and parricide cast upon him by the fullmouthed multitude, then *quia circumventus ab inimicis praeceps agor, incendium meum ruina extinguam* must needs discover the mark of his disordinate ambition and make known unto the world what massacrous and impious thoughts had, notwithstanding his smooth external carriage, anchored in his bosom.

Wherefore let every man endeavor by all means possible to calm and allay those sudden and tempestuous motions of the mind and to be that which few are, so true to himself and so settled that at no time (either upon heat, or upon bravery,ᵈ or upon kindness—as I showed before—or upon trouble of mind and weakness) he open himself or suffer his tongue to eliminate ° any part of his thoughts—no, not though he should be put to it by a counterdissimulation, which is a fashion of inquiry very current with many who will not stick, according to the Spanish adage, *dezir mentira para sacar verdad,* to tell a lie for to ᶠ extort a truth.

° *Sinister conceit:* unfavorable opinion.
ᵈ *Bravery:* bravado.

° *Eliminate:* let forth, reveal.
ᶠ *For to:* in order to.

VIII. *Of Reputation*

THERE IS nothing more hard and difficult to come by than a true and certain knowledge of the inward disposition and abilities of man. His mind is subject to many secret inclinations; 't is like a labyrinth, full of crooked windings and turnings. His deeds, words, and gestures are never lightly beautified but with some outward imposture; they are fraught with vanity and deceit and, like that specious fig tree in the Gospel, do make a glorious flourish but afford no fruits.

The silly [a] sheep, said Archidamas, can never change his natural voice; but man can alter and fashion his to as many several and sundry dialects as he please, till such time as his ambition have attained to that which it desired. Some have been thought worthy of advancement, save when they had it; and some, again, have purchased to themselves good reputation and been well esteemed in place of greatness, which before were otherwise.

It hath been often seen that such as became a meaner part well have failed in a greater and disgraced it. Hence was it that Galba *major privato visus, dum privatus fuit, et omnium consensu capax imperii, nisi imperasset,* when he was a private subject did seem to outrun the meanness of his fortune, and, by a general consent of all men was thought worthy to rule, if he had never ruled. Whereas the contrary was bruited of Vespasian, to wit, that *omnium ante se principum in melius mutatus* [*est*], of all the princes that ever did precede him he alone was changed to the better; which may be likewise instanced upon the son of Bolingbroke, entitled, after the decease of his father, Henry V of England. Ignorance, therefore, is of too dull an apprehension to censure aright the nature of men's actions. She depriveth reason of her discursive faculty and frames her judgment according to the illiterate [b] verdict that outward sense gives of them. And hence cometh it oftentimes that many are reputed wise and valiant who, were the ground of their so-conceited merit well examined, would seem the contrary.

True valor consists not in being desperately venturous. It is not the love of virtue, but the hate of life, that makes men so. Antigonus had

---

[a] *Silly:* innocent, artless. [b] *Illiterate:* uninformed.

a soldier whose forwardness upon any dangerous service he much admired and therefore, having understood that he was troubled with an imposthume ᶜ in his body, gave his surgeons express command to see him diligently cured. Which done, Antigonus perceived that he showed not himself so valiant as he was wont and thereupon rebuked him for it; but the soldier answered him that he might blame himself, for it was he that had made him less hardy than he was before in causing him to be cured of those ills which had made him altogether careless of his life. And hither may that speech of the Sibaritans ᵈ concerning the Lacedaemonians' austerer kind of living be well referred: that it was no marvel they sought death so furiously in the wars, considering how laborsome and strict a life they did endure at home. *Rebus in angustis facile est contemnere vitam*. And therefore that reputation which is purchased this way cannot possibly be of any long continuance. It is a vapor drawn out of the earthy bosom of popular admiration,ᵉ which, where the rays of clearer apprehension do shine out, is suddenly dispersed.

True virtue is always like herself; she squares ᶠ with every accident and keeps a just proportion in all her actions. She will not fear to die as Cato did, though Caesar were her dearest friend. Such, therefore, as, being in the prime and flower of their youth do seem content with every breath of honor and, after they have gained some little reputation in the world, betake themselves immediately upon it to a retired life, confining their so-begun fortune within the bounds of some solitary mansion—it is to be suspected they were generous but only in appearance and that the consciousness and distrust of their own weakness made them withdraw themselves from action, lest by their unsufficient managing of matters they might haply lose that accidental glory which, upon no certain principles, they had formerly got. For honor serves but as a sauce to whet the appetite of those whose hearts are firm and of a noble and unyielding temper. It is a gale which bears them speedily to the undertaking of every haughty ᵍ enterprise. The praise of having well conducted the course of one is a bait which draws them on to the undergoing of another.

Hercules, in his travels, will not leave so much as hell unvisited, but even upon the gates thereof will strive to erect a trophy to his triumphant merit. Yea, in military matters, the report of any one thing valorously executed, especially upon the beginning of an employment, is that which makes a smooth and easy passage for future attempts. It is a means to drive the wavering affection of ambiguous friends to

ᶜ *Imposthume:* abscess.

ᵈ *Sibaritans:* inhabitants of ancient Sybaris, noted for luxurious living.

ᵉ *Admiration:* wonder.

ᶠ *Squares:* fits, adjusts to.

ᵍ *Haughty:* high.

a certain stand and to bring forth an increase of love in the hearts and minds of such as are firm and loyal. It works a willing obedience in thy whole army and procures thee means and munition, with store of all other warlike necessaries from thy friends and allies, and that without pain and trouble to thyself; for whilst everyone contends to be thought a means in the raising of thy transcending [h] fortune thy worth cannot possibly want ladders by which to climb. And therefore Domitius Corbulo, at his first coming to the government of Armenia, endeavored to do somewhat (as Tacitus reports) *ut famae inserviret,* that in those parts might purchase him the credit and reputation of sufficiency, which in new business is most available.[i] And Julius Agricola, at his first arrival into Britain, carried himself in the like manner, *non ignarus instandum famae, ac prout prima cessissent, fore universa,* that fame was to be followed, and as he sped in the first such it was likely would his success be in the rest.

But it is here as it is in meats:[j] if taken immoderately, though never so nourishing, they prove a burden to the body rather than otherwise. It is requisite, therefore, that we sometimes clip the wings of our reputation and not suffer them to grow beyond the compass of our nest.

> *Insani sapiens nomen ferat, aequus iniqui,*
> *ultra quam satis est, virtutem si petat ipsam.*

The wiser sort will of their own accord a little now and then degrade the opinion of their worth by stripping themselves awhile of all employments. They know there is nothing lost by making themselves, for a time, less than they are. Overmuch estimation hath been the bane of many. Alcibiades, by reason of the sundry great exploits he had achieved in the behalf of his country, had got so great an opinion [k] of sufficiency that when he failed in the due performance of anything he was presently suspected; everyone was apt to judge that it was not because he could not do it but because he would not, and that wheresoever he was minded to employ himself nothing could possibly escape him.

Hence likewise was it that John Guicciardini was accused to have been corrupted by those of Lucca because he failed in the expugnation [l] of their city. The safest way, therefore, to secure ourselves from danger is to attire our worthiness in such manner as it may still be the same it was in inward substance, only altered and disguised a little in outward show.

---

[h] *Transcending:* rising.
[i] *Available:* useful.
[j] *Meats:* food.

[k] *Opinion:* reputation.
[l] *Expugnation:* siege.

It is reported of Poppaeus Sabinus that for the space of twenty-four years, and that in the days of tyranny, he was still ^m made ruler over the greatest provinces belonging to the empire, *nullam ob eximiam artem,* not for any excellent ability that was in him, *sed quod par negotiis, neque supra erat,* but that his sufficiency did no more than equal the charge which was imposed upon him. And to speak plainly, wise men, in the choice of instruments, are seldom willing to make use of such, in matters of importance, whose cunning judgment they think can sound the depth of their intent or, out of their employments, contrive anything whereby to grace themselves.

Agricola, saith Tacitus, notwithstanding his many services done to the empire, *nunquam in suam famam gestis exsultavit,* did never boast of any action to his own fame but, as an inferior planet, did modestly acknowledge the light he had to be wholly derived from a higher sun. Thus did he steal from envy and not defraud himself of his deserved glory. Germanicus likewise, having calmed and allayed the tumultuous broils and insurrections of the Germans, caused a pile ⁿ of weapons to be raised with this stately title: ^o Debellatis, Inter Rhenvm Albimqve Nationibvs, Exercitvm Tiberii Caesaris Ea Monimenta Marti, Et Iovi, Et Avgvsto Sacravisse, that the nations between Rhine and Albis ^p being overcome, Tiberius Caesar's army had consecrated those monuments to Mars, Jupiter, and Augustus—but added nothing of himself, *metu invidiae,* for fear that envy or detraction might find a subject in him for their malicious and envenomed teeth to gnaw upon, or thinking (as it is) the conscience ^q of a well-done deed to be a sufficient recompense for the doing it. And this it was that kept them upright, amidst the ruins of so many worthies, in those unworthy times.

But (alas!) the high-erected thoughts of an ambitious heart cannot possibly be brought to conceive the meaning of this principle. They will always sail by the card and compass of their own mind and rather than yield in their popular dependencies their entertainments, gifts, or public grace, most willfully hazard the distaste of all men. Caesar careth for nothing but the execution of his designs; his spirit is beyond the reach of fear. If the sea swell in waves to let his passage to Brundisium, he swells again in words and bids the mariner, "Sail on! Thou carriest Caesar and his fortune with thee." And indeed his fortune was the only thing that kept both him and his estate from being shaken and disjointed by the violent events of such resolved courses.

^m *Still:* ever, repeatedly.
ⁿ *Pile:* monumental heap.
^o *Title:* inscription.

^p *Albis:* Elbe.
^q *Conscience:* consciousness.

IX. *Of Accusation*

IT IS NO golden age in which we live, but an age so corrupted and depraved that, in comparison of others, many are esteemed virtuous at a reasonable rate. Yea, he is thought to do good enough who, when he is in place of authority, doth but little ill.

Iam pridem equidem rerum vocabula amisimus; quia bona aliena largire, liberalitas; malarum rerum audacia, fortitudo vocatur. All things have undergone an alteration, both in name and nature. Simplicity hath principled herself with stronger axioms than heretofore and hath learned to square and order the whole course of her conversation by another kind of method than that she practiced during the harmless infancy of the world. The silly dove hath been constrained, for her own security, to join in friendship with the serpent; and the lion thinks it no disparagement to case his valor (if need require) under the outside of the subtle fox. For piety now is counted but a fantastic fiction, and upright dealing but an airy apparition. True virtuous actions are never seen upon the scene but when by the necessity of laws they are enforced to show themselves. For where election abounds, and that all liberty may be used, everything is presently brought to a most irregular and confused motion. The will of man is so perverted that goodness is seldom made the scope of his designs.

It is said of Catiline that when he wanted present matter for his mischievous mind to work upon he was no way scrupulous to circumvent and kill *insontes, sicuti sontes,* those that had never purchased his hateful fury by offending him, as well as others. And lest either his heart or hand might haply wax numb for want of employment, *gratuito potius malus, atque crudelis erat,* he would be voluntarily cruel and without expectance of reward.

And what was said of him, I fear me, may be too truly justified in many. For (alas!) the conscience of a virtuous deed is too weak a motive to incite our dull affections to the doing of it. 'T is either hope of reward or fear of punishment that, in the attempt of things, orders and directs our choice. Give way but to impunity, and ye shall see how uncivility, like a ravening deluge, will on the sudden wash away the print and form of all mortality.[a] *Non sum moechus,* I am not an adulterer, saith one,

> *neque ego hercule fur, ubi vasa*
> *praetereo sapiens argentea.*

But, as the satirist affirms in the verses following,

> *tolle periculum,*
> *iam vaga prosiliet fraenis natura remotis.*

So that for the better ordering and preserving of a commonwealth, 't is very requisite there should be such ministers appointed in it as may, without respect or partiality, give justice information of the particular proceedings of private men. For by this means either the fear of being accused will curb their ambitious purposes and keep them from attempting anything against the liberty of that state in which they live or, having attempted, the accusation itself will presently suppress them. Besides, it will give air enough for the venting forth of those pestiferous tumors and inflammations which, through hatred or emulation, are bred in the crazy minds of ill-affected persons. Yea, there is nothing that can more firmly settle and establish a commonwealth than to order it in such manner that the alteration of those humors which do travail and molest it may find a recipe at home for her recovery, prescribed by law.

Wherefore, if at any time we see that in the divisions and distractions of an unsettled populace either party shall have need to rank themselves with foreign correspondency, the cause hereof may lawfully be suspected to proceed from some manifest defect in the institution of that government. But if, with us (as heretofore in Rome and suchlike popular and democratical polities of elder times) envy and malice were authorized, either by ostracism or any other such specious kind of proceedings, to top the branches of a spreading virtue, there should not an Aristides breathe amongst us but every base and illiterate groom would strive (not knowing why, perhaps) to procure his banishment.

Nothing can escape the forked tongue of detraction. Slander, we see, did fasten her envenomed teeth upon the precious body of our Saviour Christ himself and gave him not over until death, yet was his nature no way so imperfect as to offend. It was the advertisement of Medius, a damnable promoter[b] in the court of Alexander, that a man "should not spare to bite the reputation of anyone with untruths and forged accusations; for, howsoever," said he, "the hurt may haply be cured, the scar yet will still remain." And what success did follow

---

[a] *Mortality:* humanity.　　　　　　　　[b] *Promoter:* schemer, informer.

upon the practice of this diabolical position may easily be discovered in the fall of Callisthenes, Parmenio, and Philotas. Wisdom, therefore, and moderation should continually sit in the ears of greatness and there most carefully distinguish between truth and falsehood, between a lawful accusation and that which is feigned.

It was an easy matter (considering the suspicious nature of Tiberius) for Caepio Crispinus, who, as Tacitus reports, by humoring his bloody mind with close° and scandalous delations,ᵈ had set a golden outside upon his formerly dejected and ragged fortunes, to call the life of innocency itself in question. He overthrew Marcellus by accusing him to have spoken somewhat sinisterly of Caesar, which then (saith our historian) was accounted an inevitable° crime, by reason that the accuser did by continual observing gather out of the vicious carriage and disposition of the prince whatsoever was most vile and apt to be reproached, and upon that did frame and fashion his indictments, *nam quia vera erant, etiam dicta credebantur*. For everything was prone to be believed because 't was known to be deserved. But howsoever barbarous and inhuman tyrants may think by countenancing such sycophants to secure themselves and their estates, yet milder princes will warily avoid them. Ambitious usurpation hath been seen to cut the throat of lawful sovereignty and afterward to seat itself, by this means, in the chair of majesty.

King Richard's banishing of Mowbray, upon the difference between him and Bolingbroke, was his own deposing. The Emperor Valentinian II, having caused Aetius to be executed, demanded afterward of Proximus how he approved the fact; who answered that he knew not whether he had lawfully put him to death or no, but sure he was that, by so doing, with his own left hand he had cut off his right. Which happened shortly after to be very true, for he was slain by Maximus, a Roman patrician, whose treacherous attempts, during the life of Aetius, were so overawed that they durst never offer so much as once to show themselves. Alexander had deprived himself of a true and faithful physician if he had suffered himself to be led away with the reports and jealousies of others. 'T is therefore requisite some exemplary punishments should be inflicted upon those that spitefully endeavor to soil and black the reputation of any man with the filthy slime of their malicious and viperous jaws. For otherwise the silly lamb shall never drink at the fountain, but the greedy wolf will accuse him without cause and devour him without law.

Let Haman hang upon the gallows which by his command was

° *Close:* secret, whispered. ° *Inevitable:* capital, ineluctable.
ᵈ *Delations:* informings.

erected for the death of innocency; let those rank and goatish-eyed elders undergo that cruel sentence which their unsatisfied lust had wickedly contrived against a spotless chastity. Finally, let the Prophet Daniel be quit, and those which falsely did accuse him be condemned by Darius to the lions' den.

Neque enim lex justior ulla est,
quam necis artifices arte perire sua.

FINIS

PART II

Essays Moral and Theological

Essays Moral and Theological

London
Printed by I. W. for Eleazar Edgar,
and are to be sold at his shop at
the Windmill in Paul's Churchyard.
1609

To the Right Reverend Father in God, James, by the same Grace Bishop of Bath and Wells, Dean of His Majesty's Chapel, etc.

MY LORD:

Where judgment is, virtue can want no patronage. Her worth will be esteemed by such as are able to discern it; and in humanity a judicious understanding doth sometimes countenance a good endeavor, that by encouragement an intellectual or moral virtue may increase where it is or spring where yet it is not. Hence is it that these bolder lines do presume to present themselves unto Your Lordship, not doubting but you will be as kind to them as they are fond of you.

There is within your bosom, besides the hereditary virtues of a noble family, that which deservedly reports you to be πεπλασμένον ἐκ Διὸς ἔρνος, A fruitful branch of Eden's better tree.

Greatness hath matched herself with gravity, and riches (a thing not usual) with religion, to set the fairer gloss upon your glory. But I will here forbear, feeling myself distracted with a passion which by Euripides is thus expressed:

> πῶς ἄν σ' ἐπαινέσαιμι μὴ λίαν λόγοις,
> μηδ' ἐνδεῶς τοῦδ' ἀπολέσαιμι τὴν χάριν;
> αἰνούμενοι γὰρ ἀγαθοὶ τρόπον τινὰ
> μισοῦσι τοὺς αἰνοῦντας, ἢν αἰνῶσ' ἄγαν.

> How shall I praise you and not speak too much,
> Nor yet your high deserts too lightly touch,
> Nor lose the grace of my so dear intent
> By telling rudely what is kindly meant?
> Sith good men bear a kind of enmity
> To their own praise, if it too wordy be.

Your Lordship's worth is as apparent as the sun. It shines in so high a sphere that all but such as are maliciously blind must needs bear witness of his brightness. I need not hold a candle unto any. Here, therefore, in the humblest degree of awful observation, I kiss your reverend hands, unfeignedly desirous to be always reputed, as your many extraordinary favors have truly made me,

Your Lordship's most entirely devoted

D. T.

I.   *Of Learning and Knowledge*

VIRTUE delights not in impostures, neither doth she care for artificial ornaments; she is black but comely as the tents of Kedar and as the curtains of Solomon. Her stature requires not the help of any accessory raising, nor her garments the glory of any other trimming than her own rich inside can afford them. Do but behold her countenance at any time and you shall find the painting that she useth to be nothing else but dust tempered with sweat. Ye shall see that she is likely always busied in the toilsome shop of action, seldom refreshing her weariness in the withdrawing chamber of meditation unless it be now and then to make the easier and speedier passage to the other. She is full of high-built purposes [a] and labors not so much how to word them as how to work them.[1] Her thoughts are never taken up with frivolous doubts and inquisitions.[b] Time cannot pass her hands but upon great advantage. She troubleth not herself to know whether Anacreon were more lascivious than riotous, whether Sappho were more wanton than witty, or whether Hecuba were elder than the mother of Aeneas; she bequeaths the voiding [c] of these controversies, together with the search of etymologies and verbal derivations, to such as Didymus, that can stuff whole volumes only with quoting the diverse lections [d] of depraved [2] manuscripts or correcting the literal errors of the press, which long ago might have pleaded prescription for their pass. They are things the knowledge whereof torments neither her nor hers.

Those that are truly generous can no way brook their spirits should be confined within the solitary circle of such fruitless speculations. Marius did never blush to profess before the Senate his ignorance in Greek, yea, and his carelessness [e] in being otherwise, considering how little he observed it helped such as were excellent therein to the purchasing of virtue: *Graecas literas non didici,* said he, *parum placebat*

---

[a] *Purposes:* projects.
[b] *Inquisitions:* questionings.
[c] *Voiding:* settling.

[d] *Lections:* readings.
[e] *Carelessness:* indifference, lack of desire.

[1] Numerical superscripts refer to the corresponding numbered items in the Appendix.

eas discere; quippe quae ad virtutem doctoribus nihil profuerunt. The knowledge which he had was altogether operative; his heart was never at more ease than when his hands were working. And to speak truly, what is contemplation but a glorious [f] title invented only to set a gloss upon a base and idle disposition? In action a man doth better himself and benefit others. Heaven would never have infused a soul into the body, which hath arms and legs (only instruments of doing), but that it meant the mind should employ them and so attain to the knowledge of her own good and evil by practice, which indeed is the only way to increase the one and correct the other. In Rome, saith Sallust, during the days of her minority and before such time as public dissolution [3] had altered the well-composed temperature [g] of her estate, *optimus quisque facere quam dicere; sua ab aliis benefacta laudari, quam ipse aliorum narrare malebat:* there was no man esteemed it so great a glory to relate the valorous achievements of others as to achieve that valiantly himself which might afterward be related by others. To speak well was not then so generally in fashion as afterward; but to do well, more. And howsoever Caesar had that happiness from his birth as to be deemed a Caesar in them both, yet is he one alone; a phoenix without a match, a man without a mate. His worth was then unparalleled—and so is still.[4]

It is easy for a philosopher in his chair to sit and preach against the passions and perturbations of the mind that arise from the apprehension of some distasteful object; but can he instance on himself the truth of his assertions, can he undaunted and undismayed behold the hideous countenance of a disguised death? Can he deride the tyrant and his torture, Phalaris and his bull? Briefly, can he do as much for the settling of his positions [h] as every common mountebank will for the vending of his antidotes, who will not let in the face of the public market to stand and champ the flesh of living scorpions betwixt their jaws and to swallow down the juice of spiders that they may give the world a trial [i] of their sovereignty? If not, why doth he toil and labor in searching out of precepts and instructions for that which himself cannot well do with them and which others, peradventure, may better do without them? Where is the stoic that, with Mutius, dare thrust *his* hand into the fire, or venture with untutored ignorance to scale a wall, to keep a fort, to enter on a breach? This curious [j] arming of a man against fear is the only way to make him fear. We judge the greatness of a war by the greatness of the provision, and the danger of an assault by the directions that are given us for the assailing. Bring me out of love with life, and I shall never be afraid of death;

[f] *Glorious:* swaggering, pretentious.
[g] *Temperature:* (here) natural health, (generally) temper or disposition.
[h] *Positions:* principles.
[i] *Trial:* demonstration.
[j] *Curious:* oversolicitous.

take from me those imaginary sweets which I conceit to be in that, and I shall never be backward to abandon it for this. The overmuch acquaintance we have with the one makes us avoid as much as possibly may be the familiarity we might have with the other.

Dediscas vivere oportet ut discas mori: we must unlearn to live if we would learn to die. But where? It is a thing seldom effected in the schools. Cast but an eye awhile on many of your artists[k] and you shall find the knowledge which they have to be altogether in their books, seldom in their brains; a little in their memory, nothing in their minds. They must always, for the maintaining of an argument, appeal to that from their understanding; which, if it fail, you shall see them come tumbling down, like Icarus, from the height of their presumption and afterward lie grappling with their own illiterate weakness but cannot possibly recover.[5] They are like the greedy glutton that swallows much good meat, incorporates none. They labor to discern the motion of the heavens but never look how to compose[1] their own. They inquire if anything were existent before all time but think not how by such inquiries they omit the benefit of that time which is before themselves. Their disputations are whether privation be a principle; whether anything can be made of nothing; whether there be an empty space in the compass of nature; or whether the world shall have an end—and suchlike, which indeed are without end, to no end. If they be able to delude the vulgar[m] and with their sophistical elenchs and inductions drive them into some known absurdity, or if they can daunt their slower apprehension with terms of art—which neither they nor yet themselves perhaps most often rightly understand—it is sufficient.

Most of their learning is such as tendeth only to outward pomp and ostentation. Deprive them of their ornamental adjuncts, bar them the use of their Latin, take away from them their Aristotle with his commentators and you will go near[6] to take a man of their profession for one of us, if not for worse. They are altogether real,[n] nothing in complement. They let not for being more learned to be less foolish. I love and honor knowledge as much as they that are possessed with it, and in his[o] true use it is the greatest and the noblest acquist[p] that men can gain. But in those (and many such there are) that make it the fundamental base and prop of their sufficiency, that continually rely upon the faithfulness of their memory, and whose stock consists of nothing but of borrowed wares, I hate it (if I may dare say it) a little more than blockishness.

A general corruption hath overgrown the virtue of these later times,

[k] *Artists:* students of the liberal arts.

[1] *Compose:* control.

[m] *Vulgar:* common people.

[n] *Real:* self-existent, absolute.

[o] *His:* its.

[p] *Acquist:* acquisition.

that learning may now sufficiently better the means of men but not a whit their manners. If she finds them dull and heavy, she suffocates and aggraves ⁹ them; if pliable and gentle, she purifies them willingly, clarifies and sublimes them to their exinanition.ʳ It is a thing of quality well-nigh indifferent, a most profitable appendix and *aggiunta* ˢ to a soul wellborn but most pernicious and dangerous to one of a differing ⁷ strain—or, rather, a thing of most precious use, which suffers not itself ⁸ to be possessed at a low rate. In some hands it is a scepter; in other some, a beetle.ᵗ Louis XI of France caused his son Charles, entitled after his decease the Eighth of that name, to be brought up at Amboise not in any literature ᵘ at all; for, as Guicciardini reports, *àpena gli furono cogniti i caratteri delle letere,* hardly did he know the forms and characters of his letters. His father was content, according to his own humor, he should ⁹ learn this sentence alone in Latin: *Qui nescit dissimulare, nescit regnare,* he that knows not how to dissemble knows not how to reign. He had observed, belike, that learning did not so often correct that which was ill as deprave that which was good in nature; and that in a prince, unless it be qualified with a very rare and singular virtue, it is like a dangerous knife in the hands of a madman. And to speak truly, there is nothing so much to be feared as knowledge accompanied with injustice and armed with power. Such as are endued with it in any extraordinary measure do seldom suffer themselves to be guided or governed by the counsels and directions of others but run headlong of themselves and care not but to please their own fancy.

There was never any emperor (arms only excepted) more ignorant than Trajan, more learned than Nero; never any that in regard of his own worth did more despise and contemn the Senate than this, never any that did always more reverence and respect it than the other. Hence was it that our Saviour Christ ¹⁰ went not to the palaces of kings to furnish up the number of his disciples with them; he went not to the synagogues of the Jews nor to the temples of the Rabbins and Pharisees to choose of them; ¹¹ but he walks out toward the sea and sees two fishermen, Peter and Andrew: to them he saith, δεῦτε ὀπίσω μου, "Come, follow me." And hereupon St. Paul, writing to the Corinthians, "Ye see," saith he, "your vocation:ᵛ that not many wise men according to the flesh, not many mighty men, not many noble"—but τὰ μῶρα τοῦ κόσμου—"[but] the very foolish things of the

---

ᵠ *Aggraves:* adds weight to, oppresses.
ʳ *Exinanition:* exhaustion.
ˢ *Aggiunta:* (Ital.) addition.
ᵗ *Beetle:* wooden mallet or ramming instrument.

ᵘ *Literature:* study of letters, formal education.
ᵛ *Vocation:* calling, summoning.

world hath God chosen to confound the wise, and the weak things of the world to confound the mighty." He chose (saith St. Augustine) for his disciples men of mean birth, mean calling, mean learning, *ut quicquid magnum essent et facerent, ipse in eis esset et faceret,* that whatsoever extraordinary thing proceeded from them, himself might seem to be it and do it in them. The Prophet Elisha demanded empty vessels of the widow that he might fill them. The like did Christ: He sought for vessels that were empty; empty of riches, empty of worldly honor, empty of human wisdom. These were for his purpose, these he saw εἶδεν δύο ἀδελφούς—he saw two brethren that were fishers—and to them he said, δεῦτε ὀπίσω μου, "Come, follow me."

Virtue cannot endure to be an undersitter ᵂ to any; she will not live with kings and princes as an inmate.ˣ He that would entertain her as he ought must free his mind of whatsoever is superfluous. She loves not to be straited ʸ in her room; her train is greater than can be well bestowed within a narrow circuit. It is not part of a house that can content her; *totum pectus illi vacet,* the whole mansion must be at her command. She comes accompanied with a sinewy and substantial knowledge such as will both grace herself and advantage whomsoever shall receive her, yea, such as will adorn and enrich the mind not with any sophistical appearance or superficial tincture but with a solid and essential beauty that shall be always able to abide the touch. He that observes the manner of her proceedings shall grow as eminent in life as he doth in learning. She is both Martha and Mary, contemplation and action. She looks into many things but labors only in that which is necessary and convenient. Her precepts are nothing else but mere ᶻ examples. She never gives a principle to observe but she gives withal a precedent to follow. Her words and her works are children of one burden.

She is not like those Scribes and Pharisees in the Gospel that make no difficulty to lade the necks of men with heavy and unsupportable yokes but will not so much as move them with a finger of their own; nor like those hypocritical Levites of our corrupter times that aspire only to sit in the chair of Moses and care not, so they have Urim and Thummim (the outward marks of priesthood) on their breast, what ignorance or what impurity do harbor in their hearts. They are wells without water, clouds that are carried about with tempest, and, in a word, wandering stars reserved only for the black of darkness. They will not stick, like Balaam (such is the love they bear the wages of unrighteousness), to do or say whatever the Moabite shall require;

ᵂ *Undersitter:* undersettle, subtenant.　　ʸ *Straited:* crowded, confined.
ˣ *Inmate:* intimate, co-dweller.　　ᶻ *Mere:* pure.

whereas he that comes not of this adulterate and spurious generation but is the lawful and legitimate child of an untainted virtue cannot possibly be won by any such enticement to derogate^ᵃ so much either from himself or from his Maker. He is actually that which others strive to seem; what they have only in the bark, he hath likewise in the body. He brings forth fruit as well as leaves and teacheth his deed, his word, and his thought to tread one measure. He is like those cherubim of Ezekiel, that had wings and, under those wings, the hands of a man, *manus hominis subter pennas eorum.* He hath the wings of contemplation, the hands of action; the wings of faith, the hands of charity; wings whereon he raiseth his understanding, and hands wherewith he doth excite his will; wings with hands, and hands not without wings; action always with contemplation, contemplation never without action.

Practice is the only end of his theory; he cares not to know anything which adds not something to the bettering of his affections. This is the period of his painful endeavors and the *non ultra*^ᵇ of all his diligent and studious inquiries. And, indeed, *frustra sapit qui sibi non sapit:* that wisdom is but vanity that imparts no benefit to him that owns her; yea, whatsoever lies without [12] this compass is but a symptom of intemperancy and argues weakness in him that shall pursue it. And therefore, as Aeschylus affirms, ὁ χρήσιμ' εἰδώς, οὐχ ὁ πόλλ' εἰδώς, σοφός: he alone is to be counted wise whose knowledge is more for profit than for show. It is better yet for any man to know something which is needless than to know nothing at all. He that is absolutely ignorant is as Adam was before the Lord had breathed into him the breath of life—a lump of earth, a statue without a soul.[13]

---

^ᵃ *Derogate:* take away, impair.   ^ᵇ *Non ultra:* final end.

II. *Of Policy and Religion*

IT IS AS HARD and severe a thing to be truly politic as to be truly moral. There are many that obtain good fortunes by diligence in a plain way, little intermeddling and keeping themselves from gross errors. They take cities with a net and cannot err in their pursuit, would they never so fain. They are men (as Pompey was wont to say) *majore fortuna*[1] *quam sapientia,* more fortunate than wise; whether they sleep or wake, their purposes do thrive.

There are others that are not heirs to so great a happiness, who (led with a corrupt persuasion that the way to rise by honest principles is somewhat doubtful, wearisome, and tedious) do store themselves with evil and corrupt positions, whereof, as in all things, there are more in number than of the good, and by dispensing with the laws of charity and integrity they make the passage to their aims more hasty and compendious. But it is in life as it is in ways: the shortest is commonly the foulest, and surely the fairest is not much about.[2] Such, therefore, as are not clean transported and carried away with the tempestuous whirlwinds of irregular affections, but being in their own power do bear and sustain themselves, must continually set before their eyes not only that general description of the world—that all things are vanity and vexation of spirit—but many other more particular maps and cards for the directing of our course: chiefly, that being without well-being is a curse. *Non est vivere, sed valere, vita,* saith the poet.[3] It is said of Saul, *duobus*[4] *annis regnavit,* that he reigned two years over Israel; when, notwithstanding, according to the computation of men he reigned twenty. But the Scripture reckons only upon the days of grace, not counting those at all which either went before or followed after.[5] As sin itself is nothing, so is a sinner less than nothing. *Ad nihilum redactus sum, et nescivi,* said David: I was brought to nothing, and I knew it not. And hither did the words of our Saviour Christ tend, when, speaking of the treacherous disloyalty of Judas, that *apostata,* he said, "It had been better for him that he had never been born." For, as it is a higher degree of good to be a master rather than to be a servant, so is it a lesser degree of ill not to be at all than to be a sinner.

Secondly, he must observe and know that there is no greater joy and solace than a life not obnoxious^a to any base or scandalous reproach.

Hic murus aheneus esto,
nil conscire sibi, nullaque pallescere culpa.

And so of the contrary; for how can it profit a man to win the whole world and to lose his own soul?

Thirdly, he must note how God, in His eternal providence and divine judgment, subverts the wisdom oftentimes of evil plots and irreligious imaginations,[6] according to that passage:[7] "He hath conceived mischief and shall bring forth a vain thing."[8] I will not hazard my conscience, therefore, to secure my state nor do as the Jews did, who had no greater motive to crucify the heir apparent of heaven than this: ἐλεύσονται οἱ Ῥωμαῖοι, etc., "the Romans will come and take both our place and our nation from us." I desire not to climb but with Jacob's ladder, nor to mount aloft but in the chariot of Elijah; I will not soar with the pinions of a dragon but with the wings of a dove, that when my flight is done I may obtain a habitation among the blessed and glorious cherubim. I will not build upon any other foundation than that *Primum quaerite* which is the cornerstone both of divinity and philosophy. For the one saith, *Primum quaerite regnum Dei,* etc., "First seek the kingdom of God, and all these things shall be ministered unto you." And the other saith, *Primum quaerite bona animi*—"First seek the good things of the mind"—*caetera aut aderunt, aut non oberunt,* "and whatsoever is remaining, the having it shall either help thee or the wanting it shall never hurt thee."[9]

To say I will employ my fortune well though I obtain it ill doth savor nothing of a regenerate mind. These compensations and satisfactions are good to be used, never to be purposed. To take from Peter to give to Paul is mere oppression; to rob one altar to enrich another, no discretion. If my desires be not canonical^b and such as carry in their front^c the lineaments of piety, I will suppress them. If I cannot cross them in the womb, I will crush them in the cradle; if I cannot prevent them in their beginning, I will strive to hinder them in their proceedings. When reason, like a faithful counselor, shall give me notice of the baseness of their birth and quality, I will avoid them; and as before appetite was will's solicitor, so will shall now be appetite's controller. What I coveted by the one I will reject by the other. If the groundwork be sure, the building cannot fail. I will therefore lay my foundation on the rock and not upon the sands; and

---

^a *Obnoxious:* vulnerable.   ^c *Front:* forehead.
^b *Canonical:* orthodox.

while I hold my hand on the helm to direct the stern, I will heave up mine eyes to heaven and observe the stars.

Good ends are not to be compassed by evil means. If out of poison we may extract a quintessence, the words of Judas may serve us for a pattern whereby to frame our actions. It is not enough for us to seek Christ, but we must seek him till we find him; and having found him, we must lay hold on him and lead him warily.[10] κρατήσατε αὐτὸν καὶ ἀπαγάγετε ἀσφαλῶς, said that *apostata* when he betrayed the Lamb.[11] Those which do otherwise, they hold him but they lead him not warily; they offer sacrifice, but without salt; they have zeal, but they want knowledge.

III.   Of Civil Carriage and Conversation

MAN IS LIKE unto a bee, he cannot possibly live alone; his birth bewrays ᵃ it, his bringing-up confirms it. For whereas other creatures do no sooner come into the world but they are able of their own proper strength to raise themselves upon their feet, he alone hath need of outward aid and assistance. And in this regard hath nature furnished him with speech, to the end he might confer and negotiate with those of his own kind and not be any way defective in the performance of such offices as are necessarily required for the preservation of human society. He that avoideth conversation, therefore, doth nothing else, in effect, but contradict the power of his creation. *Non est bonum hominem esse solum,* said the Lord: "It is not good that man should be alone"; and therefore He supplied him with a helper. Hence then with those Athenian Timons, those Diogenical cynics, that make their private mansions the public monuments of their living carcasses and so retire themselves from all occasions of intercourse that the very doors of their habitation do seem to challenge by way of anticipation the inscription from their tombs.¹

He merits not the name of man that had rather hide his light under a bushel than set it in a candlestick, bury his talent rather than employ it, or like the fox had rather his tail should drag upon the ground than the ape should have a piece of it to help his wants withal. Our being in this world is nothing but a mere dependency; we stand in need of one another's perfections; what is wanting at home must be supplied from abroad. But by reason of the great variety and dissimilitude of natures and dispositions, the disproportion and inequality of estates and conditions which are amongst us, we must so principle ourselves as that our carriage may be pleasing and acceptable to all men, to the intent that love, peace, and charity may be preserved. Our Master hath taught us that the eye of a serpent is an ornament in the head of a dove. And therefore we may lawfully learn so to frame our own affections that they may the better fasten upon others.

There is no man but will willingly delight in him that is affected with those passions whereunto himself is subject and inclined. Experience teacheth it and reason proveth it. The wolf, the tiger, the

ᵃ *Bewrays:* reveals.

lion, and the leopard are seldom at enmity[2] with those of their own kind.[3] Alexander asked a pirate that was brought before him how he durst be so bold as infest the seas and interrupt the traffic and commerce of men in such manner as he did. "I do, sir," answered he, "with one ship but what your Majesty doth with a whole navy." This reply of his so pleased Alexander that he gave him presently both life and liberty; the similitude of action altered the king in his determination.

Likeness of manners is likely in reason to draw liking with affection. Whosoever, therefore, would estate[b] himself within the bosom of his friend, he must beware of everything that may cause either fraction[c] or division; and, as near as piety will permit him, conform himself altogether to his motions:[d] love where he loveth, hate where he hateth, and still follow the temperature of his humors. Caius Caesar maintained his reputation with his grandfather Tiberius by no means but this: he shadowed his cruel mind with subtle modesty and showed no discontent either for the condemnation of his mother or the banishment of his brethren. *Pari habitu semper cum Tiberio, haud multum distantibus verbis:* he did imitate him in his apparel, in his words, in all things as near as possibly he could.

But as this doth nourish charity[e] if well used, so doth it foster flattery if abused. He must not be obstinate and inflexible[4] either in his actions or discourse. *Fili, ne innitaris prudentiae tuae,* saith the mouth of Wisdom. He must not, likewise, be too curious and inquisitive, too vaporous[f] or imaginative; nor, with Cato, be one of the antipodes to tread opposite to the present world. He that reproveth everything shall find himself hated, nothing amended. *Ulteriora mirari, praesentia sequi, sapientes decet,* saith Tacitus: wise men must fit and accommodate themselves to the state wherein they live and, howsoever they admire what is past, subscribe to what is present.

> *Saturnus periit, perierunt et sua jura:*
> *sub Jove nunc mundus, jussa sequare Jovis.*

> Saturn is dead, his laws are all decayed:
> Jove rules the world, now Jove must be obeyed.

For *frustra niti, et odium quaerere, dementiae est:* it is madness in a man to kick against a thorn, to strive against a stream. If I see the day grow cloudy and overcast, I will betimes withdraw myself to shelter and there remain till the storm be past; nor will I greatly complain of

---

[b] *Estate:* establish.
[c] *Fraction:* a breaking off.
[d] *Motions:* conduct, principles of action.

[e] *Charity:* a favorable inclination.
[f] *Vaporous:* fanciful.

the violence of the tempest, because I know it may be followed with a worse. I often think upon that rustic who, having blamed Antigonus whilst he lived, grew after some trial had of his successor to recant his error, to recount[g][5] his crime; and, digging one day in the field, *Antigonum refodio,* "I seek," said he, "Antigonus again."

The nature as of men that have sick bodies, so likewise of the people in the crazedness[h] of their minds possessed with dislike and discontentment at things present, is to imagine that anything, the virtue whereof they hear[6] commended, would help them—but that most which they least have tried. I will not suffer my reason to be so captivated by my sensual appetite. If I frequent with greatness, I will take her as she is; and when I cannot reform her, I will by no means be induced to provoke her. I will not brave[i] her proceedings with presumptuous frowns nor humor them where I ought not with servile fawns; but, with Marcus Lepidus, *inter abruptam contumaciam et deforme obsequium, pergam iter ambitione et periculis vacuum:* I will choose a path that is void of danger and ambition and as far discoasted[j] from barbarous contumacy as deformed obsequy.[k]

Where civil government and lawful discipline do labor of intemperancy,[7] *adulatio perinde anceps, nulla, ac si nimia:* it is as dangerous not to flatter at all as to flatter too much. The courtier that goes about to raise himself a fortune must never enter into comparison with his prince; he must not question his advice, nor yet contest with his opinion. 'T is a mild and modest carriage which is pleasing and acceptable to the God of heaven and to those whom He hath placed as gods upon the earth. Kings are like lightning; they never hurt but where they find resistance. He must not strive or contend to go beyond him in apprehension, judgment,[8] or conceit, but moderate his understanding and somewhat abase the value and estimation of his worth; he shall sail with much more safety and by a surer compass than those that shall do otherwise.[9]

Emanuel, king of Portugal, having received a letter from the pope, imparted the contents thereof to Don Luis of Silveira, his principal Secretary of Estate,[1] and willed him to frame an answer to it; himself would write another and, having afterward perused both, make choice of which should like him best.[10] He, proud that his pen should run the same career[m] with his prince's,[11] employs in the composing of it all the art and skill he had. The King, having compared them, tore his own; whereupon (though indeed too late) he did perceive his

[g] *Recount:* reconsider.
[h] *Crazedness:* disordered condition.
[i] *Brave:* challenge, criticize.
[j] *Discoasted:* removed.

[k] *Obsequy:* obsequiousness.
[l] *Estate:* State.
[m] *Career:* course.

error and immediately withdrew himself from court, complaining to his wife that through indiscretion and want of judgment he had utterly overthrown himself and his estate. Which was very true, for never after could the King endure his presence.[12]

Ruy Gomez took[13] a better course; for when Charles V, with whom he played for a great sum of money, upon the encounter of a favorable card, swore by the life of his empress (which was his ordinary oath) that he would win the game, though he were sure to make him lose it, rather than he would seem to deprive his sovereign of the pleasure of his expectation, gave up his hand. Whereat the Emperor, perceiving such of his nobles as were by to smile, said nothing for the present; but afterward demanding them the reason of it, and understanding it, grew to so great a liking of him for his discretion in that one point that he made him guardian and protector of his son.

A prince can seldom times endure to see his worth checkmated by an homager.[n] Saul was mightily incensed against David because the women in their song ascribed ten thousand unto him and but one thousand to himself. *Et quid amplius praeter regnum,* "And what," said he, "can be now looked for but the kingdom?" They do easily conceit that great deserts are always attended on by great desires. Be therefore like the moon; ascribe the splendor of all thy glory only to that sun.[o] It is said of Agricola that *nunquam in suam famam gestis exultavit, ad authorem, et ducem, ut minister, fortunam referebat; ita virtute in obsequendo, verecundia in praedicando extra invidiam, nec extra gloriam erat:* he never gloried in anything he did to his own praise but, as an agent, referred the good success of his fortune to him that did employ him; and so, by his virtue in obeying, his bashfulness in boasting, he freed himself from envy and lost no part of his deserved glory.

> *Tacitus pasci si posset corvus, haberet*
> *plus dapis, et rixae multo minus, invidiaeque.*

> If so the crow but silently could feed,
> His fare perhaps would larger be by far,
> And with less envy and tumultuous jar.[14]

Service is no longer respected than it may well be recompensed, and therefore it is not good for any man to reckon upon more than he thinks his master will willingly acknowledge.

Antonius Primus overthrew himself and his whole house by nothing else than his overmuch glorying in his valiant deeds. And Caesar could not stand under the big swollen words of Silvius, who bragged

---

[n] *Homager:* subject. [o] *That sun:* i.e., the prince.

that he alone had held his army in obedience and that it would have been but ill with Tiberius if he and his legions had gone minded to have left him. *Destrui Caesar fortunam suam, imparemque tanto merito*[15] *rebatur,* saith Tacitus: Caesar imagined his fortune to be overthrown and no way equal to so great a merit.

A proud and insolent[p] carriage toward men of spirit can hardly compass anything unless in some sort or other he that useth it be able to overawe them. Physicians may converse[q] with sick men and cure them; but if their diseases be contagious they will not easily adventure on them, lest in curing others they should kill themselves. Vices are of the same nature, and vicious persons are alike as dangerous. It is good therefore to deal with them afar off and not in such places where their fits are strongest, as with the glutton at a banquet, the drunkard at a tavern, or the lustful satyr in a house of brothelry. He that walketh in the sun shall be tanned, and he that toucheth pitch shall be defiled—

> *grex totus in agris*
> *unius scabie cadit, et porrigine porci,*
> *uvaque conspecta livorem ducit ab uva*[16]

—or at least he shall be thought so. For, as[17] the Wise Man[r] saith, all flesh will resort to their like, and every man will keep company with such as he is himself.[18]

Augustus, being present at a public prize[s] with his two daughters, Livia and Julia, observed diligently what company came to court them and perceived that grave senators talked with Livia but riotous and wanton youths with Julia, whereby he came to discern their several humors and inclinations; for he was not ignorant that customs and company are cousins-german and that manners and meetings for the most part sympathize together. It is a proverb in Italy not so trite as true:

> *Dimmi con cui tu vai,*
> *E saprò quel che fai.*
>
> Tell me with whom thou wonted art to go,
> And what thou doest I presently will know.

He that talketh much before his betters cannot but be taxed of pride and arrogancy, weakness and indiscretion; and therefore it is best to speak briefly and to the point, or not at all—either a Phocion or a Pythagorean. In much talk there is much vanity; and an open mouth is a purgatory to the master.[19] The nightingale may meet with a

---

[p] *Insolent:* swollen, haughty.   [r] *Wise Man:* Solomon.
[q] *Converse:* associate.   [s] *Prize:* contest.

Laconian [t] that will not let to tell her, *Vox es, praeterea nihil,*[20] that she is nothing else but voice. Let him labor, therefore, like those of Crete, to show more wit in his discourse than words and not pour out of his mouth a flood of the one when he can hardly wring out of his brains a little drop of the other.

To converse much with inferiors, as it breedeth contempt so is it an argument of a base mind—as though the height of his conceits [u] were but proportioned to the low-built roof of their capacity.[21] But if those that be beneath us in estate do equal us in quality, it may be done without prejudice or disparagement. For as Valerius said of Metellus, that when, being consul, in requital of the love and kindness which Quintus Calidius (then tribune of the people) had shown in the repealing of his banished father, he became an humble suitor for him to the people for the praetorship and styled him always the lord and patron of his house and family, he derogated nothing from the dignity either of his place or person; *quia non humili, sed grato animo longe inferioris hominis maximo merito eximiam summittebat dignitatem:* it is not out of baseness, but nobleness of spirit that he submits his glory to the worth and worthiness of an inferior.

To enter abruptly into company, though of equals, without some compliment is mere rusticity; to depart without some courteous ceremony is uncivil and savors of contempt. To laugh overprofusely at anything begets dislike; and too much jesting, as it is a sign of lightness, so is it always followed with dissension. He that would please in doing it must be very careful and respective.[v] He must not be too comical nor too satirical. The one is currish, the other clownish and fitter for a smell-feast [w] than a man of gravity. To bite at him that is in misery is inhumanity, and he that snarls at such as are in favor and authority, he hurts himself and will repent him of his rashness. *Facetiarum, si acerbae fuerint, apud praepotentes in longum memoria est,* saith Tacitus. A bitter savor continues long[22] in a dainty palate, and a biting jest is seldom forgotten by the mighty.

He that would please in his discourse, let him not urge a man to speak of anything in which he thinks he ne'er was conversant but reduce him still to his own element. It is the way to profit himself and pleasure him. *Nemo vult latere, quod didicit:* there is no man but delights to be questioned in his own profession. He thinks he hath obtained the fruits of his labor when he finds a means to publish [x] his

---

[t] *Laconian:* Spartan.

[u] *Conceits:* ideas.

[v] *Respective:* respectfully observant of persons.

[w] *Smell-feast:* sycophant.

[x] *Publish:* make public (not necessarily in print).

learning; but then especially when, being moved thereto by others, he may seem to do it without ostentation.

I will never, therefore, talk with a divine but of his precepts, with a physician but of his practice. I will invite a soldier to relate of wars, a sailor to recount his storms. I will inquire of a falconer about his hawks, of a huntsman about his hounds; and, as near as I can, give no man occasion to blush at his own ignorance.

IV. *Of Alms and Charitable Deeds*

THERE IS no way to that eternal happiness, that celestial Jerusalem, the habitation of immortal cherubim, but either by contemplation, action, or repentance. He that would willingly, therefore, attain unto it, he must of necessity labor to be one of those three whom Christ was said to love in the Gospel. He must either sit with Mary continually at the feet of his Saviour and feed his understanding with the seeing of His works, the hearing of His words; or, with Martha, he must employ himself wholly [1] in cherishing the poor, in comforting the stranger. Or, if he have been negligent in these, he must with Lazarus arise out of the grave of sin, wherein the powers and faculties of his soul have lain putrifying for a time, and with a penitent and sorrowful intention repair the ruins of his transgression.

To imitate the first is to anticipate the joys of blessedness and, whilst we live on earth, to command the heavens. To follow the other is the only way to purchase the fee simple [a] of whatsoever the Lord hath lent us and to make ourselves absolute patrons [b] of what before we were but temporary guardians.

To give sounds [c] nothing else but gain. St. Paul confirms it when, speaking of the distribution of those of Macedonia and Achaia toward the poor saints which were at Jerusalem, he styles it by the name of fruit. And in the fourth to the Philippians, verse 17, οὐχ . . . ἐπιζητῶ τὸ δόμα, etc.[2] "I desire not a gift," saith he, "but I desire the fruit that may enlarge your account." Those that are courteous and tender-hearted toward others, ἑαυτοῖς χαρίζονται, they gratify themselves, saith the mouth of Truth. Hence is it that in Italy their ordinary form of begging is, *fate ben per voi,* do good for your own sakes. The Lord that fed five thousand could always have fed himself and his disciples, but he would be relieved by the hands of women, that their charity toward him might be an occasion of benefit to themselves. And so it is with us; we pleasure not the poor so much by our giving as we do profit ourselves by their receiving.

It is as hard for a rich man to enter into the kingdom of heaven

---

[a] *Fee simple:* outright ownership.
[b] *Patrons:* masters.

[c] *Sounds:* signifies (ME *sounen*).

as for a camel to pass through the eye of a needle. Let him follow, therefore, the counsel of our Saviour[3] and purchase friends unto himself with the Mammon of iniquity, that when he wants they may receive him not into a house of clay but into an everlasting habitation. If God have blessed him with abundance, let him not cast how to enlarge his barns but repair immediately to the bellies of such as are needy and oppressed with want and make them the storehouses of his increase. Whatsoever is given in this kind, it is not lost but lent. The Lord himself stands bound both for the use and principal; and, which is more than all, *unum accipit, et centum dat:* He receiveth one, but He repays a hundred.

Let us not, then, be backward in our alms but continually open-handed and ready to give relief where we see occasion. *Mane semina semen tuum, et vespere non cesset manus tua,* saith the Wise Man. Let us account that day as lost whereon we have not done some charitable deed and know that, whatsoever our substance be, we may afford a mite.

He that sounds a trumpet when he gives his alms, he hath in that received his reward. Popular applause was the thing he hoped for, and that he hath. God is not bound to any better payment; himself hath broken the covenants and, by the vanity of his doing, discharged Him the debt. Let us do it, therefore, in such manner as the left hand may not know what the right hand doth. *Concludamus eleemosynam in sinu pauperum,* let us convey it closely into the bosom of those that need it, and always countenance the outward action with some inward pity and compassion. "I wept," said Job, "with him that was in trouble, and my soul was heavy for the poor."

He that is truly merciful, he cannot choose but sympathize with his distressed brother and groan with him under the heavy burden of his oppression. But as Seneca saith, *lachrimandum, non plorandum,* we may weep but we may not wail; *imbecilles esse oculos scias, qui ad alienum lippitudinem, et ipsi suffunduntur.* Yet this, peradventure, would sound a great deal better in the mouth of a Stoic than a Christian, who indeed hath been instructed otherwise than to think that mercy could any way be allied to misery, which is a main and special principle in their doctrine. "Be ye merciful," said our Saviour to his disciples, "even as your Father is merciful."

If we observe the Scriptures, we shall quickly find that God is never called the Father of power, or the Father of knowledge, but the Father of mercy and compassion only, to show that such as are His children must not so much affect similitude with Him in the first, or in the second, as in the last. The Lord had three sons: Lucifer, Adam, and our Saviour Christ. The first aspired to His power and was therefore thrown down from heaven; the second, to His knowledge and was therefore deservedly driven out of Eden; the third did altogether imitate and follow Him in His mercy, and by so doing obtained an everlasting inheritance. "Ask of me, and I will give thee the nations for thy portion and the ends of the earth for thy possession," said the Lord unto him by the mouth and in the person of His servant David.

Whosoever would obtain the like, let him labor to do the like. *Invenisti patrem,* saith St. Augustine, *imitare patrem.* Let the goodness of thy works argue the greatness of thy birth; and as thy Father is merciful, so be thou. The eagle can know her chickens [d] by their eyes, and God His children by their hands. If they be closefisted He takes them not for His. They must not have them opened only but extended likewise—and that to the full length—or He reputes them but as bastards and degenerate sons and will forever disinherit them.

But if this be too weak a motive to entice us, let us behold the creatures. *Interroga jumenta,* saith holy Job to Zophar and the rest of those merciless and stonyhearted persons that were about him: "Ask the beasts, and they shall teach thee; the fowls of the heaven, and they shall tell thee; speak to the earth, and it shall show thee; or the fishes of the sea, and they shall declare unto thee." If an elephant do fall, the rest make haste to raise it; if a stork grow old, the young ones take care to feed it. The eagle eats not her prey alone but imparts it to the birds that follow her; the dolphin, if it meets with men that are drowned in the sea, it brings them to the shore. As for the earth, behold how liberal[4] it is: of all the fruits and commodities which it affords it challengeth nothing for her own use but ministers all things wholly unto thine.[5] Be not thou (whom nature hath endued with reason) more unkind to thy brother than that senseless element is to thee.

Meats, if not well concocted [e] in the ventricle [f] and afterward distributed in equal quantity according to the need and quality of the members, prove but offensive to the stomach and the whole body, whereas otherwise they feed the one and comfort the other; and so do riches to him that hath them: if he retain them greedily, they hurt him; if he bestow them graciously they purify his soul and cleanse it from what spots and blemishes soever it was polluted and defiled with. "Give of your substance to the poor," saith our Saviour Christ to the Pharisees, "and behold all things shall be clean unto you." And Daniel's counsel to Nebuchadnezzar was, *Eleemosinis peccata tua*

---

[d] *Chickens:* eaglets (here), (generally) newly hatched birds.

[e] *Concocted:* digested.
[f] *Ventricle:* stomach.

redime, that he should repair his sins by righteousness and his iniquities by giving alms.

If charity can work such powerful effects, let us not turn our faces from the poor, nor stay till such as are in distress do come unto us, but like true well-disposed Christians that have a sensible [g] feeling of one another's wants be always ready, as Abraham [6] and Lot were, to run unto them. For this is that same φιλοξενίαν διώκειν, that pursuing of hospitality, whereunto St. Paul so fervently exhorts us.

Let us not defer it till our end.[7] Do good unto thy friend before thou die[st] and according to thy means stretch out thy hand and give him.[8] The alms of a man is like a candle that giveth light: it suffereth not the soul of him that useth it to come into darkness but keeps his favor as the apple of the eye. He that bestows not his goods till then, he hath eyes when he departs from hence, but they are behind him; he hath a candle, but at his back. His own shadow is greater than that narrow path and so obscures it [that] he cannot possibly discern it.

Besides, we must so order it that the good may sooner be relieved than the bad—a Christian before a Turk, a saint before a sinner. Who would not condemn the sower that should cast his seed either upon stones, where it would wither, or among the thorns, where it would be choked, and little or none upon the good ground, which would bring forth fruit in great abundance and for every grain return a hundred?

Last of all, we must observe their necessities and not defer the salve to putrify the sore, nor keep back the potion to endanger the patient.[9] There are some that order their distributions by a calendar and think it a deadly sin to give the poor a penny but on an Easter eve, upon a communion day, or against [h] some extraordinary time; some, again, that do feed them, but (alas!) it is as the proverb saith, with a bit and a knock; othersome [10] that put it to their lips, but make them leap for it before they have it.[11] All these are barbarous and inhuman courses such as become not the birth and breeding of a Christian.

I will not, therefore, delay my alms (as moved thereto by any side respects), nor will I neglect to put my oil into the lamp till such time as I have occasion to use the light. I will not like the rich man in the Gospel cry out, *quid faciam?* what shall I do? by reason of my store, when he that is stored with nothing but with the want of store cries out *quid faciam?* in another kind. If my hand be withered, I will entreat my Saviour to restore it, that when I come into the temple I may be able to pluck my gift out of my bosom and lay it on the altar.

[g] *Sensible:* sensitive, responsive.

[h] *Against:* at, shortly before, in anticipation of.

If my neighbor's sheep do fall into a pit upon the Sabbath, I will make no scruple to run to it and lift it out. Whatsoever is good and necessary may be done at any time, and that without derogation from the holiness of the day in which it is done.

> *Rivos deducere nulla religio vetuit*
> *balantum ve greges fluvio mersare salubri,*

saith the poet. The pontifical law [1] forbade the people to wash their flocks upon a festival, yet was it done without offense to cure them of the scab. It was not lawful for them to labor in a new river, yet might they cleanse and deduce [1] the old. And by the law of God was every man strictly prohibited not to work at all upon the seventh day but to keep it holy to the Holy One, and yet priests did both cut their wood and kindle their fire on the Sabbath:

> *festis quaedam exercere diebus*
> *fas, et jura sinunt.*

To omit the performance, therefore, of those things which (besides their own goodness) are by circumstances made necessary, for fear of breaking the commandment, hath more of superstition in it than religion. The Lord hath taught us both by precept and example that mercy is always to be preferred before sacrifice, and a helping hand before burnt offering.

[1] *Pontifical law:* law of the high priests (Roman).   [1] *Deduce:* lead away, divert.

V. Of Respect and Reverence

IT IS not with virtue as with worldly princes; her pride consists not in her plumes, nor the glory of her state in the greatness of her train. She needs no outward pomp to procure respect. Her very countenance is so full of majesty that it commandeth admiration in the hearts of all men. Kings have adored her infancy and laid the ensigns of their sovereignty at her feet, even when she lay but in a manger. She hath rid as gloriously, and with as great applause, in triumph on an ass as ever did any conquering Caesar in a chariot. Tyrants have vailed [a] when she was by and been content to submit their royalty within the compass of her presence. One word from her imperious mouth hath stayed the sun, even in the swiftest of his course, and made the seas be silent [1] in their greatest rage. The lion hath stood to gaze her in the face, and the leopard hath forgot his prey with looking on her. Her beauty hath amazed [b] damnation; the very glances of it have struck such terror in the hearts of those that have conspired her overthrow that they have seemed unmindful of their wicked resolution and in an instant altered their intention. Honor attends both her and hers, and dutiful observance stirs not from [2] their elbow.

The Romans at their Floral sports were all ashamed, as long as Porcius Cato sat amongst them, to have their mimic wenches [c] strip themselves according to their ancient custom, seeming to attribute more majesty particularly to him [3] than they would challenge universally to themselves. Yet were his means but mean and his retinue small; all things in his house for use, nothing for ostentation; his authority amongst them not so great as to exact that grace. He led a life most private and retired and double-locked his doors upon ambition; no statues of his ancestors, no monuments of his descent; himself the only image of his father's family; his carriage not so pleasing as to purchase reverence. He was no friend to affectation, nor did he care for being popular; his forehead was not a throne for flattery, nor could his hands applaud that which his heart disliked. Lastly, no outward circumstance to force respect upon a multitude: 't was nothing

---

[a] *Vailed:* stooped.
[b] *Amazed:* bewitched, stupified.

[c] *Mimic wenches:* actresses in mimes.

but his virtue that amazed them—which was, indeed, so absolute in him, so well-acknowledged by them, that whosoever would have expressed an honest and worthy citizen, he did define him by the name of Cato.

Scipio, that worthy conqueror of Africa, when certain pirates were come from far to visit him at a village where he lay, stood first upon his guard and labored to repel them. But when they had assured him that their coming was not to diminish his wealth but to admire his worth, and had entreated him they might approach his presence and have a view of his person, he let them in. And immediately they went and worshiped the posts and pillars of his gates, as if his house had been the harbor of some sacred deity; and, having laid their gifts and presents at his threshold, ran hastily to his hands and kissed them. Which done, overjoyed (as it were) with so great a happiness, they returned home. Where is the king, the prince, or the dictator, with all their swelling titles and additions,[d] that can boast the like? *Delapsa coelo sydera hominibus si se offerant, venerationis amplius non recipient,* saith Valerius: should an angel descend from heaven, what could he hope for more?

Simplicity is honored by deceit, the dove is worshiped by the dragon. Virtue hath many favorers, though but few followers.

> *Quis tam*
> *perditus, ut dubitet Senecam praeferre Neroni?* [4]

Some are content to woo her that, by reason of the strictness of her life, are loath to wed her. The proudest will not let to praise her, and the profanest will not willingly displease her. Hell is no longer jaw-fallen when she is by, and Cerberus is tongue-tied in her presence.

There are none so desperately bent upon mischief but will forbear their malice in the sight of some. The lion will not always stretch forth his claws, nor will the serpent continually thrust out his sting. 'T is said of Tiberius that whilst Augustus ruled he was no way tainted in his reputation; and that while Drusus and Germanicus were alive he was content, the better to maintain a good opinion of himself in the hearts of the people, to feign those virtues which he wanted.[e] *Idem* (saith Tacitus) *inter bona, malaque mixtus, incolumi matre*—he was both gall and honey, a rose upon a thorn, till his mother was removed. And as long as he did either love or fear Sejanus, though he were taxed for his cruelty, he was not noted for his luxury. But after he had got himself out of the reach of contradiction and controlment, there was no fact in which he was not faulty, no crime to which he

---

[d] *Additions:* honorific designations.   [e] *Wanted:* lacked.

was not accessory. *Qui scire posses aut ingenium noscere, dum aetas, metus, magister prohibebant,* saith Simo to his servant, speaking of his son.

The disposition of a man is hardly known till he be out of check. He never shows himself in his own likeness till he be freed from forced respect, and then his will inclines most often to the worse. Let the gardener lay aside his knife, and his plants will riot in their growth. Hence was it that Scipio Nasica would not consent to the overthrow of Carthage, *ne ablato metu aemulae urbis luxuriari romanorum faelicitas inciperet,* lest Rome, deprived of her competitor, should surfeit in her happiness.

These later ages⁵ are corrupted and depraved. Goodness is seldom entertained but upon constraint.⁶ The times have been⁷ she could have lodged herself without a harbinger. Mortals contended only for her company and grew proud of nothing more than of her presence. Improbity was thought a wonder; sinister ᶠ dealing was like an owl among the birds at noon. *Sed genus hoc vivo iam decrescebat Homero.* But (alas!) the tares have overgrown the corn,ᵍ the venomous weed hath eaten out the wholesome herb. *Terra malos homines nunc educat, atque pusillos*⁸—the earth produceth nothing but stinking hemlock, bitter wormwood, and unsavory rue. Simplicity lies bedrid in the world. Sincerity draws near her funerals. The Cynic may go out with his lantern but repent him of his labor before he find a man according to his mind.

> *Rari quippe boni, numero vix sunt totidem, quot*
> *Thebarum portae: vel divitis ostia Nili.*⁹

> Good men are scarce, no age so many brings,
> As Thebes hath gates, or wealthy Nile hath springs.

It was a capital offense, in former times, for a young man not to rise up and reverence his elder. But now if a *friend* forswear not the thing which was committed to his trust, if he restore it as he had it, when he might have easily detained it—

> *Prodigiosa fides, et Tuscis digna libellis*
> *quaeque coronata lustrari debeat agna—*

his faith is counted as a prodigy.¹⁰ The world is become a tumbler; the head of it is in the earth whilst the heels of it are capering in the air. Not to be poor is monstrous; and to be pure is merely ominous.ʰ ¹¹ Perfection is a changeling; uprightness fades like an abortive embryo.

There are few that abstain from vice more for the love of virtue

---

ᶠ *Sinister:* crooked.

ᵍ *Corn:* grain.

ʰ *Merely ominous:* downright ill-omened.

than for the fear of punishment. All things are utterly inverted. Whatsoever is not irregular is counted so, nor is there any hope it should be otherwise.

> *Serpente Ciconia pullos*
> *nutrit, et inventa per devia rura lacerta:*
> *illi eadem sumptis quaerunt animalia pennis.*

The stork to feed her young doth serpents bring,
And lizards found in every uncouth [1] way.
They be no sooner fledged and got on wing,
But they do seek like creatures for their prey.[12]

Children can neither hear nor see, either at home or abroad, but that which is altogether unlawful and unmeet. Besides the forwardness of their own nature, they have withindoors the precepts of their parents to instruct them, their examples to encourage them; and, for the subject of their imitation abroad,

> *Catilinam*
> *quocunque in populo videant, quocunque sub axe:*
> *sed nec Brutus erit, Bruti nec avunculus usquam.*

A ruffian may they see at any time,
In every country, under every clime;
But not a Brutus treads upon the ground,
Nor can Brutus's uncle anywhere be found.

Men are curious to cleanse their houses both of dirt and dust against the coming of their friend but care not to see them hung with vices in the presence of their child. Reverence is wanting where it should most be shown. How is it possible the daughter should be chaste that cannot reckon up the adulteries of her mother, though she be never so well in breath, without a dozen stops and intermissions at the least? Such as are conscious to [j] these faults in others cannot but be culpable of them in themselves. The hearing of them told begets a willingness to try them; the seeing of them done, a willingness to do them. Many presume upon their children's indiscretion [k] and do unlawfully in their sight because themselves are persuaded they have not wit enough to discern it. But (alas!) they are mistaken in their ciphers, they do err in their accounts. The son will not let, when he is come to years, to do that in his father's sight which his father before would not forbear in his. And with what face shall he reprove him?

---

[1] *Uncouth:* unfamiliar, secret.   [k] *Indiscretion:* immaturity, innocence.
[j] *Conscious to:* aware of.

Loripedem rectus derideat: Aethiopem albus;

The crooked wretch must not upbraid the lame,
Nor must the Moor the tawny Indian blame.

It is injustice to look for reverence and respect from others when we neglect to show it toward others. There are few but desire it, though they know not how to deserve it. I will therefore esteem of men as men esteem of coin and value them not so much according to their own worth as according to what they go for. I had rather give them a little too much than come short of that which is their due. I will do by ceremonies and compliments as the tailor by his clothes, who cuts them out with advantage always rather than otherwise, yet not so far beyond all measure and proportion as that when he is to make a sleeve it should fall out to be a cloak or a mantle.

I will be wary how I reverence a man before his equal or superior, lest I purchase envy to him and hatred to myself. Tiberius could not endure that any should be reverenced whilst himself was by. The Senate had decreed to grace his mother with fresh additions of honor to her style; but he, perceiving it, labored with wise pretexts to divert their minds from that determination. The rising of her majesty made him misdoubt the setting of his own.

If greatness will maintain her state with gravity, she must not be prodigal of her presence. A prince, in the managing of his subjects, must imitate the wisdom of his Maker in the governing of the world: he must show himself but seldom in their sight, and never but with a majesty correspondent to his might. The King of Borneo never speaks but to his wife and children. If occasion of intercourse be offered him with others, he causeth a gentleman to speak unto them through a hole, holding a trunk[1] in his mouth through which he doth convey his answer to their ears, as he did not long ago to the Ambassador of Spain.[13]

But this[14] is somewhat too much affected. Howsoever, though, *majestati majore longinquo reverentia:* majesty the more retired, the more admired. The sun is seldom looked upon by any, but a comet is the amazing object of every eye. Men are by nature most ambitious and, withal, presumptuous. It is hard for a king to free his dignity from the danger of popular contempt. If the lion do but smile, the ape is ready to pluck him by the beard. But were their minds a little better seasoned with the rules and principles of virtue they would be more respective.

There is in magistrates a sacred deity.[15] To deny that honor and

---

[1] *Trunk:* speaking tube.

that reverence to their person which their place exacts is sacrilege. The censors branded a citizen of Rome with the mark of infamy, and degraded him from his order, for having yawned a little too loud in their presence. It was not lawful for a man to laugh in the Senate of the Areopagites. And Vectius was executed without process [m] because he rose not to do his duty to the tribune as he passed along. It is the part of a beast to grow respectless of authority, and the property of a block to be void of reverence.

There are some that think to make themselves esteemed by an affected carriage and are persuaded that an austere and supercilious look is the only way to work it; but their imagination moves not in her proper sphere. Their thoughts are eccentric,[n] their opinion is extravagant.[o] The ass may clothe his shoulders with the lion's skin, but whatsoever [16] he conceit he cannot affright the woods; his weakness will at length be thoroughly discovered, and his hide must pay the forfeiture of his unadvised [p] error.

[m] *Process:* trial.
[n] *Eccentric:* off-center, erroneous.

[o] *Extravagant:* off the (proper) path.
[p] *Unadvised:* heedless, ill advised.

VI.   Of Gifts and Benefits

T O SAY there were nothing so sure a man's[1] own as what he gives, in the hearing of some miserable usurer that makes his gold his god, his countinghouse his shrine, would peradventure beget no more belief than an affected paradox; but with such as are truly generous and dote not on the burnished outside of such glistering clay, it is embraced as an accepted opinion. Hence was it that Rabirius, bringing Mark Antony upon the stage, makes him, when he beheld the funerals of his best fortunes, to cry out upon the scene, *Hoc habeo, quodcunque dedi:* "Whatsoever I have given, that still is mine."

Alfonso, king of Sicily, being demanded what he would reserve for himself that gave away so many things to so many, "Even those things," answered he, "which I do give; for whatsoever is over and above I deem not in the number of what is mine." The like hath Xenophon reported of his Cyrus, and Curtius of his Alexander; and hence it was that Martial, peradventure in confirmation of this assertion, did take occasion to frame this witty epigram:

> *Callidus effracta nummos fur auferet arca,*
> *prosternet patrios impia flamma lares:*
> *debitor usuram pariter, sortemque negabit,*
> *non reddet sterilis semina iacta seges.*
> *Dispensatorem fallax spoliabit amica,*
> *mercibus extrustas obruet unda rates,*
> *extra fortunam est, quicquid donatur amicis,*
> *quas dederis, solas semper habebis opes.*

The subtle thief may break thy chest and steal thy wealth away,
Profaner flames thy household gods to ruin may betray,
Both use and principal likewise thy debtors may retain,
And barren soil no profit yield of all thy foresown grain.
A wanton and a wily lass thy steward may deceive;
Thyself the waves may of thy ship, full fraught with wares, bereave.
Those favors Fortune cannot touch, which to thy friends are shown:
That wealth alone thou giv'st away shall always be thine own.[2]

But, that the barbarous ingratitude of inhuman cannibals may not frustrate our expectation in this point, we must have a continual care that our liberalities and presents be still accompanied and ordered with discretion.[3] To give is not an easy and tumultuary [a] action. It must be done with choice, and not by chance; wisely and warily, not heedlessly and hastily.[4] It is a passage full of dangerous encounters, and which [b] cannot be avoided but with advise [c] and caution.[5]

Wisdom will either give to such as are already good or, at least, to such as may in time be made so. After a long and ripe deliberation she will choose the worthiest. Her bosom is open, but not loose; much may come out of it, nothing fall. Her bounty, though it walk, it wanders not. She endeavors herself to this man, she seeks to repay that man.[6] She succors one, she pities another. To some she gives; to some she only offers—yet not like an Italianated courtier, that hates to see his kindness entertained. To some, again, she neither [7] offers nor gives, although their wants require it, because she sees their own improvidence is such they will not let to want, whate'er she give them; and yet othersome she will both urge and press to a kind acceptance of her willing proffers. *Multi,* saith Tacitus, *silentium et paupertatem confessioni, et beneficio praeposuere:* many had rather endure their poverty with silence than by publishing their wants receive relief. *Sero dedit, qui roganti dedit:* those benefits are slow of foot that come not till I call them.

To ask is a thing both troublesome and wearisome; it is a word that lies heavy on the tongue and cannot well be uttered but [8] with a bashful and dejected countenance. I will strive, therefore, to meet my friend in his wishes if I cannot prevent [d] him. Arcesilaus had no sooner discovered the cloaked wants of his decayed associate but presently he conveyed a sum of money in very close and secret manner under his pillow, that he might seem rather to find than to receive that which he stood in need of and was ashamed to ask. Meat, though but mean, is always comfortable when the stomach of the patient is prepared to receive it; and water ministered in season doth work ofttimes as powerful an effect for the recovery of the diseased as a more costly recipe.[e] [9]

It is the manner of the giving that lends a glorious luster to the gift that comes not gratis, which is purchased by importunacy and violent entreaty. There can be nothing more overbought than that which costs us the price of so many long-winded prayers and tedious supplications.

> *Sex sestertia si statim dedisces,*
> *cum dixti mihi: sume, tolle, dono;*

---

[a] *Tumultuary:* spur-of-the-moment, unreflecting.
[b] *And which:* such as.
[c] *Advise:* advisement.
[d] *Prevent:* anticipate.
[e] *Recipe:* prescription.

deberem tibi Paete pro ducentis,
at nunc cum dederis, diu moratus,
post septem puto, vel novem kalendas,
vis dicam tibi veriora veris?
Sex sestertia, Paete perdidisti.

Six sesterces if thou hadst lent me straight [f]
When thou saidst, take, bear hence, I give it free,
I would have ought [g] thee for two hundredweight,
And thought myself withal much bound to thee.
But now, because thou gav'st it with delay,
And mad'st me, Paetus, some nine kalends stay,
Wilt give me leave of more than truth to boast?
Six [10] sesterces, dear Paetus, thou hast lost.[11]

The grace of a deed consists in the willingness of him that doth it, which cannot well be argued but by his forwardness to do it. To hold the mind of a man in suspense is but to torture it betwixt hope and fear. Such as can temporize with men's expectancies and promise anything for present satisfaction's sake are not of my garde.[h] [12]

Diligo praestantem, non odi Cinna negantem:
sed tu nec praestas, nec cito Cinna negas.

I view the granter with a cheerful eye,
And hate not him that doth my suit deny;
But Cinna, thou, the greater is thy blame,
Nor grant'st nor quickly yet deniest the same.

I had rather my hopes were clean cut off than so produced.[i]

Mutua te centum sestertia Phaebe rogavi,
cum tu dixisses, exigis ergo nihil.
Inquiris, dubitas, cunctaris, meque diebus
teque decem crucias: iam rogo Phaebe, nega.

I prayed thee, Phaebus, me a crown to lend,
When thou replied'st, "That's nothing, gentle friend."
With doubts, demurs, inquiries, and delays,
Thyself and me thou tortur'st many days.
Now therefore, Phaebus, I begin to pray
Thou would'st deny and quickly say me nay.[13]

Ἀ χάρις ἀ βραδύπους, ἄχαρις χάρις. The Graces are all of them youthful virgins, very nimble in their motion and full of spirit. They are not paced either like the crab or snail. No gout is in their feet, no palsy in

---

[f] *Straight:* straightway.
[g] *Ought:* owed.

[h] *Garde:* guard, company; but see Appendix, p. 150, number 12.
[i] *Produced:* delayed, drawn out.

their hands. Their words are full of refreshing; their countenance is Jovial¹ and like the highest heavens, always without clouds. Neither their tongues nor their eyes were ever taught how to equivocate. They bear about no faces but their own. If at any time they appear either masked or disguised, it is by their keeper's enforcing, not of their own choosing. They are fallen into the hands of some broking pander ᵏ that seeks by his malicious practices to deprave their breeding, to corrupt their blood. Of themselves they are ingenuous ¹ ¹⁴ and no way tainted with any base or servile references. He that is willing to be principled and instructed by them shall learn that what he gives he must give freely, for to stick at this were to detract from the grace of his munificence; and that when he gives he must not think on what he shall receive, for this were sordid and mechanical ᵐ and of itself sufficient to dim the gloss and glory of his action.

It is the property of a usurer not to let out his money but for interest, and of his gripping ⁿ scribe not to do any man a pleasure till he be sure of some consideration. He that will give aright must never think of gain. The profit and commodity which proceeds from hence must come unlooked for, and when the thing that causeth it is clean out of the mind of him that did it.

> *Munera magna mihi mittis, sed mittis in hamo:*
> *et piscatorem piscis amare potest?*
>
> Thou send'st me gifts, but such as baits do prove:
> And can the fish, think'st thou, the fisher love?

He must order his presents in such manner that they may be the better welcome and the more esteemed because they come in convenient time and to serve his turn to whom they are directed. I prize not the love and friendship of a surgeon who, having notice of my hurts, doth notwithstanding forslow ° his coming till my wounds be either past recovery or, at least, recovered by some other.

He must beware that his gifts be not a charge and burden to his friend, rather than otherwise, and that he do not hurt when he intends to heal.

> *Quod non argentum, quod non tibi misimus aurum,*
> *hoc facimus causa, Stella diserta tua,*
> *quisquis magna dedit, voluit sibi magna remitti:*
> *fictilibus nostris exoneratus eris.*

ʲ *Jovial:* Jovelike.
ᵏ *Broking pander:* money-grubbing procurer.
ˡ *Ingenuous:* frank, uncorrupted.

ᵐ *Mechanical:* base.
ⁿ *Gripping:* grasping.
° *Forslow:* delay.

That thee no gold or silver we did send,
'T was for thy sake we did it gentle friend:
Who great things give, do look for great again;
Our trifling toys shall ease thee of that pain.[15]

He must not send him that which is superfluous and of little use. It
were a[16] senseless oversight in any man to present a maimed cripple
with a corselet, a strong-limbed soldier with a crutch, a thresher with a
book, a student with a flail.

There must of necessity be always some even correspondency between the gift and the party's abilities to whom it is given.

> *Non est aptus equis Ithacae locus: ut neque planis*
> *porrectus spatiis, nec multae prodigus herbae.*
> *Atreide, magis apta tibi tua dona relinquam.*
>
> My land for horse is no convenient place,
> It runs not out in any even space;
> The fields are barren, and the meads are poor,
> Such as of grass afford but little store.
> I leave therefore, Atreides,[p] unto thee
> Thy gifts, far fitter for thyself than me—

saith Telemachus, the son of Ulysses.[17] *Parvum* [18] *parva decent*. Offer a
beggar gold, he thinks you mock him; give him a penny, he repays
you thanks.

He must likewise beware that while he labors to send him that
which may be pleasing and acceptable, he do not send him that which
may upbraid him with any weakness or infirmity. To proffer wine to
one that is intemperate, or a potion to him that is of a sick and crazy
constitution, would hardly, peradventure, be taken in good part. It
is no gift, but a reproach, in which the receiver may acknowledge his
defects.

He that would interest and estate himself upon some long-intended
travail[q] in the remembrance of his friend must look that the memorial
which he leaves behind him at his departure be both necessary and
durable. There are many[19] that think no longer on the giver than they
have occasion to use his gift. Their brains are subject to the symptoms
of a dangerous lethargy: they can no sooner receive a benefit but
suddenly they forget it. Their eye alone is their heart's intelligence;
they are like a glass that represents no object longer than it stands
before it. For such, therefore, we must seek out that which may be
lasting and of some continuance, the sight whereof may still incul-

[p] *Atreides:* Homeric designation for   [q] *Travail:* work.
Agamemnon and Menelaus, supposed
sons of Atreus.

cate the countenance of the author. *Extet, haereat amico meo, et convivat.* Let it be such as may be always extant,[20] such as may cleave as close unto him as his shirt and continually both bed and board with him.

But he that would not lose the benefit of his bounty must above all take heed he make not himself the trumpet of his own benevolence.

> *Quae mihi praestiteris menini, semperque tenebo;*
> *cur igitur taceo, Posthume, tu loqueris?*
> *Incipio quoties alicui tua dona referre,*
> *protinus exclamat, dixerat ipse prius.*
> *Non belle quaedam faciunt duo, sufficit unus*
> *huic operi: si vis ut loquar, ipse tace.*
> *Crede mihi, quamvis ingentia, Posthume, dones,*
> *authoris pereunt garrulitate sui.*

> I think on thy good turns, and always will;
> Then why hold I my peace? thou speakest still.
> When I begin to tell them, evermore
> Each man cries out, "He told us so before."
> Two cannot well do this; let one surcease;
> If thou wilt have me speak, hold thou thy peace.
> Believe me, Posthume, though thy gifts delight,
> Their author's prating makes them perish quite.[21]

It is the basest degree of baseness to enter our liberalities upon record, or in a calendar to register the days of our good deeds. It is for the triobolary empirics ͬ to stage themselves in the market and recount their cures.

A friend of Caesar's had preserved a certain man from the tyranny of that triumviral proscription, whom afterward he enforced to exclaim, *Redde me Caesari,* "Prithee, restore me back again to Caesar; I had rather undergo a thousand deaths than be thus continually upbraided by thee with [22] my life." *Lacerat animum et premit frequens meritorum commemoratio:* the frequent commemoration of a benefit doth rack the mind of him that did receive it.

To entertain a man with fair assurances and deep engagements of our word and promise [23] till such time as our own turns are served, and then to search occasions of dislike, may well savor of much subtlety but hath no smack at all of any honesty.[24] Here is policy without justice, a serpent without a dove.

A sudden change in him that hath a long time estranged and alienated himself from our acquaintance may minister us just occasion to suspect the soundness and sincereness of his affection.

ͬ *Triobolary empirics:* threepenny quacks.

Quel che ti fa lo che non suole,
O ingannato t'ha, o ingannarti vuole,

saith the Italian proverb.[25] Every man's look is not the map of his meaning. The siren's song is the sailor's wrack; the fowler's whistle the bird's death; and the wholesome bait the fish's bane. The wolf hath made him a cassock of a wether's skin and thinks that under the habit of this disguise he may pass without fear or danger of discovery and conceal the loathed brood of his adulterate thoughts. But let him that loves his own security ascribe no credit to the words of Davus, be they never so sententious: a man may easily be prodigal of that which costs him little. *Latet anguis in herba*—there is a canker often in a rose, and every kindness is not to be construed as the prognostic of an ingenuous love. There is no labyrinth more intricate than the mind of man; it is so full of angles, by-passages, and cross-conveyances that the wisest and nimblest apprehension cannot but lose itself in seeking out the center.

His actions that should direct us are oftentimes disguised as strangely as his words; he gives them that outward dye which he thinks fittest for the closer effecting of his intended projects and designs. Eutrapelus [26] shall serve me for an instance to verify the truth of this assertion,

cuicunque nocere volebat,
vestimenta dabat pretiosa,

saith the poet:

If he to mischief any did intend,
To him still precious garments would he send.

'T was somewhat a costly and unusual kind of proceeding, yet such as brought to pass his purpose without discovery and gave his expectation that contentment which it looked for;

beatus enim iam
cum pulchris tunicis sumet nova consilia, et spes
dormiet in lucem, scorto postponet honestum
officium, nummos alienos pascet, ad imum
thrax erit, aut olitoris aget mercede caballum.

For now grown proud with his gay clothes, new ways,
New plots, new hopes, new counsels he essays;
He'll sleep till noon and honesty forgo
For lust, not caring where or what he owe.
At length he must—his wants will so require—
Turn rogue or drive an herbwife's ass for hire.[27]

The like hath been the practice of those inhuman tyrants that heretofore have made the very earth to groan under the heavy burden of their cruelty. For when once they began to distaste the power and greatness whereunto they had advanced their favorites, considering they durst not (for fear of popular detraction) openly work their overthrow, they labored to increase the flame of their ambition by gracing them more and more with all the dignities and honors that they could, to the intent that, having puffed them up with pride and insolence, they might the better work them to a neglect of their dependency and make them slide into contempt, or some more capital inconvenience, whereby afterward they might have juster title to oppress them.

Many there are *quos insidiosa tranquillitate provectos improvisus turbo perculit,* whose woeful and unexpected shipwreck, after a long but yet deceitful and deluding calm, may give authority and countenance to this undoubted truth. It is reported of Domitian that *eum semper impensissime se diligere simulabat, quem maxime interemptum vellet,* he would seem to love them most whom he wished least should live. Nero dismissed Seneca with kisses and embracements, when, notwithstanding those his faithless flatteries, he minded [a] nothing but his death. Livius [28] Drusus was accused by a feigned friend to be a factious noveller: [b] Caesar gave ear to his indictment yet nevertheless invested him with the praetorship, invited him to his table. He did so color his displeasure that he neither seemed estranged from him in countenance nor changed in words; and when he might have stayed the slippery footing of his youthful rashness, he chose rather to see him fall by his improvidence. *Ira quae tegitur nocet,* saith the tragedian: the slowest barker is the surest biter.[29]

He that discovers unto me the anger of his heart shows that he hath no mind to do me any hurt but wisheth I would refrain his presence and give way to his distemperature till such time as the heat of it were somewhat spent; whereas,

> *gravia quisquis vulnera*
> *patiente et aequo motus animo pertulit,*
> *referre potuit:*

he that can temporize with those that wrong him, and manage his conceived displeasure with observations and respects, and now and then (to clear himself of all suspicion) present them with some testimony of a friendly mind, may make what passage he please for his

---

[a] *Minded:* intended.   [b] *Noveller:* innovator, or talebearer.

revenge. Who would imagine that a countenance so smooth and fair were only plastered? 'T is usual for men to veil a wrinkled" heart with ceremonious compliments and verbal promises, but to apparel it with the habit of actual kindnesses is seldom seen; yet therefore the more to be feared because the least suspected. There can be nothing looked for but duplicity from him that hath got[30] the mastery of his looks and can smile at that which galls him to the quick. But he that suddenly discovers the imperfections which he hath, though the world account him not very wise, he cannot be very wicked. King John of France was of so generous a disposition that he could not endure the sight of any that displeased him, yet he was never the author or the actor of any base or beastly cruelty.

As it is against the nature of love not to be violent, so is it against the nature of violence not to be inconstant. The fierceness of our passions argues the shortness of their continuance, and in those that are of a hot and fiery temper they are as easily removed as they were quickly moved. Their anger is like a flaming bavin' that crackles terribly for the time but presently consumes to ashes. Whereas Herod and those prodigious" monsters whom I named before, with divers others of the like stamp and mold, that can double-gild their malicious hatred with pleasing words and plausible appearances and that can seem out of a cold and settled temperature carelessly to neglect, as it were, the privy nips and secret glances of such as understand the course of their disguised proceedings, are oftentimes the wretched and accursed authors of many doleful and dismal tragedies. They register their discontents in sheets of brass and write them with a pen of steel; and howsoever they make no show of apprehending them, yet do they think on nothing more than on repairing them. *In animo revolvente iras etiamsi impetus offensionis languet, memoria valet,* saith Tacitus: though the force of what offends them do seem to languish, the memory thereof is strong and able.

ᵘ *Wrinkled:* devious, not well-intentioned.

ᵛ *Bavin:* a brand made up of light combustible matter.

ʷ *Prodigious:* unnatural.

VII. *Of Repulses and Denials*

I T IS no honesty to produce the hopes of men with vain and frivolous delays, nor yet civility to cut them off with harsh and barbarous denials. The wise physician doth never minister a potion which he thinks will prove unsavory to the palate of his patient but he seconds it with something that is more pleasing and delicious to the taste, wherewith he relisheth the mouth of him that doth receive it and makes his stomach the willinger to take it, the stronger to retain it. A well-complexioned countenance wants not the help of artificial insinuations.[a] Beauty is welcome wheresoever she come;[1] she needs no other usher than the mildness of her own aspect to procure her passage. But that which is of a[2] coarser grain, and seems to be defective either in show or substance, must of necessity have some addition to give it complement and make it passable.

If I cannot therefore satisfy my friend in one kind, I will strive to do it in another and make him know by real demonstration that it was not because I would not, but because I could not, that I did not[3] content him in the former. I will not offer him a serpent when he asketh bread; nor will I go about to counsel him when I should relieve him. I will not, like Dionysius, give much to him that will accept of nothing, but nothing to him that would be glad of anything. Briefly, I will not, when I suspect his wants, the better to prevent him in his demands, begin to reckon up my several debts and payments and with a whispering accent (yet such as he may easily understand) complain how weakly I am furnished for the present to discharge them. They are forms of denials which do a little savor of inhumanity, yet such as I could better brook than those barbarous interrogatories of churlish Nabal, *Quis est David? aut quis est filius Ishai?* "Who is David, or who is the son of Ishai?"[b] Yet, as the poet saith concerning the latter,

> *Durum est, Sexte, negare cum rogaris,*
> *multo durius, antequam rogeris.*

> 'T is harsh, when thou art asked, for to deny;
> But harsher far, before a man do try.[4]

[a] *Insinuations:* aids, supporting.   [b] *Ishai:* Jesse, father of David.

I would not willingly destroy a serpent in the shell. If the requests of my friend [5] be such as are at enmity with reason and hold no correspondency with religion, I will answer him, with Pericles, that I can satisfy him no further than the bounds and limits of the altar will permit me. If he have the face to demand me that which is unjust, why should not I likewise have the heart to deny it?

Agesilaus, when his father would have enforced him to have judged a certain process contrary to right and reason, "Father," said he, "you have shown me from my youth that I should always be pliable [c] to the laws. Now, therefore, I will obey you in judging nothing which is any ways against them." If vice have the boldness to offend, why should not virtue dare to reprehend? There came two men to Theocritus to borrow his bathing comb, the one a stranger, the other of his acquaintance. His answer to them both was altogether negative but somewhat differing: for, "As for thee," said he to the one, "I know thee not at all; and as for thee," to the other, "I know thee but too well." A votary of Minerva's in the town of Athens, when certain fellows that had brought some victims to the temple entreated her to make them drink, "My friends," said she, "I am afraid it would become a custom."

And thus we may without fear of scandalous imputations cut short the importunacy of such as being not known to us at all (or, at least, not known but for some notable enormity) shall notwithstanding presume to ask us that, the grant whereof may peradventure redound with loss and hindrance to ourselves. As I am not σκυθρωπός, so I would not willingly be δυσωπός; as I am not churlish, so I would not be childish. *Est inter Tanaim quiddam socerumque Viselli.* As I cannot frowningly repel a reasonable request, so I will not bashfully [d] consent to that which is otherwise. If the desires of my friend be such as may both prejudice me, endanger him, and pleasure neither, I will labor to dissuade him from them; but, howsoever, I will not yield unto him in them. *Exorari in perniciem rogantium saeva bonitas est:* it is a cruel kind of courtesy to condescend to anything that may be dangerous and hurtful to him that asks it.

If I do a good turn to any man it shall be such as I think will never turn, and whatsoever is not of this strain cannot proceed but from an affable and soothing kind of hatred. I will not give him money to maintain a courtesan, because I will not make myself an accessory to his crime. He shall never have occasion in colder blood (and when the heat of his distemperature shall be allayed) to exclaim against me and say: *ille amando me occidit,* there is the man whose loving and

---

[c] *Pliable:* conformable.   [d] *Bashfully:* timidly.

kind affection hath wrought my utter overthrow and ruin. I will shun the patronage of such unseasonable indulgence and give nothing to any which myself might be ashamed to ask of any.[6]

I will not offer much to him that sues for little. It was an error and a madness in Alexander to force a city on a soldier that thought himself too weak and base for so high a fortune. A low-built spirit will easily believe that he which goes about to overcharge his hopes would willingly discharge them, and that to proffer him more than ever he desired were but a subtle kind of practice to make him fail of what he had deserved.

The glory of humility, Christ Jesus, when he came to wash the feet of his disciples, he was repelled by Simon Peter in a threefold manner. First, by an interrogatory reprehension: Κύριε, σύ μου νίπτεις τοὺς πόδας, "Lord, dost thou wash my feet?" Secondly, by an absolute negation: οὐ μὴ νίψῃς μου τοὺς πόδας εἰς τὸν αἰῶνα, "Thou shalt never do it." And lastly, by too liberal and free a grant: Κύριε, μὴ τοὺς πόδας μου μόνον, etc., "Lord, not my feet only, but my hands and my head also." And I know not if in this latter his opposition were more relenting than in either of the former.

Unwillingness can alter her fashion and disguise her habit as often as she please. She is never unprovided of excuses. Antigonus hath an evasion at all hands. If the Cynic ask him a penny, οὐ βασιλικὸν τὸ δόμα, "It is not a gift for a king"; if a pound, οὐ κυνικὸν τὸ λῆμμα, "It is not an alms for a beggar," when indeed he might have given a penny as to a beggar, a pound as from a king. I cannot but wonder much at that which histories report of Titus, the son of Vespasian: that he never suffered any man to depart with discontent out of his presence.

A prince that doth exceed in grants shall find his subjects exceed in their demands. Men fashion not themselves[7] by reason, but example. They never look on what they have received, but continually fix their minds on what they may receive. The easy purchasing of one suit is but a motive to the setting forward of another. And where is the exchequer that can afford contentment unto all? *Quod cunctis tribuat, non habet arca Jovis.*[8] It was nothing else but the sweetness of his conversation that did correct the bitter and malignant quality which all denials and repulses are wont to carry with them. If I cannot therefore satisfy my friend in his desires, I will so manifest my love to him by circumstance that he shall never have occasion to tax me of unkindness.

VIII. *Of Reprehensions and Reproofs*

THIS WORLD is nothing else but a retiring place for all infirmities. The most things that are in it are perfectly imperfect and the best things but imperfectly perfect. It is *casa d'Iddio,* a house of charity erected by the hand of heaven for the receipt [a] of weakness. All that are in it are either mad or maimed, diseased or distempered; there is not one amongst us absolutely sound. Our essence and existence is in itself but an unequal mixture of crazy and sickly qualities. We are altogether defective in our functions and fail exceedingly in the performance of our operations. It is frailty that supplies our being both with matter and form; he, therefore, that is most upright in his proceedings may at some times stumble if not fall.

There are some that offend but know not their offense; some that know it yet let not to proceed in it; and some, again, that will not seem to know it because they are ashamed to confess it. Correction, therefore, is necessary to reform our ignorance, to remove our bashfulness, and to prevent our perseverance. But then it must not proceed from any passion of the mind, but from a compassion of the heart. "I prithee," said Plato to Speusippus, "do thou correct my servant, for I am angry." It must be done with the spirit of mildness, not of madness; of love and lenity, not of choler and severity.

And that we may the better prevail in this so charitable an action, we must first of all vouchsafe a little now and then to turn the discussion of our judgment from outward objects to those that are within. We must take a diligent survey of our own weaknesses and consider well if ourselves be no way tainted with the contagion of those corrupt affects [b] and putrefactions which we observe in others:

> *teipsum*
> *concute, num qua tibi vitiorum inseverit olim*
> *natura, aut etiam consuetudo mala.*[1]

It is hard when he that cannot order his own life shall be made the judge of another's. He must form himself that would reform his friend. It is impossible for any man to discern aright the mote which

---

[a] *Receipt:* reception.   [b] *Affects:* inclinations.

is in his brother's eye when there is gravel in his own. The hand can never cleanse the body unless itself be clean.

First, therefore, physician cure thine own ills and break not out into passion against intemperancy when thou thyself art more intemperate than any. Glory not like an hypocritical Pharisee in the fulfilling of the law, when thou dishonorest God by nothing more than by the transgression of the same:

> *castigas turpia, cum sis*
> *inter Socraticos notissima fossa cynaedos.*[2]

Thou that rebukest others for adultery, abstain from it thyself; and thou that hatest images, commit not sacrilege. Such as cannot disguise their imperfections nor blanch their errors with some show of purity, as they are gently to be pitied, so are they generally to be pardoned: *his furor ipse dat veniam*—their own weakness doth sufficiently excuse them—

> *Sed peiores, qui talia verbis*
> *Herculis invadunt, et de virtute locuti*
> *clunem agitant,*
>
> But they are worse that stoutly such upbraid,
> Or giantlike with swaggering terms invade,
> And, whilst they speak of what is good and just,
> Practice the motions of lascivious lust.[3]

But if he be not for the present the subject of those infirmities which he discerns in others, let him call to mind if theretofore[4] he were not; and as then he would willingly have received help from others, let him be now as forward to afford it in the like proportion to others. Let him not scorn the lameness of his friend but grant that pity which he sought for then; let him make it his own case and handle the ulcerous inflammations of his neighbor as nicely and with as much respect as he would his own.

But if he be not polluted in the like kind, nor ever was, let him think with himself time is not so far spent but hereafter he may be. We are all of us the children of corruption; and, as the Mimic[e] saith, *Cuivis accidere potest, quod cuiquam potest:* that may happen to every man which can happen to any.

Security is not a creature of this world. Our life is nothing else but a temptation. There is oftentimes in men an ebb and a flow, a reciprocal change and alternation both of humors and qualities. Their minds are subject to the accessions and intermissions of a tertian;[d] sometimes

[e] *The Mimic:* a writer of classical mimes (here, Publilius Syrus).

[d] *Tertian:* recurrent fever.

they grow from bad to good, sometimes again they fall from better to worse. It is said of Saul, *non erat melior illo,* there was no man like him among all the people; yet in a little space he became a reprobate. David was a man according to God's own heart, yet falls into the sins of murder and adultery.

Peter was a disciple and apostle, so far in love with his Master that he promised to follow Him to the prison, to the death, and never to be offended by Him, never to deny Him; yet a maid seduceth him, he renounceth Him, he forswears Him, he detests Him.[5] Let no man, therefore, in regard of his own strength triumphantly insult over the imperfections of his weaker friend, but with modesty seek to reduce ° his wandering feet into the way. *Ne glorietur accinctus, aeque ac discinctus.* He that persuades himself he stands, let him beware he do not fall.

But if he do not labor of the like infirmities, nor ever did, nor yet is like to do, let him consider if the party that merits reprehension, as he may be taxed for his deficiency in some things, may not be likewise praised for his proficiency in othersome and, for those good parts which he hath deserved, be borne withal for such as he wants.

> *Amicus dulcis, ut aequum est,*
> *cum mea compenset vitiis bona, pluribus hisce,*
> *si modo plura mihi bona sunt, inclinet, amari*
> *si volet.*[6]

The reprehensions wherewith emperors and wise commanders have heretofore been accustomed to note the factious and rebellious contumacy of their soldiers have always been interwoven with many praises and approbations of their former merit. *Tu tot praeliorum socia, tot praemiis aucta,* saith Germanicus to that seditious legion which was the principal cause of all those troubles and commotions in Pannonia. *Nimia pietas vestra,* saith Otho likewise to his tumultuary soldiers, *acrius quam consideratius tumultus hosce excitavit:* "Your overkind affection hath more eagerly than advisedly excited these disorders."

Yea, God himself, intending to reprove the Bishop of Ephesus, tells him that he had abandoned and forgone his former charity. "But thou hast this in thee," saith He, "thou hatest the doings of the Nicolaitans, which I likewise hate." *Ad reprehendenda aliena facta aut dicta, ardet omnibus animus; vix satis apertum os, aut lingua prompta videtur, quae meditata pectore evolvat,* saith Sallust: "We run with open mouths to reprehend the sayings and the deeds of others, and think our tongue too backward in uttering what we have

___
° *Reduce:* lead back (L., *reducere*).

conceived." But if we did descend sometimes into ourselves, and not always fasten our eyes upon the wallet which hangeth at his back that goes before us, we might peradventure find a means to cure ourselves of this intemperancy.

The mind of man is of a weak and tender constitution; we must take heed we do not chafe it but feel and handle the wounds of it with dexterity. Let us observe but with what modesty Christ in the fourth of John doth work the woman of Samaria to a free confession of her fault and afterward how discreetly he reproves her, πέντε ἄνδρας ἔσχες, etc., "Thou hast had five husbands, and he whom thou now hast is not thy husband"; and with what art he brings the two disciples of Emmaus to bewray themselves, ἡμεῖς [δὲ] ἠλπίζομεν, etc., "We believed that it was he that should deliver Israel"; and that howsoever he rebuke them sharply—"O ye fools, and slow of heart"—he doth at all hands allege his reasons, ἀρξάμενος ἀπὸ Μωυσέως, etc., beginning from Moses and from all the prophets.[7] Lastly, how after he had reproved his disciples for sleeping whilst he himself was praying in the garden, he doth immediately upon it excuse their error: "The spirit," saith he, "is willing, but the flesh is weak."

Whosoever, therefore, would reclaim his friend and bring him to a true and perfect understanding of himself, he must never reprehend him but he must *t* quote his reason and second it with the sweetness of some kind and friendly consolation. He must not do it publicly and before such as peradventure would but entertain themselves with laughter, to the great disparagement of his sufficiency.[8] An open admonition is an open disgrace. He that doth it, I account him no better than mine enemy; he seeks not to correct my passions but to please his own. He must avoid all rashness of words, all harshness of voice. He must temper his vinegar with oil; and when he hath given the stroke, apply the balm. In us it is a part of charity; in ministers, a point of duty.

There was placed by God's appointment in the Ark of the Covenant the rod of Aaron, a pot of manna, and the Tables of the Law to show us that the minister (who indeed, [if] rightly called, is nothing else but the ark of God's testament) should have in him the manna of pleasing consolation for the good, the rod of correction for the wicked, and the Tables of the Law (that is, the tables of understanding and discretion) for all. Solomon, to instruct us in the like, caused both lions, oxen, and cherubim to be engraven upon the bases of the temple. Lions to signify unto us the severity which a minister is to exercise against the bad, oxen to denote the mildness wherewith he

---

t *But he must:* unless he.

ought to practice such as are good, cherubim to express the knowledge
that should accompany his words to make them pleasing and profitable to all.[9]

To a heart fully resolute, counsel is tedious and reprehension loathsome. It will not be amiss, therefore, to give him leave a little to
vent [g] his heart and then to set upon him when he is more calm, more
capable of reproof. If contraries encounter, the conflict must needs
be dangerous.[10] There can be no agreement between Caesar and
Pompey, but one of them must vail. If a house be on fire, we seek not
so much to quench it with water as by pulling down the next to
make the want of fuel diminish the flame. But if a superior, or a
magistrate, shall perceive one that is under his command and jurisdic-
tion ready to plunge himself into some vile extreme, he may boldly
threaten and reprove him. One passion doth often cure another. A
gentle potion works but a weak effect in a strong body. It is in sins
as it is in sores: some cannot be cured but with corsives,[h][11] nor some
amended but with menaces. The way to overrule them in their disordered motions is to overawe them.

Argue sapientem, et diliget te, correct a wise man and he will love
thee; but he that is void of understanding will laugh thee to scorn.
To reprehend a fool is to cast pearl before swine; he knows not the
benefit of correction, and therefore he refuseth it; but (alas!) it hap-
peneth to him thereafter. Adam and Eve, because they did reply
when God reproved them, their punishment was greater than it
should [i] have been. He cursed Cain because he kicked against Him
when he said, *Numquid ego sum custos fratris mei?* "Am I my
brother's keeper?" He chased Saul out of His presence because he
contradicted Samuel but pardoned David because he yielded to the
rebuke of Nathan. And Christ, when He saw how patiently His
Disciples did submit themselves to His reproofs in the twenty-sixth
of Matthew, *Dormite iam, et requiescite:* "Now sleep," saith He,
"and take your rest."

The reprehensions of a friend are like sweet balls [j] wherewith he
washeth away the spots and stains of sin from out our souls; there is
nothing that brings us to a truer knowledge of ourselves. It is an
axiom in philosophy that *posito sensibili super sensorium non fit
sensus:* there can be no sense unless the object be somewhat removed
from the instrument. We can hardly see those imperfections and defects which harbor in our own bosom; but others may easily discern
them.

[g] *Vent:* ease, give relief to.

[h] *Corsives:* strong medicines; an obsolete form of "corrosives."

[i] *Should:* would.

[j] *Sweet balls:* perfumed soaps.

A just reproof is like the rod of Aaron. If we hold it in our hands it flourisheth; that is, if we esteem of it, it doth us good. But if we cast it on the ground it becomes a serpent; that is, if we neglect it carelessly it doth increase our fault, it multiplies our sin.[12] If vices have attained to their full strength and stature, and consist not so much individually in some as generally in all, I should think it better, with Tiberius, to pass them over with a sponge than by painting them out with a pencil, *hoc assequi, ut palam fiat, quibus vitiis impares simus,* make the world a witness of our weakness, and withal show such as are our enemies [13] how they may assault us with advantage to themselves and prejudice to us.[14]

IX. Of Injuries and Indignities

TRUE VALOR is not headstrong. Obstinate opinions are not of her company, nor self-willed resolutions of her counsel. She stands not upon terms of honor and reputation with her fortune but willingly treads the path to which necessity doth drive her. She discommends that courage which, rather than strike sail, would perish in the storm. Her mettle is more pliable than so; she had rather bow than break. If her passage be so low that she cannot through it upright, she will not let to stoop; and when a tempest threatens her with shipwreck, she delays not to cast out something to secure the rest. If her designs succeed not one way, she essays another and thinks it better to lose a little than endanger all. She will not, like Aesop's dog, for greediness of the shadow forgo the substance.

The beaver, when he hears the hounds, he knows for what they hunt; and immediately, to secure his skin, he biteth off his stones. Nature hath taught both it and us how to preserve ourselves; and who can tax her precepts as deficient?

That spirit is prodigious which, rather than shake hands with inconvenience, would cast itself into the jaws of danger.[1] It is the part of a wise man to make a virtue of necessity and, with a settled countenance, to swallow down upon an urgent extremity the bitter potion of indignity. If, when the winds do storm, he cannot harbor where he would, he will anchor where he may.

Augustus had advanced Agrippa to so high a sphere that, as Maecenas most wisely did advise him, he must either put himself upon the dice by killing him or be content to take him for his son-in-law, which could not but much obscure the splendor of his imperial[2] majesty. His beginnings were so base and descent so mean that Caligula was wont to deny him to be his mother Agrippina's father and to affirm that Augustus had incestuously begot him upon Julia, rather than he would acknowledge himself to be his grandchild; yet Caesar, to free his crown from check, subscribes to his demands.

Led with the like respects was Alfonso d'Este, duke of Ferrara, when he took to wife Lucrezia Borgia, the daughter of Pope Alexander VI. Her brother Valentine most greedily hungered after his dominions; he had no choice but either he must marry her or mar himself.

There is courage even in retreat, and to be valorous is not always to be venturous.[3] A generous and heroic spirit will yield to Fortune as he sees occasion. He will not strive to swim against the wave, to sail against the wind. The greatness of his mind gives place to the weakness of his means when he cannot what he would; he wills but what he can and thinks those plots and counsels to be best which, though they be inglorious and want that luster which prosperity might lend them, are yet convenient to be followed in regard of circumstance.

> *Non sumit, aut ponit secures,*
> *arbitrio popularis aurae—*

he fears not the adulterate censure of a senseless multitude,[4] nor doth he care how preposterously the vulgar comment upon his proceedings. Let them construe his meaning as they will; whether they take it with the right hand or the left, he is still the same. He will not be ashamed to bias [a] when he sees there is no hope of attaining to the mark by running right.

King Charles VII, to work a reconcilement between himself and Philip, duke of Burgundy, his homeborn homager, did think it no disparagement to his person (considering the state of the present) to send unto him the Lord High Constable of France, the Chancellor, the Marshall, and divers others of his peers; who, in the name of the King their master, before a great assembly, demanded pardon of him for the death of John of Burgundy, his father, excusing the vileness of the fact upon the unadvisedness of their prince; who thereupon pronounced before them all that, for the honor which he bare to God and the compassion which he had of the people, he was content to pardon him. This degrading of his dignity was the raising of his estate. The difference between the Duke and him was a blot which the English played upon. He knew that if they entered upon it he might bid farewell to the gain;[5] and therefore well and wisely were all means embraced that might afford him any means to avoid it.

Eversio rei familiaris dignitatem, ac famam praeceps dat, saith Tacitus: there is no worship where there is no wealth. Honor depends not upon fortune, but in her transcendence.[b] Respect is never to be found where there is no revenue. The reputation of a man is grounded on his rents, and from the quantity of his coin proceeds the quality of his credit. Where honesty, therefore, is not offered

---

[a] *Bias:* swerve.   [b] *Her transcendence:* surmounting her.

violence, nor piety enforced to complain of prejudice, a man may
lawfully and without fear of any scandalous or ignominious attaint
mortgage his titles to redeem his state; for, being peaceably possessed
with this, he may easily recover the other.

If an injury be offered me by my superior I will receive it and return him thanks. To take notice of it as a wrong is to invite him to
do it again. I will shadow my discontents with smiles when they
proceed from those whose fortunes are higher by many stories than
mine own. *Facient iterum, si se fecisse crediderint,* saith Seneca. And
what avails it the lamb to have the better cause ᵉ if the wolf have the
stronger teeth? ⁶ Justice is overawed by violence; greatness takes
pleasure in oppression; nor can poor innocency find a counselor to
plead her cause against the mighty. 'T is madness to kick against a
thorn, to spurn ᵈ against a stone. He that shoots at the stars may hurt
himself but not endanger them. I will shun their anger, therefore, like
a storm—but yet so warily and with so good advise that I may not
seem to do it.

One part of security consists in this: not to profess the seeking of it.
This fearful avoiding of a thing infers ᵉ a secret taxation of the same;
and to decline ᶠ from any man upon suspicion is nothing, in effect,
but to accuse him. He must be therefore very circumspect that goes
about to settle his own safety. If the ruin of it be threatened from the
clouds, opposition is vain; and to expostulate is very doubtful. The
earthen pipkin, when it encounters with the brazen pot, must never
hope for other than a tragical catastrophe; and he that contesteth with
the mighty cannot but be the fatal subject of a bloody scene.

If an affront be done me by an equal I will confront it with a more
open spirit. *Veterem ferendo injuriam invitas novam,* saith the Mimic:
"To pocket up one wrong is to allure another." Malice delights to set
her foot upon the throat of mildness, and insolence is not ashamed to
trample on the neck of patience. The ass doth never want a burden,
because he never denies to bear one. Alcibiades reports of Socrates,
his fellow soldier, that after the discomfiture of the army he found
him in the rearward ᵍ of those that fled, marching his ordinary pace
and viewing friend and foe with such a countenance as encouraged
the one and signified to them that he would not part with his blood
but at an honorable rate to whomsoever should attempt the purchase
of it; and, by his fearless neglect of them,ʰ he saved himself. Men do
not willingly fasten upon these; they leave ¹ the lion to pursue the

ᵉ *Cause:* case (at law).
ᵈ *Spurn:* thrust, kick.
ᵉ *Infers:* implies.
ᶠ *Decline:* fall away.
ᵍ *Rearward:* rear guard.
ʰ *Them:* i.e., the foe.
¹ *Leave:* abandon, neglect.

hare. There is nothing betrays a man so much to danger as an inconsiderate desire to avoid it. We must take heed that our fears bring us not within the compass of contempt, *et ne dum nolumus calcari, videamur posse calcari,* and that whilst we are unwilling to be trodden on we show not mischief the way to tread upon us. There are many that in nature are like the nettle: if thou touch them fearfully they sting thee, but if thou handle them roughly thou deprivest them of that offending and hurtful quality.

If such as are below me labor to disgrace me, I will neglect them and, like the noble sort of beasts that are not moved with the barking of lesser curs, I will onward still and scorn either to change my path or alter my pace. He that complains of wrong disableth himself and gives in derogation of his own sufficiency and worth a wealthy argument of superiority in him that did it. For to grieve that he had the worst is nothing else but to grant that he was the weakest. Witness that common proverb [7] of our own, which without exception affirms that such as those go always to the wall.

The end and scope of an injury is to affect with ill the person of a third. Wisdom prevents the effect thereof in hers. Nothing is ill to them but that which is dishonest; and as for that, it never quarters where virtue keeps,[1] it ne'er presumes where piety prevails. He that is thoroughly settled and composed in himself moves in so high an orb and at so far a distance from the earthy bosom [8] of malicious and ill-disposed men that their unsavory belchings and exhalations cannot possibly annoy him. Marcus Cato, when a certain fellow that unawares had struck him in the bath came afterward to give him satisfaction, "I remember not," said he, "that I was ever struck." He thought it better *non agnoscere, quam ignoscere,* not to acknowledge than [to] forgive. And when Lentulus had spit in his face as he was pleading, he wiped it off and said he would maintain such were deceived as did deny that Lentulus had a mouth. Socrates received a blow upon the head and said no more but that it was great pity men did not know when they should need a helmet.[9] They found no fault with these indignities, because they did not feel them.[10] Their minds were elevated a pitch above the reach of contumely. The abuse of their person did no more offend them than the violating of an image doth endanger the Deity.[11]

¹ *Keeps:* dwells.

X.   Of Temptations

M AN'S LIFE is a continual warfare.[1] He cannot pass from the
womb to the cradle but one or other of his enemies will still
assault him. There is no country but can yield a Pharaoh to destroy
him, no clime but can afford a Herod to pursue him. *Nascitur ad
laborem sicut avis ad volandum:* it is as natural for him to suffer
hardness as it is for a fish to swim or for[2] a bird to fly. His birth is
but an entrance into this life, where, in the sight of heaven, he must
endure for a trial of his valor the furious shock of many fierce encounters. And whilst he sojourns in this camp he must not hope for
any holiday; his travails can have no rest, his labors can have no end.
The hatred which his adversaries bear him is so great that he must
never look for any peace, for any truce or interim at all.

If he sound not an alarm in his own tents, he shall hear the sum-
mons to a dangerous conflict from the midst of theirs. He must never,
therefore, be unarmed but stand continually upon his guard, with the
shield of faith in one hand and the sword of the Spirit in the other.
For it is not with flesh and blood alone that he must wrestle, but with
principalities and powers,[3] with worldly governors, and with the
Prince of Darkness, that worketh in the children of disobedience.
Nor is the reward which is propounded[4] corruptible, that he should
grow careless, but a crown of immortal glory which God himself
hath prepared to beautify therewith the temples of the conqueror.
There is no man that shall enjoy it but he that combats as he ought to
do, saith Paul to Timothy.

The skill of a pilot is unknown but in a tempest; the valor of a
captain is unseen but in a battle; and the worth of a Christian is
untried but in temptation.[5] We press the grape for to express ª the
juice; and when we cheapen ᵇ an earthen vessel we knock upon it
with our hands and judge of the soundness of it by the sound. This
earthly globe is but a theater on which the Lord hath placed us to
get some proof from hence of our sufficiency. Death will assail us; the
world will entice us; the flesh will seek to betray us, and the Devil to
devour us. But let not this deject our spirits. Let us consider that the

---

ª *Express:* press out.   ᵇ *Cheapen:* bargain for.

King of Kings is our spectator, and that His son, Christ Jesus,[6] hath already undergone these trials for our encouragement. He hath marched upon the bellies of our enemies and upon their heads erected the trophies of His victories. He hath plucked the sting out of the mouth of death; she is not now so dangerous as she hath been. The way to shun the violence of her fury is to strip ourselves of worldly pleasures and to offer her the combat even in our shirts. She is like a pirate, that never sets upon a ship but when there is hope of spoil. Job wooed her in his misery, but then he could not win her; whereas the rich man in the Gospel did no sooner solace himself in his abundance and bid his soul make merry with her store but presently[7] she fastened on his collar, she cut his throat. Malicious death (yet less malicious than thy companion, the world) is treacherous and deceitful.

A man may easily secure himself from open and professed enemies, but from such as under a pretense of amity do go about to overthrow his safety there is no sanctuary. Being gulled with shadows and impostures, he draws up the portcullis of his heart and lays the gates thereof wide open to his own ruin. Who would imagine that a pleasing countenance could harbor villainy, or that a smile could sit upon the face of mischief? Yet such is the world. *Arridet,* saith St. Cyprian, *ut saeviat; blanditur, ut fallat; allicit, ut occidat; extollit, ut deprimat.* She is like a courtesan that for her own advantage can entertain thy appetite with wanton dalliance but of a settled love will make thee no assurance; when thou thinkest thyself most interested in[c] her, then is it likely thou art farthest from her. She is like Absalom's mule, that went from under him in his greatest need and left him hanging in the midst of danger.

Some have compared her to the sea in three respects. First, for her unquietness—*Impii quasi mare fervens, quod quiescere non potest,* saith the Psalmist: The wicked are like an ocean, that cannot rest from raging. It happens oftentimes that in the church of God, where the waters of Siloam should run with silence, there is nothing heard but the tempestuous roaring of some gulf[d] or catadupe.[e] Such as bear office in the same are partly cause of it. Their hearts and minds were never so thoroughly seasoned with the salt of heaven as was requisite and convenient. They suffer themselves to be seduced by vanity and care not to be trodden under by temptation.

Secondly, she is likened to the sea because of her unsatiableness. All rivers do repair to that, and yet it riseth not; all vices do resort to

---

[c] *Interested in:* intimately involved with. [e] *Catadupe:* waterfall, cascade.
[d] *Gulf:* whirlpool.

this, and yet it swelleth not. For whatsoever is faulty and defective, be it in the words or in the works of men, is either hatched by avarice or pride; or if by neither of these, it is the spurious issue of incontinency. And these are those three infernal lakes which rise out of the very mouth of hell and fall into the bosom of the world but cannot satisfy her, *quo plus sunt potae, plus sitiuntur aquae.*

Thirdly, she resembles the sea by reason of her bitterness. A distempered palate cannot but judge preposterously of dainties,[8] nor a depraved understanding of delights. That which it thinks is pleasant is not so. The fishes perceive not the saltness of the one because they are nourished[9] in it, nor worldlings the unsavoriness of the other because they are accustomed to it. But I will step from hence to give a touch at a homebred rebel, a factious noveller and a domestical [t] disturber of our weal.

The Devil is unable of himself to compass his desires. *Debilis est hostis, et non nisi volentem vincit:* He is too weak an enemy, saith St. Jerome; he cannot vanquish any but such as are willing to be overcome. Yet lets he not to manage all occasions for his own advantage and to benefit himself by our negligence. He goes about, saith Peter, like a roaring lion and seeks continually whom he may devour. His craft is to incense the subject against the sovereign, the flesh against the spirit, that this little commonwealth of ours, being severed and divided into factious partialities, may no longer stand. It is hope of her assistance that emboldens him. Those that can keep her under and in awe need never fear what he can do unto them. But this (alas!) is both difficult and painful and cannot be effected but with watchful observation. She lulls our Samson in her lap and, like a flattering Delilah, when the eyes of it are closed with sleep she deprives it of the gifts of grace and then betrays it to the Philistine. Man of himself is noway able to resist the force of her allurements, but he that trusteth in the Lord, *sicut mons Sion non commovebitur in aeternum,* shall stand as immovable as the mount of Zion, which shall remain forever. But not to move too long about one center, we must not so rely upon the providence of heaven as to grow slack or negligent in the purchase of our own safety.

Vita ista, sine tentatione duci non potest: We cannot live without temptation, saith Saint Augustine. If it were wanting, what would become of patience and the rest of those heroic virtues, *quae versantur circa difficilia,* that love not to walk but up a rough and craggy rock, nor to try mastery but with a stern and stubborn foe? *Marcescunt sine adversario:* they languish without an adversary. Motion

[t] *Domestical:* native.

is of the soul, which gives them life; and rest is the worm which doth consume them. God, therefore, to maintain them in the breasts of His, doth still employ them. He loves not to make a wanton of a righteous man; He will never suffer him to want occasions to keep himself in breath. Some accident or other shall take the wall of his prosperity and with affronts provoke him to the combat. He will omit no means to harden him: He strikes him to see if he be sound; He shakes him to see if he be settled.

The captain selects the choicest of his soldiers when there is doubt or danger in the service; and, as for them, they think it an honor rather than a wrong and redouble their valor to legitimate his judgment. The like doth he that [10] hath the Lord of Hosts for his commander and his general. He will answer the proudest challenge [11] that can be sent him by temptation—but yet without presuming upon the weakness of his foe or upon the assistance of his leader. He will not dally with his adversary nor endanger himself to show him play, but seal him his bloody passport out-of-hand and send him to his fatal rendezvous at first.

Wisdom will build upon a sure foundation. Οἱ τεθνηκότες οὐ δάκνουσι sounds better here than in the throat of murder, and may be practiced with more lawfulness than in the way to greatness. It is not amiss to make all sure and, with that kingly shepherd, to wound Goliath in the head before he can advance his hand. Our Saviour Christ hath taught us by His own example that, in these conflicts, to fight upon advantage is not dishonorable. Our warrant is His word, our precedent His practice. Temptations could no sooner peep out of the shell but He destroyed them; Satan could no sooner approach Him but He repelled him with a *Scriptum est*. And so must we.

Sin is a slippery serpent, saith an ancient Father, *et nisi in capite teneatur, totus statim illabitur,* if the head of it be in thy throat, the rest thereof will in. He that gives way to the suggestion of an evil thought can hardly [g] stop the consent of a depraved will or stay the working of a wicked hand. The head of this same hellbred snake is wriggled in, and woe is he; the body and the tail thereof must follow after.

There are some that against an Easter suspend the rage and fury of their malice; they make that blessed and that glorious day the Sabbath [h] of their inveterate and brutish hatred, intending (as appeareth in the sequel) as soon as it is past to spread again the colors of their indignation and breathe a fresh defiance in the face of their adversary. These for the time deprive him of his tail, but the head and

---

[g] *Hardly:* with difficulty.   [h] *Sabbath:* truce, rest day.

the body live within them still. There are others that will not do that which is evil, nor yet consent to the doing of it; but nevertheless their thoughts are foolish, their imaginations vain.[1] They have hacked his body, they have cut his tail; but yet his head is moving. He that would vanquish him outright must bruise him there; if that be sound, he will still be meddling.

The shepherd cannot step aside but the wolf is ready to seize upon his flock. Our Saviour, when He retired Himself into the garden to pray apart from His Apostles, He knew the Prince of Darkness would assault them and try if, by threatening them with the Jews, he might not move them to abandon and forsake Him; or if of themselves, by seeing those vile and base indignities whereunto He was subject, they would not slumber in the belief of His divinity; or, last of all, if oppressed with terror they might not forget to repair for succor to the rock of their defense. Afore [12] He left them, therefore, He gave them arms and showed them how they should resist the thief: καθίσατε, "Sit down," said He, γρηγορεῖτε καὶ προσεύχεσθε, "watch and pray, that ye enter not into temptation." But they, like *vere galeati lepores,* stout in their words but cowards in their deeds, no sooner saw the approach of the devourer but, instead of sitting still, they fled; instead of watching, they slept; and when they should have prayed, the chief of them denied Him. Wretched had they been, in general, if by His prayers they had not been relieved.

Such as are strong in faith may well be tempted, but the gates of hell cannot prevail against them. They understand not the dialect of fear, nor do they know the sense [1] of a retreat. Their courage is like their captain's: they have their grave at their back, nor will they fall but into that. But all men are not of this making.

Some there are that, howsoever the enemy cannot vanquish them, he getteth ground of them; and these are like the daughter of the Canaanite, somewhat sorely tempted with a devil. Others again that, having yielded themselves his prisoners in the assault, can never be redeemed but by repentance; and these are figured by that same dumb demoniac in the Gospel. Last of all there are some that, having ransomed themselves from his captivity, do fall into it again; and the end of them is worse than their beginning. He will be sure they shall not escape him then: seven spirits more—and every one more raging than himself—are hired to detain him. But there are many means to dispossess them all—as by humility and charity, by prayer, and [by] fasting, which, indeed, if accompanied with the rest, is most powerful

---

[1] *Vain:* empty.   [1] *Sense:* meaning.

and effectual in this case. Adam stood fast in Paradise as long as he did fast; the apple was no sooner in his mouth but the Devil was in his maw. Through gluttony we lost the joys of heaven; by being abstinent we must recover them again. Satan is like a fish: *natat in fluviis, moritur in sicco,* he lives in the sea but he dies upon the shore.

XI.   Of Reconciliation and Peace

HURTS are not healed with hurts, nor wounds with wounds. To wrong another is not the way to right thyself. It is rather a means to discover thy weakness than to recover thy wants.

Jerusalem is new erected; among her citizens there is now no thirsting for revenge.[1] The law of retribution is disannulled [a] amongst them. It is not a *dictum est antiquis* but a *dico vobis* which they follow. An eye no longer for an eye, a tooth no longer for a tooth. That impious exclamation of a more impious wretch, ἤ μ' ἀνάειρ', ἢ ἐγώ σε, resounds not within the compass of her walls. She thinks it strange and barbarous for men to combat without mission [b] and to bury their contentions but in the ashes of each other's ruin.

The Sun of Righteousness hath shined upon her face and with His beams enlightened so the minds and understandings of her inhabitants that now they do not only restrain their hands from hurting but their hearts from hating. He that smiteth anyone of them upon the right cheek shall see that he will not grieve to turn to him the left; and when he sues him for his coat, he will withal surrender him his cloak. The doctrine of the Scribes and Pharisees is condemned amongst them as defective. They know that if their zeal exceed not theirs, they cannot enter into heaven. Their anger, therefore, shall not outlive a day. The sun shall never go down upon their wrath, nor shall the stars be witness of their fury. They know that vengeance is the Lord's and that He will repay it; they likewise know that for man to practice it is to usurp upon His majesty [2] and unadvisedly to snatch the sword out of His hand. But (alas!) there are many sheep in the flock that are not of the fold.

Strangers and foreigners have gotten in and seated themselves amongst them that think it a sign of valor to lay aside the countenance of peace till such time as they be able to cry quittance [c] with their adversary; whereas indeed, according to the saying of the satirist,

> *minuti*
> *semper, et infirmi est animi, exiguique voluptas*
> *ultio —*

---

[a] *Disannulled*: rendered void.

[b] *Mission*: ceasing.

[c] *To cry quittance*: to be upon equal terms, to be avenged upon.

It is a petty, faint, and feeble mind
That in revenge doth any pleasure find.

Hence is it that none are so much delighted with it as weaker women and such as are not seasoned with the spirit of knowledge.

James and John, when the Samaritans would not receive their Master, grew presently impatient. "Wilt thou that fire," said they, "come down from heaven and destroy them all?" But He rebuked them and said they knew not of what spirit they were. When He himself, therefore, was brought unto the cross and there reviled by those Jewish cannibals that were about Him, He was so far from being moved and incensed against them that howsoever the least breath of His mouth could in an instant have brought destruction to devour them, yet His revenge is only this: "Father, forgive them"; οὐ γὰρ οἴδασιν, τί ποιοῦσιν, "for they know not what they do."

Under the Law truth took a strict examination of offense, and justice did severely punish it. But since the gracious coming of the Gospel, mercy and peace have always been at hand to temper their proceedings. If truth examine the delinquent, mercy adviseth her to look if he did not fall through ignorance, through weakness, or temptation; for wicked facts are oftentimes extenuated by circumstance. If justice go about to punish him, then presently comes peace and wills her not to confound him but to reconcile him to his Maker, to his neighbor, to himself. And thus is verified that saying of the Psalmist: Mercy and truth have met; righteousness and peace have kissed each other.

The language of the Lord is peace. "He will speak peace," saith the Prophet David, "to His people and to His saints." [3] In a word, our God is the God of peace, so much delighted in unity that if thou bring Him an offering and art at enmity with thy brother, He sends thee back immediately from His altar and is content to forbear thy service till thou be reconciled. If thou deny to do it He waxeth wroth and clean annihilates and makes void the grant of those spiritual graces which He had before bestowed upon thee, as did the Master by that merciless and cruel servant in the Gospel.

The promise of remission is conditional: He shall not have it that will not give it. Of all the petitions which our Saviour Christ hath taught us in that form of prayer which He prescribed to his disciples, this alone is to be asked comparatively and with reference to our own facility: "Forgive as we forgive." So that he which remitteth nothing must never hope that anything should be remitted him. In vain shall he pray for it; for whilst he prays, he prays against himself. He may know by what he giveth out what is to be received in. There is a *si* and a *sicut* in it—an *if* and an *as*. The first denotes [4] unto us the action itself, and the second the manner of performing it. I will therefore pardon that I may be pardoned, and so pardon as I would be pardoned. Let mine enemy be as inflexible and obstinate as he will, my mind shall not be fashioned by his example. I will omit no means that may afford me means [5] to pluck the sting out of the mouth of hatred.

There are three things that mitigate the raging of a distempered man. The first is an humble carriage; the second is a friendly gift; and the last is a powerful and overawing threat. If he be proud, humility will please him; and therefore David in I Samuel, to pacify the wrath of Saul, did so abase himself that when he might have cut the thread of his life, he did but snip the lap of his garment and (in disgrace of himself) pronounced that he hunted after no better than the carcass of a dog and did pursue no other than a flea. If he be covetous, a gift may happily prevail. Jacob, in his return from Laban, fearing the discontentment of his brother Esau that came out against him, bethinks himself how to avoid his anger; and in the end, *Placabo illum muneribus, quae praecedunt, postea videbo illum:* "I will first," said he, "appease him with a present and afterward see his face."

> *Aurea sunt vere nunc saecula; plurimus auro*
> *venit honos; auro conciliandus amor.*
>
> These golden times do gold so much admire
> That none will lend their friendship but for hire.

A dog will not be stilled but with a bone. And Cerberus will swell against Aeneas till wisdom cast into his jaws *melle saparatem, et frugibus offam,* a morsel that doth like him; and then *immania terga resolvit,* he forgets his malice,[6] he forgoes his rage.

But if thine adversary be timorous and more in vaunts than in valor, a threat may sooner peradventure bring him in. His courage will be overwhelmed with fear; and, like the Gibeonites, he will purchase his peace by stratagems before he will encounter with a Joshua. The flesh likes well of this, and when necessity requires can be content to use the other.[d] The first is somewhat harsh and goes against the hair; it thinks it a dishonor to submit so far. But the practice of our Saviour Christ in the reclaiming of a devil—for so he counted Judas, that apostate—doth censure this opinion as erroneous. It was the first He tried. For (not to flatter ourselves in false conceits) what greater humility could there be than for the Master to prostrate Himself before the servant and to wash his feet? But when He saw

[d] *Other:* second.

this did no good, He tried the second. And what richer present could He give him than Himself for food? The last, which men delight in most, the mildness of the Lamb approved least. He did not use it till He was enforced; and then He came upon him with a *Vae; vae homini,* etc.: "Woe be to that man," said He; "well had it gone with him if he had ne'er been born." But nothing could revoke ° him, for he was a devil.

There are some that, when they see themselves to be the weakest, are willing for the present to reconcile themselves unto their adversary, but it is with an intent to take the advantage of the future and with hope that they shall afterward effect that which they cannot then. If I perceive this humor in a man, and know the ground of it to be distrust, I will deal with him as Augustus did with Cinna: "Once more," said he to him, "I give thee life, first as to an enemy, now as to a traitor and a parricide. Let love and friendship from this day forward begin betwixt us; let us contend *utrum ego meliore fide vitam tibi dederim, aut tu debeas,* whether the creditor or the debtor be the honester man." Or I will use him as the Venetians did the Duke of Mantua, their deadly enemy, when, instead of depriving him of his estate, they made him their Captain General. I will tie him so fast unto me with cords of kindness and humanity that he shall never be desirous to go from me. Though he deceive my trust at one time, I will try him at another. The soldier receiveth many wounds and yet abandons not the wars; the sailor endureth many storms and yet forsweareth not the seas. A rock will in time relent; and Troy, though it stand out long, it yields at last. Whilst there is a sun to set, I will not despair of a good issue; *non omnium dierum sol occidit* shall be my comforter. But if I must needs shoot (as who can always shun the occasion?), I will shoot as Jonathan did at David, either short or gone,ᵗ that wheresoever I hit I may not hurt; because I will not seem desirous to cut off the hope of reconcilement or build my safety on the neck of his.

° *Revoke:* call back (L., *revocare*).   ᵗ *Gone:* long, over the mark.

XII. *Of Poverty*

THE WORLD is near her tomb; her spirits are clean spent, and now, like a decrepit wretch, she dotes upon the treasure which she scorned in her youth. The time hath been when, among the Romans, the possession of a little gold was counted a capital offense, *et levis argenti lamina crimen erat,* and to be master of a piece of plate[a] was punished as a censorial[b] crime. Cornelius Rufinus had been dictator in the commonwealth, yet did Fabricius degrade him for no other cause. He thought him unfit to be a Senator that sought to deprave good discipline by bad example.[1] Their glory then—and then it was at highest[2]—consisted nowhere more than in their poverty. Honor did think it no disgrace to court a virgin virtue at the plow, nor to visit an untainted valor under a smoky roof. But now there is a change of all things. For, as the poet saith,

> *Procedat vel Numa, vel qui*
> *servavit trepidam flagranti, ex aede Minervam*
> *protinus ad censum.*[3]

What need they question his behavior? He that is clothed in purple cannot but be honest, and he that wears a mine upon his back must of necessity be deemed a man of worth.

Manners are wanting where there are no means; wit never harbors where there is no wealth. Can any good thing come out of Nazareth? Is he not the son of a carpenter? Is not his mother called Mary? And are not James and Joses, Simon and Judas his brethren? Are not his sisters here amongst us? And do we not know his breeding and his bringing up? These are the censures[c] of a gaudy[d] weakness that hath nothing to boast of but a glorious[e] outside in derogation of a more able and sufficient spirit.

Wisdom, if she be poor, is ne'er respected.[4] The client looks upon the lawyer's train and taketh him to be the better counselor that wears the better clothes; let the best pleader of the world be present, if he once perceive his coat to be threadbare he will none of him:

[a] *Plate:* silver.
[b] *Censorial:* subject to the judgment of the censor.
[c] *Censures:* strictures, judgments.
[d] *Gaudy:* pretentious.
[e] *Glorious:* flashy.

Ciceroni nemo ducentos
nunc dederit nummos, nisi fulserit annulus ingens—

On him alone large fees he will bestow,
That can most rings upon his fingers show.

And hence it is that, as the satirist affirms,

Conducta Paulus agebat
sardonyche; atque ideo pluris quam Cossus agebat,
quam Basilus.

Paul hired still, ere he approached the bar,
Some precious stone that might be seen from far;
Howe'er he pleaded, he was sure of more
Than Coss or Basil ever got before.[5]

Desert, if she be mean, may to the cart; there is no room for her in court, where judgment looks asquint and casts her eyes but upon outward adjuncts. Unless she be perfumed and ruffle [f] in her silks, let her avoid the gates of greatness. Few of these earthly suns do shine upon a wretched worm or impart their brightness to a waning moon. The lamp shall have no oil put into it to maintain her light till they themselves have occasion to use it. Their expenses are preposterous.[g] Their ephemerides [h] do much resemble that of Crates the Theban: to some buffoonery parasite, six thousand crowns; to a courtesan, six hundred; *et philosopho, triobolum*—and scarce three farthings to a man of merit. Virtue they care not for; she smells too strongly for their company. *Exeat,* away with her; she defiles the place. Her outside is not velvet, and that is it which offends their stomach.[i] Such as can clap a lordship on their back, and bury more in one rich suit than the revenues of a crown came to in former times, shall still be sure of passage. No groom shall interrupt them; all hats are vailed at their approach, all knees are bowed. Let them be what they will—*lenonum pueri, quocunque in fornace nati,* the sons of bawdry, hatched in any stews [j]—it matters not; the coast is clear, and who is it but gives him way?[6] But, with the poet,

Fingimus haec, altum calamo sumente cothurnum,
scilicet, et finem egressi, legemque priorum,
grande Sophocleo quiddam bacchamur hiatu,
montibus ignotum Wallis, coeloque Britanno.

These things our pen but feigns, and writes the while
She fits the lofty buskin to her style;

---

[f] *Ruffle:* strut.
[g] *Preposterous:* disproportioned, upside down.

[h] *Ephemerides:* daily accounts.
[i] *Stomach:* taste.
[j] *Stews:* brothels.

And, having passed the scope of an essay,
And gone beyond such as have traced that way,
Tragedian-like, dishonored acts doth quote
And storms at things with Sophocles his throat,
Not known to Wales' high mounts at any time,
Nor ever heard of in our British clime.[7]

Howsoever[8] (to return from whence we strayed), so great is the corruption of the world in general that if a man be never so rich in mind, if he be poor in means his heart must languish in obscurity.[9] The princes of the Philistines will never call for Samson but to make them pastime. Pied[k] ignorance must be advanced whilst true sufficiency doth perish in her wants. There is no preferment to be had for her but by some slavish dejection or more servile observation. Men's ears are in their heels when she is to speak, and unless she stoop she cannot possibly be heard.

There are some, saith Tacitus, *quibus Fortuna pro virtutibus,* the goodness of whose stars[l] supplies the want of good deserts; and these sometimes, in their ascent, cast back a look on such as they know more able than themselves, but (alas!) 't is but a look of jealousy and with the eye of one that runneth a race. They are afraid lest they should hasten after them. Their help extends itself to none but such whose bosoms are more naked and unfurnished of all abilities than their own. They know there is no danger in a meteor—it may shine without prejudice in the presence of a star; but the brightness of a rising sun obscures them both. All men do cherish wisdom when they are to use her. They speak her fair for their own advantage, but when their turns are served they do estrange their countenance and talk not of her but in their ancient dialect. She is poor—away with her; she cannot but be ignorant and unfit to have the managing of any matter of importance; nay, though she be able to effect it, they will not trust her with it. It is impossible she should be otherwise than irreligious and profane[10] and make a conscience to preserve her honesty by discharging her duty. Let her protest, she shall not be believed; let her offer to be deposed,[m] her oath shall not be taken.

> *Contemnere fulmina pauper,*
> *creditur atque deos.*

The poor is thought, though she be just and wise,
The gods to scorn, their thunder to despise.

---

k *Pied:* checkered, spotted (in allusion to the fool's motley).

l *Stars:* fortunes, destinies.

m *To be deposed:* to be placed under oath.

A lie is well accepted if it be uttered by authority, but truth itself is scandalized [n] if it proceed from the mouth of poverty. Nor must she dare to speak in her defense:

> *Libertas pauperis haec est:*
> *pulsatus rogat, et pugnis concisus adorat,*
> *ut liceat paucis cum dentibus inde reverti.*
>
> Now all the freedom a poor man can have,
> Is to take blows and yet take pains to crave;
> And, after many knocks, humbly to pray
> With some few teeth he may depart away.

And hence it is that many fall into temptation. A spirit that is not seasoned with the spirit to free itself from these indignities will set his life upon a blot and, in a desperate resolution, hazard his part of heaven but procure his ransom.[11] *Flectere si nequeat superos, Acheronta movebit:* If he cannot compass it by lawful means, he will try how to prevail by other; and then that Spanish proverb must defend him—

> *A tuerto, ò a derecho,*
> *Nuestra casa hasta el techo—*

he cares not if what he do be either right or wrong, so it make for the raising of his fortune. And thus hath vice, by the contempt of poverty, been entertained.

Oppression hath played the rodomont;[o] and unjust dealing, since riches were in credit, hath kept her revels in the hearts of men. No crime so hateful, no attempt so lustful, but is both known and practiced. Greedy desire brooks no limit; there is no end of her pursuit. A world is not sufficient for our [12] Alexander:

> *Aestuat infoelix angusto limite mundi,*
> *ut Gyarae clausus scopulis, parvaque scripso.*
>
> The narrow bounds thereof do him displease,
> As he were shut in Guildhall's Little Ease.

Hence cometh it to pass that now in every town one part of it is nothing else but prisons. The number of malefactors, since to be poor was counted ignominious and reproachful, hath so much exceeded that, as the satirist exclaims,

---

[n] *Scandalized:* looked upon askance.

[o] *Rodomont:* swashbuckler (cf. Rodomonte in Ariosto's *Orlando Furioso*).

Qua fornace graves, qua non incude catenae?

Now bolts, now chains, now heavy fetters been
In every forge, on every anvil seen;

whereas, before, one petty [P] jail sufficed a kingdom, so harmless and innocuous were the hearts and hands of those meaner and lowborn times.[13]

I could add more. But the humor of essays is rather to glance at all things with a running conceit than to insist on any with a slow discourse; and I fear in earnest what Martial spoke in jest or out of modesty:

Iam lector queriturque, deficitque;
iam librarius hoc et ipse dicit,
ohe tam satis est, ohe libelle.

FINIS

[P] *Petty:* small.

Appendix

Appendix

SIGNIFICANT ADDITIONS, omissions, and variants in the *text* of the 1629, 1631, and 1638 editions (*Vade Mecum*) of Tuvill's *Essays Moral and Theological* are listed here. Prefatory matter has been disregarded. As in the present text of these essays, the additions and variants have been modernized. In general, only the first edition in which a change has been made is cited, though meaningful additions to, or deletions from, these changes are recorded.

Essay I

1. 1631 *adds:* She admits no nominals but reals in her grammar; no mutes in her alphabet, no ciphers in her arithmetic are acceptable [some copies of 1638 omit "grammar; no mutes in her"].

2. 1629 *reads:* praved.

3. 1631 *reads:* dissention.

4. 1629 *adds: Dic mihi musa virum:* show me such another.

5. 1631 *adds:* yet look as big as Aesop's long-eared beast in a lion's skin. They will take upon them to dispute *de omni scibile cum nihil scirent* and in the end stroke their beards five times, as the Doctors of Sorbonne did who disputed with Erasmus.

6. 1629 *reads:* you to go near; 1631 *reads:* you go near.

7. 1629 *reads:* different.

8. 1631 *reads:* itself not.

9. 1631 *reads:* that he should.

10. 1629 *reads:* our blessed Saviour Christ.

11. 1629 *adds:* such as the puff-paste titulados of these our times were not they he looked for.

12. 1629 *reads:* dies without.

13. 1629 *adds:* Yet as there is a foolish knowledge, so there is a wise ignorance in not prying into God's ark, not inquiring into things not revealed. I would fain know all that I need and all that I may: I leave God's secrets to himself. I may be *pius pulsator,* but not *temerarius scrutator;* I may knock at God's Privy Council door, but if I go farther, I may be more bold than welcome.

Essay II

1. 1629 *reads: fornatu.* Corrected in 1631.
2. 1629 *adds:* His late Majesty of blessed memory considered this well. [1631 *margin also adds:* K. James; 1631 *text also adds:* He would ever say that "honesty is the best policy."] For his entrance unto the crown of England, it may be avowed truly that he hath [*margin:* Sir Walter Raleigh] received it from the hand of God and hath stayed the time of putting it on howsoever he were provoked to hasten it. He entered not by a breach nor by blood, but by the ordinary gate which his own right set open; and into which by a general love and obedience he was received. And howsoever His Majesty's preceding title to this kingdom was preferred by by [*sic;* corrected in 1631] many princes (witness the Treaty at Cambrai in the year 1559), yet he pleased not to dispute it during the life of that renowned lady his predecessor; no, notwithstanding the injury of not being declared heir in all the time of her long reign.
3. 1629 *adds:* Had the Duke of Gloucester [1631 *margin:* Richard III], that great master of mischief, well considered this he had not made his way to the crown through such an ocean of blood royal.
4. 1609 *reads: duobis.* Not corrected until 1631.
5. 1629 *adds: Non tam multum sed tam bene:* a musician is commended not for playing so long, but for playing so well.
6. 1629 *adds:* and turns them upon the very heads of the actors themselves,.
7. 1629 *substitutes quotation and adds:* "The wicked have digged a pit for others, and have fallen therein themselves." Little did Hastings think [*margin:* Sir Walter Raleigh], when by his own advice the Earl Rivers and Grey and others were, without trial of law or offense given, executed at Pomfret in the North, that the selfsame day, and (as I take it) the selfsame hour, his own head should have been in the same lawless manner stricken off in the Tower of London.

This was Richard III his policy, and by this we see that the doctrine which Machiavelli taught unto Cesare Borgia, to employ men in mischievous actions and afterward to destroy them in the selfsame manner when they have performed the mischief, was not of his own invention. All ages have given us examples of this goodly policy; the latter have been apt scholars in this lesson to the more ancient, as the reign of Henry VIII [*margin:* Sir Walter Raleigh] here in England can bear witness; and therein especially the Lord Cromwell, who perished by the same unjust law that himself had devised for the taking away of another man's life.
8. 1629 *omits:* He hath conceived . . . thing.
9. 1631 *adds:* Men often seek *bona,* good things, *non bene,* not in a good manner; many fail in their *quando,* as Joseph sought Christ after a day's journey, who is too precious to be missed one hour; others in the right *ubi,* as Mary sought her son in *cognatione carnis,* who was *in domo patris* in the

temple. The papists seek him in pictures, but he hath promised to be found in the Scriptures; some seek honor in pride, but true nobility is grounded on humility; divers seek reputation in bloody revenge, alas, that's to be had in patience. It is the glory of a man to pass by an infirmity.

10. 1629 *adds:* lest he slip from us.

11. 1629 *omits:* κρατήσατε . . . the Lamb.

Essay III

1. 1609 *reads:* tomb. I follow 1629.
2. 1609 *reads:* emnity. Not corrected until 1638.
3. 1629 *adds: Similis simili gaudet,* birds of a feather will flock together.
4. Some copies read "influxible."
5. 1631 *reads:* and recount.
6. 1629 *reads:* neere [= never?]; 1631 *reads:* nere.
7. 1629 *reads:* contemperancy.
8. 1629 *reads:* in apprehension, in judgment.
9. 1629 *adds:* When Charles V had the repulse at Algiers [*margin:* Sir Walter Raleigh] in Africa, Ferdinando Cortese [Hernán Cortés], one of the bravest men that ever Spain brought forth, offered unto the emperor to undergo the siege at his own charge. But he never lived good day after it, for they that envied his victories and conquest of Mexico in the West Indies were bold to style his love and liberality, pride and presumption, and persuaded the emperor that Cortés sought to value himself above him; and to have it said, that what the emperor could not Cortés had effected and was therefore consequently more worthy of the empire than he that had it.
10. 1629 *margin reads:* Portugal Hist.
11. 1631 *reads:* with the prince's.
12. 1629 *adds:* Cardinal Wolsey's *Ego et Rex meus* was somewhat too saucy.
13. 1629 *reads:* But Ruy Gomez took.
14. 1631 *omits:* Latin quotation and translation.
15. 1609 *reads: tanto me- / merito.* Not corrected until 1631.
16. 1629 *omits:* quotation.
17. 1629 *omits:* as.
18. 1631 *adds:* A man can hardly converse with such as are infected and yet rest free from all contagion. Joseph was but a while in Egypt, yet he had learned to swear by the life of Pharaoh, Exod. 34:5. [This is repeated in *Christian Purposes and Resolutions,* sig. F7r-v. Tuvill's biblical reference, incidentally, is in error for Gen. 42:15.]
19. 1629 *adds:* Loquacity is the fistula of the mind, ever-running and almost incurable. A prating barber asking King Archelaus how he would be trimmed, the king replied, "Silently."
20. 1629 *margin reads:* Feltham's *Resol[ves].*
21. 1629 *adds:* wert thou a king, it would rob thee of thy royal majesty

[*margin:* Feltham]. Who would reverence thy sway when like Nero thou shalt tavern out thy time with wantons, triumph with minstrels in thy chariots, and present thyself upon a common stage with the buskined tragedian and the pantomime?

22. 1629 *reads:* continues something long.

ESSAY IV

1. 1609 *reads:* holy. I follow 1629.
2. 1629 *omits:* Greek.
3. 1629 *reads:* our blessed Saviour.
4. 1609, 1629 *read:* literal. I follow 1631.
5. 1631 *adds:* Fruit-bearing trees spend not all their sap and moisture upon themselves or the increase of their own magnitudes; but the principal or purer part is concocted into some pleasant fruits which neither themselves nor their young springals ever come to taste of but proffer them to us and, being come to maturity, voluntarily let them fall at their master's feet. Never did the olive anoint itself with the [i.e., its] own oil, nor the vine make itself drunk with the own grapes: the one spends itself to comfort thy temples, the other to exhilarate thy heavy heart. [1629 *also adds:*] The least pile of grass which thou treadest on, is able to afford instruction.
6. 1629 *reads:* holy Abraham.
7. 1629 *reads:* our last end.
8. 1631 *adds:* The covetous man is like a Christmas box, whatsoever is put into it, nothing can be taken out of it till it be broken. He soaketh up the waters like a sponge, and till Death doth come and squeeze him with his iron grasp, he will not yield one drop of that which he hath received. [1629 *also adds:*] What thanks is there for a man to put off his clothes when he goeth to bed? To give thy goods to charitable uses when thou canst no longer hold them is not praiseworthy.
9. 1629 *reads:* portion. 1629 *adds:* A penny given now may do more good than a pound hereafter.
10. 1629 *reads:* othersome be.
11. 1629 *adds:* Some again instead of alms give them good words as if men could eat precepts and drink good counsel.
1631 *also adds:* Rich men do good turns to themselves as they play at tennis, tossing the ball to him that will toss it to them again; seldom to the poor, for they are not able to bandy it back again. Pride cuts and riot shuffles, but betwixt them both, they deal the poor a bad game.

ESSAY V

1. 1629 *reads:* seas to be silent.
2. 1629 *reads:* stirs not a jot from.
3. 1629 *reads:* particularly unto him.

4. 1631 *omits:* quotation.

5. 1629 *reads:* These latter ages.

6. 1629 *adds:* It is a rare thing to find goodness in greatness.

7. Some copies of 1629 read "time hath been."

8. 1631 *omits:* quotation.

9. 1609 *reads: Thebanum.* Not corrected until 1638. For *vix* (1638), 1609 *reads: non;* 1629 and 1631 *read: nam.*

10. 1629 *adds: Terras Astraea reliquit* to the beginning of the succeeding sentence.

11. 1629 *adds: Omnia religiosa nunc ridentur;* he that maketh conscience of his ways is accounted one of God Almighty's fools. We are all (in effect) become comedians in religion; and while we act in gesture and voice theological virtues, in all the courses of our lives we renounce our persons and the parts we play. For charity, justice, and truth have but their being in terms like the philosopher's *materia prima.* Religion and the truth thereof be in every man's mouth, yea in the discourse of every [*margin:* Sir Walter Raleigh] woman who for the greatest number are but idols of vanity. What is this other than an universal dissimulation? We profess that we know God, but by works we deny him; and herein we go not so far as the devils themselves, for they know him better than we do.

12. 1629 *omits:* quotation and translation.

13. 1629 *adds:* There are some noblemen in France, that are hardly of four nobles' rent, that glory in saying "Speak to my servants," thinking thereby to imitate great princes. But I [*margin:* Comines] have often seen their servants so make their profit of them, that their folly hath openly appeared to the world. [This is almost word for word from Thomas Danett's translation, *The History of Comines* (1596), I, x.]

14. 1629 *omits:* But.

15. 1629 *reads:* kings and magistrates. 1629 *adds:* Their title and claim is in the best tenure, they have it in *capite,* even from God alone, not from prince or people: "By me kings reign, and princes decree justice" saith the Spirit of Truth. I say,.

16. 1629 (and some copies of 1609) *reads:* howsoever.

Essay VI

1. 1609 *reads:* so sure as man's. Corrected in 1631.

2. 1631 *omits:* all after "Alexander."

3. 1629 *adds:* He that where he should not gives too much, shall where he would have too little to give [*margin:* Feltham's *Resolves*]. 'T was a witty reason of Diogenes why he asked a halfpenny of the thrifty man, and a pound of the prodigal: The first, he said, might give him often, but the other ere long would have none to give him.

1631 *also adds: Est modus in dando, etc.,* there are certain bounds to be observed in the disposition our [*sic;* but 1638 *corrects to:* of our] gifts; we must look that we do not dispose of another man's gifts, but honor the

Lord with our own substance. The Devil would give all the world to our Saviour, a liberal gift, but out of God's exchequer; and Alexander VI would give America to Spain, a bounteous largess, but out of the Indians' freehold.

4. 1629 *adds:* Henry VII could [*margin:* Sir Walter Raleigh] never endure any mediation in rewarding of [1631 *omits:* of] his servants, and therein exceeding wise; for whatsoever himself gave, he himself received back the thanks and the love, knowing it well that the affections of men (purchased by nothing so readily as by benefits) were trains that better became great kings, than great subjects.

5. 1629 *adds:* Louis XI was very liberal. He gave to Clothier his physician in five months' space 54,000 crowns, besides the bishopric of Amiens [*margin:* Comines, p. 210] to his nephew, and conferred divers offices and lands upon him and his friends; but this was done more for fear than love, and therefore cannot be called bounty.

6. 1629 *reads:* repay that same man.

7. 1629 *reads:* never.

8. 1609 *reads:* both. Corrected in 1629.

9. Some copies of 1609 read "receipt," others read "recepi."

10. 1609 *reads:* Sex.

11. 1629 *omits:* quotation and translation.

12. 1631 *reads:* garb.

13. 1631 *omits:* both quotations and both translations.

14. 1629 *reads:* ingenious. 1631 restores original reading.

15. 1631 *omits:* quotation and translation.

16. 1631 *omits:* a.

17. 1631 *omits:* quotation and translation.

18. Some copies of 1609 read *Parvam.*

19. 1629 *reads:* There are a great many.

20. 1629 *omits:* such as may be always extant,.

21. 1631 *omits:* quotation and translation.

22. 1631 *reads:* for.

23. 1631 *reads:* promises.

24. 1629 *reads:* sincerity. 1629 *adds:* How many servants did Henry VIII [*margin:* Sir Walter Raleigh] in haste advance, but for what virtue no man could suspect, and with the change of his fancy ruined again, no man knowing for what offense? To how many others of more desert gave he abundance of flowers from whence to gather honey, and in the end of harvest burnt them in the hive?

25. 1631 *omits:* proverb. 1629 *adds: Fronti nulla fides* at the beginning of the next sentence.

26. 1609 *reads:* Eutrapolus. Corrected in 1631.

27. 1631 *omits:* quotation and translation.

28. 1609 *reads:* Livo. Corrected in 1631.

29. 1631 *adds: Crudelitatis horridus habitus, truculenta facies, violentus spiritus, vox terribilis.* Let cruelty look and speak like itself, and I shall be warned to avoid it. Tamburlaine his bloody tents made open profession

what his meaning was, but where cruelty and craft are coupled together, *venite, sapienter opprimamus eum,* they will be cruel in oppressing, yet they will do it wisely. Where subtilty is ingenious to invent, cruelty barbarous to execute; where subtilty giveth counsel, cruelty giveth the stroke; where subtilty hideth the knife, cruelty cutteth the throat; where cruelty and subtilty, like Simeon and Levi, sisters in evil, are combined and confederate to bring to pass, how fearful is that man's plight that is thus assaulted? Joab killeth not Amasa like an open foe: *Estne pax mi frater* — "Brother is all well?" — was the unsuspected train to make way for his fatal weapon; else what doth Judas with a kiss, and all hail in his mouth, in the very forefront of his treason? They carried both the fox and the lion in their breasts, as Carbo spoke of Scylla [i.e., Sulla] (the Scylla indeed and wrack of the Roman people). In imitation of whom rather than of St. Peter they write of Alexander VI that *intravit ut vulpes,* there is subtilty, *regnavit ut leo,* there is cruelty (for he was termed, *spongia sanguinis,* a very sponge of blood), and to make up the period all [1638 *reads:* of all] his acts and monuments, *mortuus ut canis,* he died like a dog. [Tuvill elsewhere relates this final illustration not of Alexander VI but of Boniface VIII; cf. *Essays Politic and Moral,* p. 28.]

    30. 1631 *reads:* gotten.

Essay VII

1. 1631 *reads:* comes.
2. Some copies of 1609 omit "a."
3. Some copies of 1609 omit "that I did not."
4. 1631 *omits:* all after "son of Ishai?"
5. 1609 *reads:* friends. I follow 1631.
6. 1629 *reads:* another.
7. 1629 *adds:* (in these days).
8. 1631 *omits:* Latin.

Essay VIII

1. 1631 *omits:* Latin.
2. 1631 *omits:* Latin.
3. 1631 *omits:* quotation beginning *Sed peiores* and translation.
4. 1629 *reads:* heretofore.
5. 1629 *adds:* A fit foundation [1631 *adds:* he proved] for the Church to be built on, whom the breath of a silly damsel shall thus make to deny his Master.
6. 1631 *omits:* Latin.
7. 1629 *reads:* the holy prophets.
8. 1629 *adds:* That man is not to be blamed which shunneth to make

[*margin:* Feltham's *Resolves*] the vulgar his confessor, for they are the most uncharitable telltales that the burdened earth doth suffer.

9. 1629 *adds:* To reprove a man in the height of his passion is to call a soldier to counsel in the heat of a battle: let the combat slack and then thou mayest expect a hearing.

10. 1629 *reads:* be very dangerous.

11. 1631 *reads:* corrosives.

12. 1629 *adds:* In all thy reprehensions, or reproofs, have a care thou meddle not with a nest of hornets, they will sting thee: take thou heed of awaking a sleepy lion, lest thou repent thy unadvised error. The diseases of great ones are *noli me tangere,* it is no touching of them. Princes do rather pardon ill deeds than bad words. Alexander the Great forgave many sharp swords but never any sharp tongues, no, though they told him truly of his errors. [1631 *adds:* Undutiful words of a subject often take deeper root than the memory of ill deeds do. The Duke of Biron found it when the king had him at advantage: for,] Henry IV of France had his heart more inflamed against the Duke of Biron for his overbold and biting taunts that he used against him before Amiens than for his conspiracy with the Spaniard or Savoyard: for he [*margin:* Sir Walter Raleigh] had pardoned a thousand of such as had gone farther and drawn their swords against him.

The contemptuous words that Sir John Perrott used of our late Queen Elizabeth were his ruin, and not the counterfeit letter of the Romish priest produced against him. So fared it with some other, greater than he, that thereby ran the same, and a worse fortune presently after [1631 *omits* this sentence].

And [1631 *omits:* And] certainly it belongs to those that have warrant from God to reprehend princes, and to none else, especially in public [*margin:* Sir Walter Raleigh].

13. 1629 *reads:* our own weakness *and* our mortal enemies.

14. 1631 *adds:* With my superior will I fear; with my equal will I blush; with my inferior will I scorn to contest. Hath one or other offended me? If he be under me, I will be so good as favor him; if above me, I will be so wise as to favor myself. I will wink at the child and old man, for the weakness of their age; at the woman, for her sex [1638 *omits:* at the woman . . . sex]; at the fool and madman, for their condition: yet so as to let them know it was not well done, but rather taken so.

Essay IX

1. 1629 *adds:* The French king, Francis I, wisely considered that it was less dishonor to dislodge his army [*margin:* Sir Walter Raleigh] from be [*sic;* 1631 *reads:* before] Landersey in the dark than to be beaten in the light.

2. 1631 *omits:* imperial.

3. 1629 *adds:* It is the observation of a good man of war, *Si certamen quandoque dubium videatur, tacitam miles arripiat fugam: Fuga enim*

aliquando laudanda, which must be understood in this sort: if a general of an army, by some unprosperous beginnings, doubt the success or find his army fearful and wavering, it is more profitable to steal a safe retreat than to abide the uncertain event of battle.

The French in a battle before Moncontour, standing upon their reputation not to dislodge by night, lost [*margin:* Sir Walter Raleigh] their reputation indeed by dislodging by day and were enforced to fight upon great disadvantage. But Spinola took a better course in his retreat from Burgenozp-some [*sic;* 1631 *reads:* Berghen-op-zome]: he made use of former precedents and so saved himself and all his army.

4. 1629 *adds:* That *bellua multorum capitum,* which like so many dogs barking at those they know not and, as it is their custom, to accompany one another in their clamors.

5. 1631 *reads:* game.

6. 1631 *adds:* It is an old country proverb, that might overcomes right; a weak title that wears a strong sword commonly prevails against a strong title that wears but a weak one: otherwise Philip II of Spain had never been Duke of Portugal, nor Duke of Milan, nor King of Naples and Sicily.

7. 1629 *adds:* or saying.

8. Some copies of 1609 read "the earthly bosom."

9. 1629 *adds:* Here discretion sat as Lord Keeper, and as a judge did moderate their affections.

10. 1631 *adds:* Yet every injury is more grievous, [1638 *adds:* as] proceeding from some especial friend, ηἰ ου τέχνον? "What, will Brutus stab Caesar? What, my son Brutus that stabs him to the heart?" And our Saviour to his apostles [*margin:* John 6], "Will you also forsake me?"—you that grieve His spirit.

11. 1629 *adds:* I never loved those salamanders that are never well but when they are in the fire of contention. I will rather suffer a thousand wrongs, than offer one. I will suffer an hundred, rather than return one. I will [*margin:* Dr. Hall] suffer many, ere I complain of one and endeavor to right it by contending. I have ever found that to strive with my superior is furious; with my equal, doubtfull; with my inferior, sordid and base; with any, full of unquietness. 'T is the only valor to remit a wrong, and the greatest applause that I might hurt and would not.

Essay **X**

1. 1629 *adds:* Like an Irish Sea, wherein there is nought to be expected but tempestuous storms and troublesome waves.

2. Some copies of 1609 omit "for."

3. 1629 *reads:* dominions, principalities, and powers.

4. 1629 *adds:* (by the Spirit of Truth).

5. 1629 *reads:* in trial and temptation.

6. 1629 *reads:* his son, our only Lord and Saviour Christ Jesus.

7. 1629 *adds:* with an *habeas corpus, stulte hac nocte,.*
8. 1629 *reads:* of delicates, or dainties.
9. 1629 *reads:* they are bred and nourished.
10. Some copies of 1609 omit "doth he that."
11. 1629 *reads:* challenger.
12. 1631 *reads:* Before.

Essay XI

1. 1629 *adds:* No lying in wait to kill the innocent, no Jesuitical Mariana [1631 *reads:* Martana] to persuade it [1631 *reads:* persuade treason], no treacherous Ravaillac to perform it.

2. 1629 *adds:* saucily to seat themselves upon his tribunal,.

3. 1629 *adds:* And his late vicegerent here on earth was a king of peace. [1631 *adds: rex pacificus* a very *vinculum pacis, communis terminus* betwixt nation and nation, that hath pulled down the wall of partition, and came over on this side of Jordan, and planted the tribes of his Israel, his people on both sides the river, and joined not roses but realms together: the Augustus of this latter world that hath broken swords into scythes and mattocks, the stiller of wars and extinguisher of rebellions; *nec timens bella nec provocans,* seeking after peace, not shunning his enemies.] He knew well that the blood of man violently spilt [*margin:* Sir Walter Raleigh] doth not bring forth honeybees as that of bulls doth, which stings but the fingers or the faces, but it produceth that monstrous beast, *revenge,* which hath stung to death, and eaten up of several nations so many noble personages. In preventions whereupon [1631 *reads:* prevention whereof] he hath done a most kingly and Christianlike deed which the most renowned of all his predecessors could never compass; in beating down and extinguishing that hereditary prosecution of malice called the deadly feud, a conquest which shall give him the honor of prudency and kingly power for evermore.

4. 1609 *reads:* devotes. Corrected in 1631.

5. Some copies of 1609 omit "that may afford me means."

6. Some copies of 1609 omit "he forgets his malice."

Essay XII

1. 1631 *adds:* Methinks I yet see how Crates threw his gold into the sea: *Ego perdam te ne tu perdas me.* Fabricius thought it a kingdom to contemn the wealth of a king.

2. 1629 *reads:* at the highest.

3. 1629 *adds:* Fastidious Brisk, Sir Petronell Flash, my lady's tailor, his lordship's barber, or some such gull, let him have but a good outside, he carries it and shall be adored for a god as Cyrus was amongst the Persians, *ob splendidum apparatum,* for his gay outside.

4. 1629 *adds:* Fools have the fortune, and that not without good reason for they have the most need of it.

5. 1629 *omits:* "And hence it is that, as the satirist affirms," quotation, and translation.

6. 1629 *adds:* It is a thing exceeding rare to distinguish virtue and fortune; the most impious (if prosperous) have ever been applauded, the most virtuous (if unprosperous) have ever been despised. For as fortune's man rides the horse, so fortune herself rides the man; who when he is descended and on foot, the man taken from his beast and fortune from the man, a base groom beats [1631 *reads:* bears] the one and a bitter contempt spurns at the other with equal liberties [1631 *reads:* liberty].

7. 1629 *omits:* "But, with the poet," quotation, and translation.

8. 1629 *reads:* But.

9. 1629 *adds: Ibis Homore* [1631 *reads: Homere*] *foras:* Homer may go sing ballads and scrape for his living like a blind fiddler.

10. 1629 *reads:* irreligious, prophane, and abominable.

11. 1629 *adds:* Turn rogue, parasite, villain, *necessitas cogit ad turpia:* poverty alone makes men thieves, murderers, assassinates; because of poverty we have sinned. Eccles. 27 [i.e., Ecclus. 27:1].

12. 1631 *reads:* one.

13. 1631 *adds:* I will not adventure my conscience too far in the pursuit of mammon lest I make a shipwreck before I touch at *Cape de bona speranza.* I will not, with that fool in the Gospel, lay up for many years when I am not sure my years shall be many. The little I have may (for what I know) outlast my life. I have (I know) but a little way home; I do not mean to make a burden of my provision. I will have my shoe fitted to my foot; a cloak too large or long will but tire me to travel in. I have sufficient for today, let tomorrow take care for itself. Why should my care be for the morrow, when I am not sure the morrow shall be mine? He that liketh not my resolution, let him read my warrant, and understand it: Take no thought for the morrow; for the morrow shall take thought for the things of itself, etc.

Notes

CLASSICAL EDITIONS

The following editions of classical works were consulted by the editor. References to these works in the Notes may be located in these editions, and translations and quotations of the original sources included in the Notes have been taken from them, unless otherwise noted.

Aeschylus. *Plays,* in *Aeschylus.* Ed., with an English translation, by Herbert Weir Smyth and Hugh Lloyd Jones. 2 vols. Loeb Classical Library. London: William Heinemann; Cambridge, Mass.: Harvard University Press, 1963.

Cicero. *The Letters to His Friends.* Ed., with an English translation, by W. Glynn Williams. 3 vols. Loeb Classical Library. Cambridge, Mass.: Harvard University Press; London: William Heinemann, 1952.

———. *De oratore.* Ed. (Bks. I, II), with an English translation, by E. W. Sutton; completed by H. Rackham. 2 vols. Loeb Classical Library. Cambridge, Mass.: Havard University Press; London: William Heinemann, 1942.

Diogenes Laertius. *Lives of Eminent Philosophers.* Ed., with an English translation, by R. D. Hicks. 2 vols. Loeb Classical Library. London: William Heinemann; New York: G. P. Putnam's Sons, 1925.

Euripides. *Plays,* in *Euripides.* Ed., with an English translation, by Arthur S. Way. 4 vols. Loeb Classical Library. London: William Heinemann; New York: G. P. Putnam's Sons, 1916–25.

Gellius. *The Attic Nights of Aulus Gellius.* Ed., with an English translation, by John C. Rolfe. 3 vols. Loeb Classical Library. London: William Heinemann; New York: G. P. Putnam's Sons, 1927–28.

Horace. *Satires, Epistles, and Ars poetica.* Ed., with an English translation, by H. Rushton Fairclough. Loeb Classical Library. London: William Heinemann; New York: G. P. Putnam's Sons, 1929.

———. *Odes,* in *Horace, the Odes and Epodes.* Ed., with an English translation, by C. E. Bennett. Loeb Classical Library. London: William Heinemann; New York: G. P. Putnam's Sons, 1930.

Juvenal. *Satires,* in *Juvenal and Persius.* Ed., with an English translation, by G. G. Ramsay. Loeb Classical Library. London: William Heinemann; New York: G. P. Putnam's Sons, 1928.

Livy. *Ab urbe condita,* in *Livy.* Ed., with an English translation, by B. O. Foster (and others). 13[14] vols. Loeb Classical Library. London: William Heinemann; New York: G. P. Putnam's Sons, 1925 *et seqq.*

Martial. *Epigrams.* Ed., with an English translation, by Walter C. A. Ker.

2 vols. Loeb Classical Library. London: William Heinemann; New York: G. P. Putnam's Sons, 1930.

Menander. *The Principal Fragments*. Ed., with an English translation, by Francis G. Allinson. Loeb Classical Library. London: William Heinemann; New York: G. P. Putnam's Sons, 1921.

Ovid. *Ars amatoria* and *Metamorphoses*, in *Corpus poetarum latinorum*. Ed. William Sidney Walker. London: George Bell and Sons, 1889.

Persius (*see* Juvenal).

Pindar. *The Odes of Pindar*. Ed., with an English translation, by Sir John Sandys. Loeb Classical Library. Cambridge, Mass.: Harvard University Press; London: William Heinemann, 1961.

Propertius. *Elegies*, in *Propertius*. Ed., with an English translation, by H. E. Butler. Loeb Classical Library. London: William Heinemann; New York: G. P. Putnam's Sons, 1916.

Publilius Syrus. *Sententiae*. Ed. R. A. H. Bickford-Smith. London: C. J. Clay and Sons, 1895.

Sallust. *Bellum Catilinae* and *Bellum Iugurthinum*, in *Sallust*. Ed., with an English translation, by John C. Rolfe. Loeb Classical Library. London: William Heinemann; New York: G. P. Putnam's Sons, 1921.

Seneca. *Epistulae morales*. Ed., with an English translation, by Richard M. Gummere. 3 vols. Loeb Classical Library. Cambridge, Mass.: Harvard University Press; London: William Heinemann, 1961–62.

——. *Plays*, in *Seneca's Tragedies*. Ed., with an English translation, by Frank Justus Miller. 2 vols. Loeb Classical Library. London: William Heinemann; New York: G. P. Putnam's Sons, 1927–29.

——. *Moral Essays*. Ed., with an English translation, by John W. Basore. 3 vols. Loeb Classical Library. Cambridge, Mass.: Harvard University Press; London: William Heinemann, 1958.

Tacitus. *The Histories*, ed. and trans. Clifford H. Moore, and *The Annals*, ed. and trans. John Jackson. 4 vols. Loeb Classical Library. Cambridge, Mass.: Harvard University Press; London: William Heinemann, 1962.

——. *Agricola*, in *Tacitus: Dialogus, Agricola, Germania*. Ed., with an English translation, by Maurice Hutton. Loeb Classical Library. Cambridge, Mass.: Harvard University Press; London: William Heinemann, 1963.

Terence. *Plays*, in *Terence*. Ed., with an English translation, by John Sargeaunt. 2 vols. Loeb Classical Library. London: William Heinemann; Cambridge, Mass.: Harvard University Press, 1947.

Valerius Maximus. *Valerii Maximi, dictorum factorumque memorabilium exempla*. Venetiis: haeredes Petri Ravani, 1545.

Vegetius. *Epitoma rei militaris*. Ed. Carolus Lang. 2d ed. Leipzig: Teubner, 1885.

Virgil. *Aeneid* and *Georgics*, in *Virgil*. Ed., with an English translation, by H. Rushton Fairclough. Revised ed. 2 vols. Loeb Classical Library. Cambridge, Mass.: Harvard University Press; London: William Heinemann, 1947.

Other Works Frequently Cited
(including classical authors consulted only in translation)

Aesop. *The Fables of Aesop as First Printed by William Caxton*. Ed. Joseph Jacobs. 2 vols. London: David Nutt, 1889.

Agrippa, Henry Cornelius. *Of the Vanity . . . of Arts and Sciences*. Englished by James Sandford. London, 1569. *STC* 204.

Bacon, Francis. *The Advancement of Learning*. Ed. William Aldis Wright. 5th ed. Oxford: Clarendon Press, 1926.

Barnes, Barnabe. *Four Books of Offices*. London, 1606. *STC* 1468.

Bodin, Jean. *The Six Books of a Commonweal*. Trans. Richard Knolles. London, 1606. *STC* 3193.

Browne, Sir Thomas. *Pseudodoxia epidemica*, in *The Works of Sir Thomas Browne*. Ed. Charles Sayle. 3 vols. Vols. I–II, London: Grant Richards, 1904; vol. III, Edinburgh: John Grant, 1907.

Cornwallis, Sir William. *Essayes*. Ed. Don Cameron Allen. Baltimore: Johns Hopkins Press, 1946.

Feltham, Owen. *Resolves*. Ed. James Cumming. London: J. Hatchard, 1806.

Guazzo, Stefano. *The Civile Conversation*. Ed. Sir Edward Sullivan. 2 vols. Tudor Translations, 2d series. London: Constable; New York: Knopf, 1925.

Guicciardini, Francesco. *The History of Guicciardini, Containing the Wars of Italy*. Trans. Sir Geoffrey Fenton. London, 1599. *STC* 12459. London, 1618. *STC* 12460.

Heywood, John. *A Dialogue of the Effectual Proverbs in the English Tongue Concerning Marriage*. Ed. John S. Farmer. London: Gibbings & Co., 1906.

Hooker, Richard. *The Laws of Ecclesiastical Polity, Books I–IV*. Ed. Henry Morley. Morley's Universal Library. London: George Routledge and Sons, 1888.

La Primaudaye, Pierre de. *The French Academy*. Trans. Thomas Bowes. London, 1602. *STC* 15236.

Machiavelli, Niccolò. *Discourses on the First Ten Books of Titus Livius*, trans. Christian E. Detmold, in *The Prince and the Discourses*. Ed. Max Lerner. New York: Modern Library [1940].

Montaigne, Michel de. *The Essayes of Montaigne. John Florio's Translation*. Ed. J. I. M. Stewart. Modern Library Giant, G11. New York: Modern Library, 1933.

Oxford Dictionary of English Proverbs. Comp. William George Smith, with Introduction and Index by Janet E. Heseltine. Oxford: Clarendon Press, 1935.

Perkins, William. *The Combat between Christ and the Devil Displayed*. London, 1606. *STC* 19748.

Plutarch. *The Lives of the Noble Grecians and Romans*. Trans. John

Dryden [?] and revised by Arthur Hugh Clough. Modern Library Giant, G5. New York: Modern Library, 1932.

———. [*Moralia*]. *The Philosophy, Commonly Called the Morals.* Trans. Philemon Holland. London, 1603. *STC* 20063.

Rich, Barnabe (or Barnaby). *The Honestie of This Age.* Ed. Peter Cunningham. London: T. Richards for the Percy Society, 1844.

Sidney, Sir Philip. The *Arcadia* (1590), in *The Complete Works of Sir Philip Sidney.* Ed. Albert Feuillerat. 4 vols. Cambridge, England: University Press, 1939.

Spencer, John. Καινα και παλαια: *Things New and Old.* 2 vols. London: William Tegg, 1869.

Suetonius. *The History of Twelve Caesars.* Trans. Philemon Holland. London, 1606. *STC* 23422.

Whitney, Geoffrey. *Whitney's "Choice of Emblemes." A Facsimile Reprint.* Ed. Henry Green. London: Lovell Reeve & Co., 1866.

Wright, Thomas. *The Passions of the Mind in General.* London, 1604. *STC* 26040.

Unless there is indication to the contrary, citations in the following Notes rest upon these editions. Other works, cited less frequently or but a single time, are given full bibliographical description in the note where they are first mentioned.

Notes

Essays Politic and Moral

Page 5] *Anne Harington:* Wife of John Harington, first Baron Exton. To her and to her daughter, Lucy, Countess of Bedford, John Florio dedicated the First Book of his translation of Montaigne, *Essays; or, Moral, Politic, and Military Discourses* (1603).

I Of Opinion

In the edition of 1608 this essay, through oversight, is entitled "Of Persuasion," which should be the general caption for the first three essays. In it first appears that dual influence of Montaigne and Tacitus which remains strongly marked throughout both series of Tuvill's essays. Montaigne, indeed, may have been the source of the very title of Tuvill's first series, either by way of the title of Florio's translation of his *Essays* or through his characterization of the *Histories* of Tacitus as "a seminary of moral, and a magazine of politic discourses" (*Essays*, p. 850).

Page 7] *As concerning . . . himself:* See Montaigne, *Essays*, pp. 642–43; Plutarch, *Morals*, p. 351; Aulus Gellius, *Attic Nights*, XVIII, iii. In *Peace with Her Four Gardens* (1622), by the Spenser-imitating Robert Aylett, the idea is thus versified (p. 53):

> A Spartan lewd, in serious consultation,
> Giving his good advice, was followed
> Of all the Senate in their convocation;
> And the decree in his name entered:
> A grave old man them better counseled,
> That they their honor would not so defame,
> To have decrees in such names registered:
> The sentence might continue still the same,
> Changed only from a lewd, unto a grave man's name.

Those active and working spirits . . . on work: See Sallust, *Bellum Catilinae*, xxi, 1; phrasing modified. Although naming Sallust in the text, this passage is drawn from bk. I, chap. 7, of Richard Hooker's *Laws of Ecclesiastical Polity*, p. 75, as the exact correspondence of phrase in the English translation shows.

Page 8] *Magno in populo,* etc.: Virgil, *Aeneid*, I, 148–52; for *cumque* (l. 150) read *iamque*. But Tuvill could have found this often-quoted passage in his favorite, Jean Bodin, *The Six Books of a Commonweal,* pp. 533–34.

A custom among the Spaniards: See Francesco Guicciardini, *The History of Guicciardini Containing the Wars of Italy* (1618), pp. 443–44. On churchmen as negotiators, compare John Saltmarsh, *The Practice of Policy in a Christian Life* (1639), policy 101, sig. E7r.

Ostracisms: Defined by John Bullokar, *An English Expositor* (1616), as "a banishment among the Athenians for ten years, so-called because they used to write the names of the party so condemned, in oyster shells. This punishment was chiefly used, to abate the overgreat power of noble men."

Page 9] *Malus, ubi bonum,* etc.: Marginal reference to Publius, i.e., Publilius Syrus; see *Sententiae,* l. 351. For *ubi bonum,* Bickford-Smith reads *bonum ubi.*

Cause of distaste: Some copies read "cause of *disease.*"

Τὸ καλὸν, etc.: Translated in the following sentence.

Good things lose . . . propounded: Ecclus. 20:19 reads (Genevan version): "A wise sentence loseth grace when it cometh out of a fool's mouth: for he speaketh not in due season."

Invisum semel principem: Tacitus, *Histories,* I, vii—slightly misquoted, as it is likewise in Bacon's *Essays* (1625), "Of Seditions and Troubles." The whole passage provides an instance of the rhetorical amplificatory device of *acclamation*—"these scraps of policy which men nowadays gather out of Polybius and Tacitus"—fundamental to the elaboration of Tuvill's thought. See John Hoskins, *Directions for Speech and Style,* ed. H. H. Hudson (Princeton, N.J., 1935), pp. 34–35 and note on pp. 84–85 .

Vitellius, who, as Tacitus reports: Histories, II, xci. Tuvill offers adequate versions of the Latin.

Ego me P.C., saith he, . . . mansurae: Tacitus, *Annals,* IV, xxxviii. The initials *P.C.* abbreviate *patres conscripti,* i.e., members of the Roman Senate.

That I am mortal . . . remain forever: A good translation of the foregoing Latin. But is it Tuvill's? Probably; at least it bears little resemblance to that of Richard Grenewey (1598), the only English rendering available when Tuvill was writing.

Page 10] *So likewise . . . agreeable hereunto:* Tacitus, *Histories,* I, v. Bacon also knew and quoted this passage in Tacitus; see *Essays* (1625), "Of Seditions and Troubles."

And hence it is . . . iniquity: Marginal reference to II Tim. 2:19.

Non est enim, saith Theophylact . . . peccatoris: "Praise in the mouth of a sinner, however, is not seemly."

And why Paul likewise: Marginal reference to Acts 16:[17–]18.

The Pythonist: A pythoness, or priestess, "a certain damsel possessed with a spirit of divination" (Acts 16:16).

Quasi nolens, etc.: "As if not wishing the holy to be praised by an impure mouth."

Neither was it without reason . . . strain: Cf. Diogenes Laertius, *Lives of Eminent Philosophers,* VI, 4 ("Antisthenes").

This corrupted and depraved age: Compare the statement in *Essays Moral and Theological,* p. 102: "These later ages are corrupted and depraved." The idea was a Renaissance commonplace.

The salt of the earth: See Matt. 5:13.

They run: Some copies omit *they* and read *do run.*

PAGE 11] *Boundless dissolutions of some churchmen:* Marginal reference to Rom. 2:24.

Wherefore I cannot choose . . . Jew again: A similar incident, under but slightly different terms, is related in Montaigne, *Essays,* p. 389. This is followed, *loc. cit.,* by another anecdote which Montaigne seems to have drawn from Boccaccio, *Decameron,* Day 1, Novel 2. Tuvill has blended the two.

Facta mea, etc.: Livy, *Ab urbe condita,* VII, xxxii, 12. Trans.: "Soldiers . . . it is my deeds and not my words I would have you follow, and look to me not only for instruction but for example. . . . with this right hand, have I won for myself three consulships and the highest praise."

Suddenly turn conqueror: Newberry copy omits *turn.*

The other . . . in lingua sua: The Latin (Vulgate) is found in Ps. 14.

Whereof Christ saith: Marginal reference to John 10:25. The full text (Vulgate) runs: *opera, quae ego facio in nomine Patris mei, haec testimonium perhibent de me.*

Whereat St. John the Baptist aimed: See John 1:19–23.

PAGE 12] Ἐγὼ φωνὴ . . . *desert:* John 1:23.

And therefore . . . the altar: See Isa. 6:6–7. *Isaias* is the common seventeenth-century form of Isaiah.

To encourage Jeremie: Jeremie is, of course, Jeremiah; see Jer. (Vulgate) 1:5.

Spiritu principali . . . converted unto thee: Ps. 51:12–13 (or, Vulgate, Ps. 50).

Wherefore . . . redress thine own: See Luke 4:23.

Clodius accusat moechos, etc.: Juvenal, *Satires,* II, 27; adapted. Translate, freely: "Kettle calls pot black."

That concent of spheres: The delectable "music of the spheres" predicated upon Ptolemaic astronomy, and too refined to be heard by sinful human ears. Montaigne (*Essays,* p. 74) speaks somewhat whimsically about "what philosophers deem of the celestial music, which is, that the bodies of its circles, being solid smooth, and in their rolling motion, touching and rubbing one against another, must of necessity produce a wonderful harmony: by changes and intercaperings of which, the revolutions, motions, cadences, and carols of the asters and planets are caused and transported."

Hannibal will but scorn: Not Hannibal, but Eudamidas; see Plutarch, *Morals,* pp. 425, 457, and Montaigne, *Essays,* p. 642.

Cleomenes will account: Like the preceding, probably drawn immediately from Montaigne, *Essays,* p. 642. The original is Plutarch, *Morals,* p. 460; but compare also Stefano Guazzo, *Civile Conversation,* I, 152, and note that Tuvill re-uses the illustration in *The Dove and the Serpent* (1614), sig. A4r.

Qui de virtute locuti, etc.: Juvenal, *Satires,* II, 20–21: "[who] after discoursing upon virtue, prepare to practice vice."

Page 13] *Vitellius, Gracchus:* An adaptation of Juvenal, *Satires,* II, 24.

Manus, quae sordes abluit, etc.: Probably drawn from Thomas Wright, *The Passions of the Mind,* sig. M7r., "as St. Gregory well noteth, *Manus quae sordes abluit, munda esse debet:* the hand which washeth filth away, should be clean."

Quis coelum terris, etc.: Juvenal, *Satires,* II, 25–26. Loeb text omits *aut* in line 26.

As St. Paul saith: Marginal reference to I Cor. 9:[24–]27.

It is said of Vespasian: Tacitus, *Annals,* III, lv.

And hence it came . . . authority: Although the mention of Theodoric may suggest Cassiodorus (cf. *Variae,* bk. III), the whole passage was supplied by Bodin, *Of a Commonweal,* p. 503: "Yea, Theodoric, king of the Goths, writing unto the Senate of Rome passeth further, using these words, *facilius est errare naturam, quam dissimilem sui princeps possit rempublicam formare,* an easier thing it is (said he) for nature to change her course than for a prince to frame a commonweal unlike unto himself."

For Sulla, being a disordered liver: Plutarch, *Lives,* "Comparison of Lysander with Sylla," p. 575.

II OF AFFECTION

The fundamental discussion of the relation between persuasion and the affections is found in Aristotle, *Rhetoric,* II, iii–xvii; but see also Bacon's comments in *The Advancement of Learning,* pp. 207–9. Much of the Renaissance psychology of this and the following essay finds its way to Tuvill through the medium of Thomas Wright's *Passions of the Mind in General* (ed. pr., 1601).

PAGE 14] *Witness Pisistratus:* Plutarch, *Lives,* "Solon," p. 115.

And the reason hereof: The following discussion of passions, reason, wit, will, senses, and imagination is based upon Wright, *Passions of the Mind,* sigs. E1v-E3v; see also bk. II, chap. ii, "How Passions Seduce the Will," sigs. E5r-E6r.

During her weaker nonage: Newberry copy adds "or minority."

PAGE 15] *Neither can the soul . . . followers:* The phrasing here clearly indicates the derivation of this passage from Wright's *Passions of the Mind,* sig. E1v.

It was a saying of a prince: Plutarch, *Lives,* "Agesilaus," p. 720; *Morals,* p. 424.

PAGE 16] *Brutus and Cassius contending:* Plutarch, *Lives,* "Caesar," p. 890; "Marcus Brutus," p. 1190.

But with this caution: Saying attributed to Pericles. The Greek phrase is Plutarch's; see *Morals,* p. 166. See also Aulus Gellius, *Attic Nights,* I, iii, 20.

And this Agesilaus knew: Plutarch, *Lives,* "Agesilaus," p. 720; *Morals,* pp. 424, 446.

Make those things make with them: That is, "make those things work to their advantage," etc.

Would turn the bias: "Bias," a term from the game of bowls, describes the swerving path of a rolling ball produced by off-centering or imperfect sphericity.

Compared to a green glass: The equivalent of our "looking through rose-colored glasses."

That forealleged Spartan . . . chance: The account is in Plutarch, *Lives,* "Agesilaus," p. 718, but the brother is *Pisander,* not Lysander.

It is said of Agrippina . . . and hers: Tacitus, *Annals,* XII, iii; Tuvill has slightly modified the quotations, opposite the second of which he has a marginal reference reading "*Lib.* 12. 240 *et* 267."

PAGE 17]   *And hence it was . . . daughter:* Tacitus, *Annals,* XII, iv.

That excellent saying of the Greeks: From Menander, *Monosticha* 123. *The Oxford Dictionary of English Proverbs,* p. 578, without noting the present instance, cites as the first occurrence in English that in the 1586 Pettie-Young Guazzo, *Civile Conversation,* II, 172.

PAGE 18]   *And thus did Absalom . . . justice:* II Sam. 15:1–6.

The only harbingers: With Tuvill's figurative use of *harbinger,* compare John Downame, *Spiritual Physic* (1600), sig. D7r-v: "their unquiet and turbulent thoughts are fit harbingers to prepare a lodging in their hearts to entertain anger." See also Tuvill's own *Asylum Veneris* (1616), sig. B6v.

The Scripture doth assure us: II Cor. 11:14.

He told our first parents: Gen. 3:5.

PAGE 19]   *For, saith he,* etc.: Gen. 3:4–5. Vulgate: *nequaquam morte moriemini.*

III   OF THE FORCE OF REASON

The religious emphasis of the ending to the preceding essay serves to remind us that Tuvill was, after all, a preacher and that his interest in rhetorical persuasiveness was a practical one. In this third, and shortest, of the "rhetorical" series, anecdote and apothegm—Tuvill's chief stock in trade, as with his masters Plutarch and Montaigne—again figure heavily. But his chief indebtedness for ideas is still to Wright's *Passions of the Mind.*

PAGE 20]   *Out of probable conjectures:* Compare the phrasing of Hooker, *Laws of Ecclesiastical Polity,* p. 116.

Witness Caesar . . . absolve him: Plutarch, *Lives,* "Cicero," p. 1064; also related in Bodin, *Of a Commonweal,* p. 510.

And for a further confirmation . . . seen: The saying had wide circulation. See Plutarch, *Lives,* "Pericles," p. 188; *Morals,* p. 353. See also Eunapius, *The Lives of Philosophers and Orators* (1579), sig. K4v; H. C. Agrippa, *Of the Vanity . . . of Arts and Sciences,* sigs. F1v-F2r; and Montaigne, *Essays,* p. 263.

An incongruity committed by Marcus Brutus: Plutarch, *Lives,* "Marcus Brutus," pp. 1197–98.

PAGE 21]   *Lend an ear:* This phrase inevitably calls to mind Mark Antony's oration in Shakespeare's *Julius Caesar,* III, ii, 78 ff.

Rhetorical enthymemes: Holland (Plutarch, *Morals,* p. 1370) defines these:

"unperfect syllogisms, or short reasonings, when one of the premises is not expressed yet so understood, as the conclusion nevertheless is inferred."

Demosthenes did attribute . . . no other: Cicero, *De oratore,* III, lvi, 213; Plutarch, *Morals,* p. 932; Valerius Maximus, *Dictorum factorumque memorabilium exempla,* VIII, x; see also Bacon, *Essays* (1625), "Of Boldness." But Tuvill's immediate source is Wright, *Passions of the Mind,* sig. M8r-v.

For in an orator . . . gestures: Wright, *Passions of the Mind,* sig. M6v: "Orators, whose project is persuasion, have two principal parts wherewith they endeavor to compass their purpose, *Ornate dicere, & concinne agere,* To speak eloquently and to act aptly."

So that when I consider . . . misdeed: Plutarch, *Lives,* "Cicero," p. 1055.

The dust . . . cast into the eyes: Proverbial, and earlier than the instances cited in *Oxford Dict. Eng. Prov.,* p. 548.

Aeschines, after his banishment . . . adversary: Tuvill's source is Wright, *Passions of the Mind,* sig. H2r; Wright's marginal direction indicates that *he* is following Erasmus, *Apophthegmata,* bk. VIII; and Erasmus, in turn, draws upon Plutarch, *Morals,* p. 927, or Cicero, *De oratore,* III, lvi, 213 — or both.

Wherefore he . . . madman's hand: Still Wright, *loc. cit.;* but compare Guazzo, *Civile Conversation,* I, 211: "a sword is put into a madman's hand, when an office is bestowed upon a naughty person."

It is an instrument . . . deceitful art: A loose paraphrase, in jumbled order, of bits selected from the opening of Montaigne's essay, "Of the Vanity of Words"; see *Essays,* pp. 263–64.

PAGE 22] *But it is not my purpose . . . patient:* The phrasing clearly indicates Tuvill's source as Wright, *Passions of the Mind,* sig. N4v.

For the learned . . . none at all: Tuvill's faith in the formulae of classical rhetoric is similarly illustrated by a passage in *The Dove and the Serpent,* sig. I3v: "Whatsoever is the subject or occasion of intercourse and debatement is either judicial, deliberative, or demonstrative. The first consisteth in accusing and defending, in demanding and denying; and comprehendeth under it all such speeches as are either conquestory, expostulatory, or refutatory. The second, in exhorting and dehorting and compriseth such as are gratulatory, complemental, or officious. The third and last is altogether exercised in praising and dispraising and containeth in it such as are petitory, commendatory, deprecatory, consolatory, objurgatory, and the like. So that nothing is at any time in question or controversy between man and man but it may well be referred to some one of these. And therefore having once discovered to what kind of cause the matter which he is to treat of, be it by letter, by personal conference, or howsoever, doth naturally belong, he may straightway know to what topics, heads, and commonplaces he should repair for arguments, examples, and inductions, with other such preparatory store, wherewith to strengthen and corroborate his plea."

Arsenals and storehouses of persuasive provision: Compare *The Dove and the Serpent,* sig. G4v: "Those writings, wherein the arts of men are registered, are as the arsenals and storehouses of politic directions."

An example of the former . . . respective: As the phrasing proves, this passage is again drawn directly from Wright, *Passions of the Mind,* sigs. L6v-L7r.

Contemn the forces: Some copies read *force.*

Of the latter, in Sejanus . . . purposes: Tacitus, *Annals,* IV, lix. The Latin is translated as: "and, fatal though his advice might be, yet, as a man whose thoughts were not for himself, he found a confiding listener."

Page 23] *Let Delphidius assure himself,* etc.: See Johann Gast, *Convivalium liber* (Basel, 1566), tom. II, sig. p1v. Robert Burton, *Anatomy of Melancholy,* ed. Floyd Dell and Paul Jordan-Smith (New York, 1941), p. 550, ascribes Julian's answer to Ammianus Marcellinus.

IV OF PRAISES

This is the longest, best-developed, and most variously illustrated of Tuvill's essays. It may be compared for interest with some of those of Montaigne himself, from whom Tuvill, as usual, has drawn with an over-liberal hand. Much that is typical of Tuvill's other writings can be seen here in epitome: his strong interest in history, his admiration of individual *virtù,* his sense of present moral decay, his delight in proverbial and epigrammatic statement, certain individual modes of expression—to which attention will be called in the following notes. Here too, it seems to me, Tuvill achieves a more successful blending of the preacher and the "man of the world" than is the case elsewhere. This balance, together with the division of interest between ancient and modern illustrative instances, could only have proved toothsome to the "gentlemanly" seventeenth-century reader.

Encomia, as rhetorical and poetic "kinds," under various forms and with differing degrees of sobriety, have been popular from antiquity to the present; that "love of praise" about which Tuvill writes was by one of his contemporaries described as "that last infirmity of noble mind." For the general treatment of this theme in the Renaissance, see Lorenzo Ducci, *Ars aulica,* tr. Edward Blount (1607), the long chap. xx, "Of Praise and Flattery," probably known to Tuvill; and, among modern books, Isabel Rathborne, *The Meaning of Spenser's Fairyland* (New York, 1937) and O. B. Hardison, *The Enduring Monument* (Chapel Hill, N.C., 1962).

PAGE 24] *The love of praise . . . altissima cupiunt:* Tacitus, *Annals,* IV, xxxviii, adapted. For *Optimi n quique* Loeb reads *Optumos quippe.* The two passages may be translated: "Contempt of fame, contempt of virtue" and "Best men desire highest things."

Some extraordinary genius: In Roman religion the Genius was the *numen,* or personal *virtù,* of each individual.

Witness that undaunted Curtius: See Livy, *Ab urbe condita,* VII, vi, 1–6; Valerius Maximus, *Dict. fact. memorab.,* V, vi; Pierre de la Primaudaye, *The French Academy,* pp. 96–97.

So Brutus . . . victory to us: Lucius Junius Brutus, consul and patriot; see Livy, *Ab urbe condita,* II, v, 5–9.

Vicit amor patriae, etc.: A variant reading of Virgil, *Aeneid,* VI, 823. Trans.: "Yet love of country shall prevail [*vincet*], and boundless passion for renown."

PAGE 25] *Compertum ego habeo . . . hortere:* Sallust, *Bellum Catilinae,* lviii, 1–3, the beginning of Catiline's final speech: "I am well aware . . . that words do not supply valor, and that a spiritless army is not made vigorous, or a timid one stout-hearted, by a speech from its commander. . . . It is vain to exhort one who is roused neither by glory nor by dangers."

Quem quisque vivus . . . tegebat: Sallust, *Bellum Catilinae,* lxi, 2. Tuvill's translation is adequate, although the Latin text in Loeb reads *vivos* where Tuvill has *vivus.*

That worthy martialist Gonsalvo: Gonzalvo Fernández de Córdova y Aguilar (1453–1515), otherwise called *el gran Capitán.* For the origin of the title, see Guicciardini, *History* (1618), p. 83.

When his captains advised . . . hundred years: Guicciardini, *History* (1618), p. 237. See also Bacon, *Advancement,* p. 192, and Sir William Cornwallis, *Essays* (Pt. II; 1601), sigs. Gg6v-Gg7r.

Would have desired rather, etc.: The figure is repeated in Tuvill's *Christian Purposes and Resolutions* (1622), sig. I5v.

The forealleged historian . . . properabat: The paragraph follows Sallust, *Bellum Catilinae,* vii, the Latin quotations being a jumbled reproduction of vii, 6: *Sed gloriae maxumum certamen inter ipsos erat; se quisque hostem ferire, murum ascendere, conspici dum tale facinus faceret, properabat; eas divitias, eam bonam famam magnamque nobilitatem putabant. Laudis avidi, pecuniae liberales erant; gloriam ingentem, divitias honestas volebant.* "Nay, their hardest struggle for glory was with one another; each man strove to be first to strike down the foe, to scale a wall, to be seen of all while doing such a deed. This they considered riches, this fair fame and high nobility. It was praise they coveted, but they were lavish of money; their aim was unbounded renown, but only such riches as could be gained honourably."

Opposite the last sentence of the Latin, Tuvill's margin reads: *Laudatas ostendit avis Iunonia pennas: Si tacitus spectes illa recondit opes.* He uses this quotation from Ovid, *Ars amatoria,* I, 627–28, again in *The Dove and the Serpent,* sig. C2v, with the translation: "Her praised plumes great Juno's bird spreads forth, / But viewed with silence, she conceals her worth."

PAGE 26] *A certain Laconian . . . before the king:* Plutarch, *Lives,* "Lycurgus," p. 67.

Witness the Ottomans, etc.: See Bodin, *Of a Commonweal,* p. 613. Turkish military might and discipline were still matters of grave interest to the Christian world.

And by this means . . . nations: Almost certainly a rephrasing of René de Lucinge, *The Beginning, Continuance, and Decay of Estates,* tr. John Finett (1606), sig. b1v: "naked and unarmed, they have marched victorious over the bellies of the most warlike nations under the heavens." The same work illustrates (sig. D11-v) and is perhaps the source of Tuvill's following remarks (pp. 26–27) on the encouragement given by the Turks to their common soldiers.

It is no principle in their philosophy: A characteristic turn of phrase in Tuvill; compare *Christian Purposes and Resolutions,* sig. E8v: *"Farewell friends so foes may perish,* is no principle in his politics, no precept of his propounding."

No, the greatest . . . manger: With this statement concerning virtue compare *Essays Moral and Theological,* "Of Respect and Reverence," opening lines, p. 100.

PAGE 27] *Qualem commendes . . . pudorem:* Horace, *Epistles,* I, xviii, 76–77: "What sort of a person you introduce, consider again and again, lest by and by the other's failings strike you with shame."

Polyperchon . . . commend him: Plutarch, *Morals,* p. 169. Polyperchon (or, correctly, Polysperchon) was a general under Alexander the Great.

Could testify of Nathanael: See John 1:47.

Fallimur, et quondam, etc.: Horace, *Epistles,* I, xviii, 78: "At times we err and present someone unworthy."

Quem sua culpa premet, etc.: Horace, *Epistles,* I, xviii, 79: "if taken in, forbear to defend him whose own fault drags him down."

That restraint of Plato . . . change: Plutarch, *Morals,* p. 169, where the letter is attributed to *Cato.* But note that there is no Greek in Holland's text; Tuvill was evidently following the original.

PAGE 28] *Such a one enters . . . like a dog:* See Montaigne, *Essays,* p.

292. T. B., *Historia de donne famose* (1599), sig. E4v, applies the saying to Hildebrand (Gregory VII).

Cato, Vatinius, Curius, Fabricius, etc.: Egregious Roman exemplars of the virtues or vices here variously attributed to them.

So great and difficult . . . same pace: Both the idea and the Latin phrase occur in Montaigne, *Essays,* p. 298.

This corrupted age: See above, note to p. 10.

That fantastical musician: Tigellius. The two Latin quotations are from Horace, *Satires,* I, iii, 9–15 and 15–19.

Elkanah, Samuel's father: See I Sam. 1:1 ff. (Vulgate, I Regum 1:1).

PAGE 29] *Solyman the Great,* etc.: Details and sequence indicate that this paragraph derives from Bodin, *Of a Commonweal,* p. 718, with some possible assistance from Lucinge's *The Beginning, Continuance, and Decay of Estates* (1606), especially in the opening (cf. Lucinge, sig. O3r-v) and closing lines. I find this same account also in George More's *Principles for Young Princes* (1611), fol. 31v. Solyman's inhuman treatment of his sons is retold in Tuvill's *St. Paul's Threefold Cord* (1635), sigs. K6r-K7r. See also Thomas Newton, *A Notable History of the Saracens* (1575, tr. from Celio Agustino Curione), fol. 139; and Fulke Greville's *The Tragedy of Mustapha* (1609), V, ii.

So little could he . . . empire: Compare Lucinge, *The Beginning, Continuance, and Decay of Estates* (1606), sig. E2v: "the ambition of rule strives to be alone and brooks no fellowship, no not between brothers; as little between father and son."

PAGE 30] *I could instance . . . many:* A verbal formula repeated identically at the opening of the final paragraph of this essay. Tuvill is fond of such patterns.

And come to Tiberius . . . his own: Tacitus, *Annals,* I, xiv. For Tiberius' envy of his mother, Livia, see also Suetonius, *The History of Twelve Caesars,* sig. LIV. Tuvill again refers to the matter in *Essays Moral and Theological,* p. 104.

Alexander will . . . admit comparison: The idea that kings cannot abide paragons is quaintly illustrated in Barnabe Barnes, *Four Books of Offices,* sig. K1v: "*Unum et enim arbustum non alit duos Erithacos:* one bush will not admit two ruddocks [robins] at once upon it. Neither can the empire or kingdom of any brook two phoenixes to live at once."

Dionysius, because . . . son of a cobbler: Although he has scrambled their order, Tuvill clearly derives all these illustrations from Montaigne, *Essays,* "Of the Incommodity of Greatness," pp. 828–32. Notes on the individual illustrations may be found in editions of the *Essays* by Pierre Villey (Bordeaux, 1906–20), IV, 403–5, and Jacob Zeitlin (New York, 1934), III, 370–71.

Favorinus, therefore . . . thirty legions: Also related in Bacon, *Advancement*, p. 27.

It is no wisdom . . . proscribe: A manuscript marginal note in one Folger copy reads: "*non est tutu scribere contra eum qui p^t [= potest] proscribere.* Petrarch." Trans.: "It is not safe to write [*scribere*] against him who is able to proscribe [*proscribere*]."

Page 31] *That witty saying of Carneades:* Montaigne's original is probably Plutarch, *Morals,* p. 96, where Tuvill also would have seen it; but compare Guazzo, *Civile Conversation,* I, 88.

Regibus, saith Sallust, etc.: Sallust, *Bellum Catilinae,* vii, 2. Tuvill's translation is a trifle free; see Loeb.

One only accident . . . occasioned the action: Guicciardini, *History* (1599), pp. 269–70.

Page 32] *Cincinnatus, when he took . . . unadvised error:* See Livy, *Ab urbe condita,* III, xii, 8. Caeso, caught in the quarrel between Senate and plebeians, went into voluntary exile, forfeiting his surety, which was then exacted from Cincinnatus.

Non omnis fert omnia tellus: This seems to be adapted from Virgil, *Georgics,* II, 109: *nec vero terrae ferre omnes omnia possunt.*

Did not stick to instance on himself: Compare the phrasing of *The Dove and the Serpent,* sig. C3v: "there are some that will not let to instance many feigned matters on themselves."

Page 33] *Enyalios, Mantoos, Kerdoos:* = Ἐνυάλιος, "the warlike"; μαντῷος or μαντεῖος, "the foreseeing"; κέρδος, "the thievish" or "the wily one" (a fox).

But that we may . . . interpret them: Roughly, the content of I Cor. 12:1–11.

The reason whereof . . . same body: I Cor. 12:12–30.

Moses, howsoever . . . the other: For Aaron, see Exod. 4:10 ff.; for Jethro, Exod. 18.

There is the like . . . recompense: Fundamental idea of Juan Huarte's *Examen de ingenios* (Baeza, 1575), one of the most influential of Renaissance books. There was an English translation by Richard Carew, *The Examination of Mens Wits,* in 1594, very likely known to Tuvill.

Castor gaudet equis, etc.: Horace, *Satires,* II, i, 26–27: "Castor finds joy in horses; his brother, born from the same egg, in boxing."

To beautify and adorn that Sparta: "Let us adorn this Sparta of ours" is used proverbially in Plutarch; see *Morals,* "Of Tranquillity of Mind," p. 155, and "Of Banishment," p. 273.

Antony, angling one day . . . instrument: Plutarch, *Lives,* "Antony," pp. 1120–21. Plutarch's account has some amusing details omitted by Tuvill.

PAGE 34] *Hence is it . . . in none:* Like the following statement, this idea has taken on proverbial form: "Jack of all trades, master of none."

And it is a proverb . . . least: A popular motto in emblem books; see Geoffrey Whitney, *A Choice of Emblems,* p. 55. See also Guazzo, *Civile Conversation,* I, 139: "I holding nothing fast, of all things fasten hold."

Philip, hearing his son . . . otherwise: In Montaigne, *Essays,* p. 200. Plutarch (*Lives,* "Pericles," p. 183), who is Montaigne's source, has Alexander *playing* music, not singing.

And this Demosthenes . . . a sponge: Plutarch, *Lives,* "Demosthenes," p. 1031. The anecdote also occurs in Montaigne's *Essays,* p. 200, but without mention of Aeschines and Philocrates. In this instance Tuvill seems to have gone directly to the original.

PAGE 35] *A wise distrust . . . wisdom:* See Bacon, *Advancement,* p. 229: "We will begin therefore with this precept, according to the ancient opinion, that the sinews of wisdom are slowness of belief and distrust." That Tuvill is drawing from Bacon, not from "ancient opinion" (= Cicero), is indicated by the fact that in *The Dove and the Serpent,* sig. C1r-v — a work heavily indebted to the *Advancement*—he restates Bacon's "precept."

Many there are . . . their hearts: A modified proverb; see below, p. 47, for the more usual form.

Like unto our oarsmen: Compare Montaigne, *Essays,* p. 717: "as rowers, who go forward as it were backward." But the comparison was proverbial.

Which Alfonso . . . contrary note: Alfonso V (Alfonso the Magnanimous), king of Aragon and Sicily (1416–58) and (as Alfonso I) of Naples (1443–58). The incident is related by Panormita (Antonio Beccadelli), *De dictis et factis Alfonsi,* III, 15 — see his *Speculum boni principis: Alphonsus Rex Aragoniae,* ed. Johannes Santes (Amsterdam, 1646), pp. 73–74.

Fronti nulla fides: "Put no trust in appearances." This is Juvenal's *frontis nulla fides, Satires,* II, 8; from its form, however, and from its appearance here, so close on the heels of another phrase of Bacon's, I conclude that Tuvill probably drew this motto from the *Advancement,* p. 230.

Harpies have . . . like a foe: One of Tuvill's occasional lapses into euphuism.

This world . . . personated fashion: Compare *The Dove and the Serpent,* sig. B4r: "The world affords us almost nothing now, which is not personated and disguised." See also, *Essays Politic and Moral,* p. 56, and *Essays Moral and Theological,* p. 109.

Look into Epeus's horse . . . Troy: Homer, *Odyssey,* VIII; Virgil, *Aeneid,* II, 264. Tuvill apparently found his inspiration nearer home; compare Stephen Gosson, *The Schoole of Abuse . . . 1579,* ed. Edward Arber (London, 1868), p. 20: "But if you look well to Epaeus horse, you shall find in his bowels the destruction of Troy."

The lion is a lion: Proverbial.

There be many . . . effect it: Marginal reference to Ecclus. 13[:3–7].

PAGE 36] *Tacitus, making a brief . . . commended him:* Tacitus, *Agricola,* xli, [2–5], with brief omission.

And indeed . . . quam ex mala: Tacitus, *Agricola,* v, [17–19]. Marginal reference reads: *"In vita Agric."*

Those inhuman cannibals: The phrase is repeated in *Essays Moral and Theological,* p. 106.

Hence it was . . . author: Tacitus, *Annals,* XIV, lvii; related also in Bacon, *Advancement,* p. 233. Tuvill's marginal note at this point reads: *"Annal. lib. 14."*

In fenny regions . . . diseases: Varro, *Rerum rusticarum,* I, xii, 2. Tuvill's marginal reference reads, inexactly, "I. De re Rust. 15."

Thus in the head . . . basil: Although citing Holerius (i.e., Jacques Houllier, d. 1562; margin reads: *"Cap. I. Praxis Medic."*), Tuvill draws both the illustration and the documentation from Thomas Cogan, *The Haven of Health* (1605), sig. D1v. See also Sir Thomas Browne, *Pseudodoxia epidemica* (or *Vulgar Errors*), II, vii, 9.

PAGE 37] *The fencer sometimes . . . head:* An illustration perhaps suggested by Guazzo, *Civile Conversation,* I, 86: "behold a fencer, who, making at his enemy's head, striketh him on the leg, or somewhere else."

PAGE 38] *Another kind of sinister praisers,* etc.: See the long section on flatterers and flattery in Guazzo, *Civile Conversation,* I, 76–90.

And as the ivy: Tuvill repeats this comparison in *Asylum Veneris,* sig. C6v: "It [jealousy] resembleth in effect the ivy, which doth always hurt that most which it most embraceth." Compare also Montaigne, *Essays,* p. 912: "the ivy, which corrupts and ruins the walls it claspeth."

V OF PAINS AND INDUSTRY

Although Montaigne provides much at the beginning of this essay, the temper—as well as a substantial part of the text—derives from Seneca. The idea that virtue must be achieved through hard contest in unfriendly surroundings would have been congenial to Milton; the correlative notion, also expressed here, that effort is in itself virtuous, contains the germ of what Carlyle later developed into his characteristic "gospel of work." From the biblical decree, "In the sweat of thy brow," to Aesop's fable of Hercules and the carter, down to the mowing of yesterday's lawn, *Dii laboribus omnia vendunt* remains one of the immutable facts of life to be accepted, endured. It requires a more positive and creative attitude to add, with Tuvill: "Without pains and industry nothing can be got; *and with it, most things may.*" No doubt much of Tuvill's preaching, after the immemorial manner of sermons, fell upon deaf ears and stony hearts; but in an age that rejoiced in the virtuous triumphs of a Simon Eyre and a Golding, of self-made merchant and industrious apprentice, this particular sermon could only have met with rapt attention.

PAGE 39] *Ingrata quae tuta:* "Safe things are unpleasing." The phrase is lifted, perhaps unconsciously, from Tacitus, *Histories,* III, xxvi.

No accidents have power . . . not appall: This passage is an adaptation, with omissions, of Montaigne, *Essays,* pp. 309–10.

Duris ut ilex . . . strength again: Horace, *Odes,* IV, iv, 57–60, quoted in Montaigne, *Essays,* p. 309. Tuvill does not follow Florio's translation of the verse.

Si fractus . . . appall: Again in Horace, *Odes,* III, iii, 7–8 (and again in Montaigne, p. 310). This time Tuvill *has* followed, and modified, Florio's translation.

Avida est periculi virtus: "Virtue is eager for dangers"; Seneca, *Moral Essays,* "De providentia," iv, 4—but probably drawn here from Montaigne, *Essays,* p. 209.

Edward III . . . overthrow: See Montaigne, *Essays,* p. 221. It may be doubted that Tuvill had recourse to Montaigne's source, cited by Villey and by Zeitlin as Froissart, *Chroniques,* ed. Siméon Luce (Paris, 1869–99), III, 182–83.

PAGE 40] *Witness the first just battle,* etc.: Montaigne, *Essays,* p. 44. The phrase "a troop of well-nigh ten thousand footmen" is identical with Florio's.

Julius Caesar made known . . . possessed: The phrasing of this paragraph seems to indicate that Tuvill was following the account in Philemon Holland's translation of Suetonius, *History of Twelve Caesars,* sig. C1v. See also Plutarch, *Lives,* "Caesar," p. 874.

Cries, "Have at all!": Tuvill has modified Caesar's traditional phrase but has followed decorum in retaining the language of dicing; see Henry Parrot, *The Mous-Trap* (1606), Epig. 20:

> Tush hang it: have at all (says Curio,)
> Comes not deuce ace, as soon as six and three?

PAGE 41] *That virtue is but weak . . . whatsoever:* Compare Milton's famous declaration in *Areopagitica:* "I cannot praise a fugitive and cloistered virtue, unexercised and unbreathed, that never sallies out and sees her adversary, but slinks out of the race where that immortal garland is to be run for, not without dust and heat." Quoted here from *Selected Essays by John Milton,* ed. Laura E. Lockwood (Boston, 1911), p. 70.

Pelopidas, being advertised . . . the more: Plutarch, *Lives,* "Pelopidas," p. 365.

The Lacedaemonians . . . advantages: The saying of King Agis; see Plutarch, *Morals,* p. 423.

It was Scipio's opinion, etc.: "Way should be prepared for enemies whereby they may flee"; see Vegetius, *Epitoma rei militaris,* III, 21, 11–12.

Those of Gaunt [i.e., Ghent], etc.: Reference not located.

The Earl of Foix . . . unsevered: Guicciardini, *History* (1599), p. 449.

[Fortuna] vitrea est, etc.: Quoted by Montaigne (*Essays,* p. 216) as from Seneca. The original, however, appears to be Publilius Syrus; see *Sententiae,* p. 13. Florio translates:

> Fortune is glasslike, brittle as 't is bright:
> Light-gone, Light-broken, when it lends best light.

The French proverb . . . lose it: Compare Edward Forsett, *A Comparative Discourse of the Bodies Natural and Politic* (1606), sig. G2r-v: "The stirring nature of man is like the quickness and slipperiness of the eel, *si laxes erepit,* but *si stringas erumpit:* so that (though he be hardly by either way detained in steadiness) yet by the feeling of himself to be too much gripped, he the more enforceth all his strength and motion for his enlargement."

Many have had the victory snatched, etc.: Compare Barnabe Barnes, *Four Books of Offices,* sig. Cc3v: "And hereupon note by the way, that if thine adversary turn his back toward you, pursue not in further heat and greediness of victory, but rather according to the proverb, *Make him a silver bridge to be gone:* lest being constrained to fight upon necessity they become desperate, of which there is infinite example of divers being pursued after the fight which have upon that example finished in much effusion of blood and victorious conquest had of them that followed."

PAGE 42] *Una salus victis,* etc.: "For the defeated the one safety [is] to hope for none"; Virgil, *Aeneid,* II, 354.

Those which Vectius . . . hand of them: Vectius (= Vettius Messius) was a Volscian rebel leader; see Livy, *Ab urbe condita,* IV, xxviii, 3–5.

Catiline's seditious followers . . . hands: See Sallust, *Bellum Catilinae,* lviii, 8; adapted from Catiline's harangue to his troops.

Witness those several inundations . . . crown of France: Most of this information could have been found conveniently gathered in the second chapter of Richard Verstegen's (i.e., Richard Rowlands') *A Restitution of Decayed Intelligence* (Antwerp, 1605), sigs. F2r-F3r.

The Longobards: Langobardi (or *Longibarbi,* "long beards"), a Suevian people who invaded northern Italy about the middle of the sixth century. Their mythical or traditional island home was called Scadinavia or Scandavia, not Scandinavia. For a fuller account, see Paolo Diacono (= Paulus Diaconus), *Della origine et fatti de i re Longobardi,* tr. Lodovico Domenichi (Venice, 1558), bk. I.

PAGE 43] *Charles, surnamed the Gross:* Charles II (of France) or Charles III (the Fat), emperor 839–88. The ceding of Normandy to the Northmen, however, took place in 911 and was the act not of Charles "the Gross" but of his successor, Charles the Simple (= Charles III of France).

Imperia . . . saith the Tragic: "Do away with harsh commands—what then will valor be?"; Seneca, *Hercules Furens,* l. 433.

Inveniet viam . . . or make one: Seneca, *Hercules Furens,* ll. 276–77. Compare Hannibal's statement in crossing the Alps: *Viam inveniam aut faciam.*

The gladiator thinks . . . not dangerous: A translation of Seneca, *Moral Essays,* "De providentia," iii, 4: *Ignominiam iudicat gladiator cum inferiore componi et scit eum sine gloria vinci, qui sine periculo vincitur.*

Bellum cum captivis . . . said Alexander: "I cannot wage war against captives and women; he must be armed whom I shall hate." See Quintus Curtius Rufus, *Historiarum libri X* (Amsterdam: Elzevir, 1630), bk. IV (p. 96); for Tuvill's *non possum* read *non soleo.*

He would not run . . . victory: Plutarch, *Lives,* "Alexander," p. 803.

Paulus Aemilius . . . a foe: Plutarch, *Lives,* "Aemilius Paulus," p. 337. See also La Primaudaye, *French Academy,* pp. 115–16.

In tauros ruunt, etc.: Martial, *Epigrams,* XII, lxi, 5–6.

The like doth Fortune . . . disdain: Another direct translation of Seneca, *Moral Essays,* "De providentia," iii, 4: *Idem facit fortuna: fortissimos sibi pares quaerit, quosdam fastidio transit.*

Transit tutos Fortuna sinus, etc.: Seneca, *Hercules oetaeus,* ll. 697–99. For *suppara* Loeb reads *sipara.* Trans.: "misfortune passes by quiet ports, and seeks for ships sailing the open sea, whose topsails smite the clouds."

PAGE 44] *She seeks a Mutius . . . is pleased:* Tuvill appropriates this stock catalogue of variously virtuous ancients from Seneca, *Moral Essays,* "De providentia," iii, 4.

Had he been a Samson: See Judges, chaps. 14–16.

Had he been a David: See I Sam. 17:34–50.

Did the all-seeing . . . whole world: Compare *Christian Purposes and Resolutions,* sigs. D1ov-D11r: "Sloth shall not consume their mettle; nor ease effeminate their minds. He will make them sweat even upon holy days. One accident or other shall provoke their valor and keep it from growing sluggish through want of exercise." See also *Essays Moral and Theological,* p. 131.

Had not Rutilius been wronged, etc.: See Seneca, *Epistulae morales,* XXIV, 4; also *Moral Essays,* "De providentia," iii, 7.

Illustrat fortuna aliquos, dum vexat: Tuvill's translation is adequate; source not found.

Zeno knew himself . . . philosophy: See Seneca, *Moral Essays,* "De tranquillitate animi," xiv, 3; Plutarch, *Morals,* pp. 238, 275.

Languet per inertiam saginata virtus: Adapted from Seneca, *Moral Essays,* "De providentia," ii, 6.

PAGE 45] *How quickly sundry arts,* etc.: See Gen. 4:20–22.

Want was their mother: Compare "Necessity is the mother of invention."

Quis expedivit . . . conari: Persius, *Satires,* Prol. 8–9. The Latin reads: *picamque . . . verba nostra.* Tuvill was perhaps quoting from memory — as was Bacon, *Advancement,* p. 151.

Magister artis . . . voces: Persius, *Satires,* Prol. 10–11.

The immortal gods: An echo of the often-recurring classical *dii immortales.*

The Grecian proverb, etc.: "With Athena's aid also to move (one's) hand."

That rustic in the apologue: One of the most widely diffused of the "Aesopic" fables, although not included by Caxton. See *The Fables of Aesop,* ed. Joseph Jacobs (London and New York, 1894), pp. 145, 214; Gabriello Faerno, *Fabulae centum* (London, 1743), no. XCI.

For, as Cato said . . . with thee: Sallust, *Bellum Catilinae,* lii, 29. Minor differences of text.

PAGE 46] *Ceres, when she showed,* etc.: See Robert Graves, *The Greek Myths* (Baltimore: Penguin Books, 1968), I, 92; with references.

Charles the Emperor: Charles V (1500–58), king of Spain and "Holy" Roman emperor.

Dii laboribus omnia vendunt: "The gods sell everything at the price of labor." Compare Montaigne, *Essays,* p. 608: "The gods sell us all the goods they give us; that is to say, they give us not one pure and perfect, and which we buy not with the price of some evil."

Demosthenes had many . . . another: Valerius Maximus, *Dict. fact. memorab.,* VIII, vii, fol. 174a.

Feras quod laedit . . . perferas: Publilius Syrus, *Sententiae,* p. 13. Tuvill, perhaps quoting from memory, seems to have conflated two different "sentences": *Feras difficilia ut facilia perferas* and *Feras quod laedit, unde quod prodest feras.*

Sour accidents . . . quiet calms: Another slice of well-worn euphuism. For copious illustration, see Thomas Proctor, comp., *A Gorgeous Gallery of Gallant Inventions,* ed. Hyder Rollins (Cambridge, Mass., 1926), p. 167.

That herb moly: Homer, *Odyssey,* X, 302 ff.

VI CAUTIONS IN FRIENDSHIP

Few themes, through the ages, have been more popular with essayists and moralists than has that of Friendship. Tuvill's essay, more strictly limited than most, makes no notable contribution to the theme; but then, the same statement is true of the marshaled platitudes authorized to walk abroad under the protection of many names more resoundingly famous. Here is nothing of the generous or genial, nothing of idealism. Instead, the emphasis falls upon the niggling "Cautions" of the title. We travel in the cold realm of practicality, of calculated gain; and our companions along the road are Bacon, Machiavelli, Guicciardini. As usual, the slender scaffolding of Tuvill's thought is almost overwhelmed with the weight of example, quotation, and digression.

"Cautions in Friendship," rather more than the preceding essays, offers phrasal and thematic connections linking it with others of Tuvill's writings, as the following notes demonstrate. The substance of the opening page, for instance, is almost totally repeated in *The Dove and the Serpent.* Characteristic Tuvillian expressions and constructions abound. Here, too, begins that heavy dependence upon Juvenal and Martial which is to be noted elsewhere in these essays. Although "Cautions in Friendship" concludes with quotations from the sunnier Horace, they are still from Horace in one of his more negative moments. The essay remains an ungracious assessment of one of man's greatest felicities.

This essay is much drawn upon by Edward Sutton in his *Anthropophagus: The Man-Eater* (1624). Sutton was also indebted to Tuvill's 1609 volume of essays.

PAGE 47] *It was not . . . the other:* Plutarch, *Morals,* p. 195; repeated in *The Dove and the Serpent,* sig. C1r.

For there are many . . . market: Compare *The Dove and the Serpent,* sig. B2v.

There are few . . . within him: See Guazzo, *Civile Conversation,* I, 71; repeated in *The Dove and the Serpent,* sig. C1r.

It is an ancient saying: See John Heywood, *A Dialogue of the Effectual Proverbs in the English Tongue Concerning Marriage,* p. 6.

Many have honey . . . girdles: Proverbial; see Guazzo, *Civile Conversation,* I, 68, 137. See also *The Dove and the Serpent,* sig. B4r, and "Of Praises," p. 35.

Multis simulationum involucris, etc.: Cicero, *Epistulae ad Quintum fratrem,* I, i, 5, 15. "There are many wrappings and pretences under which each individual's nature is concealed and overspread, so to speak, with curtains; the brow, the eye, and the face very often lie, but speech most often of all."

The Marquis of Pescara . . . greatness: Guicciardini, *History* (1599), p. 759. Fenton calls him "Pesquiero."

It was not mine enemy, etc.: Ps. 55:12–14. A similar use of the passage is made by Henry ("Silver-tongued") Smith in "A Glass for Drunkards," *Works* (Edinburgh, 1866–67), I, 306.

The kingly prophet: David. Tuvill uses the phrase earlier, p. 12, and in *The Dove and the Serpent,* sig. F3r. It is the common epithet for David in Thomas Fitzherbert's *First Part of a Treatise concerning Policy and Religion* (Douai, 1606).

Page 48] *Antigonus, in his prayers . . . protection:* Compare *Essays Moral and Theological,* p. 129: "A man may easily secure himself from open and professed enemies, but from such as under a pretense of amity do go about to overthrow his safety there is no sanctuary."

Veil a wrinkled heart: The identical phrase recurs in *Essays Moral and Theological,* p. 114.

The secret practices of Judas: Matt. 26:47–50; Mark 14:10–11, 43–45; Luke 22:1–6, 47–48.

Joab . . . to kill him: II Sam. 20:9–10.

As the poet witnesseth: Marginal reference to Ovid, *Ars amatoria,* I [, 585]. (For *per amici* some texts read *per amicum.*) Tuvill quotes the same Ovidian line in *The Dove and the Serpent,* sig. D3r. For the sentiment compare also Barnabe Barnes, *Four Books of Offices,* sig. V4v, "that saying of Sallust, *Per maximam amicitiam maxima est fallendi copia;* that where greatest friendship harboreth, there hath deceit most power and force to practice."

And Socrates thereupon exclaimeth: The Greek corresponds to Diogenes Laertius, *Lives of Eminent Philosophers,* V, 21 ("Aristotle"). Montaigne, *Essays,* p. 150, refers to "the saying *Aristotle* was wont so often to repeat,

Oh you my friends, there is no perfect friend." I have not found the saying elsewhere attributed to Socrates.

But not in every soil: See p. 32.

Hunc quem . . . amicus eris: Marginal reference to Martial, *Epigrams,* IX, xv (i.e., xiv in Loeb). For the influence of Martial on Tuvill, see especially *Essays Moral and Theological,* "Of Gifts and Benefits." In the first line of the passage quoted here, for *cena* read *mensa,* for *mensa* read *cena.*

Page 49] *There is no man . . . or no:* Compare Henry Smith, "The Heavenly Thrift," *Works* (1866–67), I, 343: "As they which try a vessel first put water into it, to see whether it will hold water, then they commit wine into it."

Alcibiades conveyed the image, etc.: A form of this tale appears as the first exemplum in the famous *Disciplina clericalis* of Petrus Alphonsus. See *Disciplina clericalis,* ed. Alfons Hilka and Werner Söderhjelm (Heidelberg, 1911). With some modifications, this classic test of friendship reappears in the 129th tale of the *Gesta Romanorum,* tr. Charles Swan (London, 1877), pp. 232–33. See also La Primaudaye, *French Academy,* p. 134.

Yet, in those things . . . the white: Plutarch, *Lives,* "Alcibiades," p. 248.

Page 50] *The Italian proverb witnesseth:* Compare Guazzo, *Civile Conversation,* I, 71.

Unity never passeth . . . common report: Plutarch, *Morals,* p. 198.

And howsoever the Florentine, etc.: Niccolò Machiavelli, *Discourses,* bk. III, chap. 6. For the duplicity of Saturninus, see Plutarch, *Lives,* "Caius Marius," pp. 512–13; but Tuvill's source remains Machiavelli throughout this passage.

Duels and combats . . . assigned by princes: Trial by "wager of battle," or single combat, as a recognized instrument of "justice," lasted well beyond the age of chivalry in Europe and was the ancestor of revenge by private duel. The latter, in England, was suppressed through proclamation by King James in 1613, almost on the heels of Tuvill's essay.

Page 51] *A serpent in my bosom:* The reference is perhaps to Aesop's fable of serpentine ingratitude; see *Fables* (1889), bk. I, fable 10, II, 15.

Stoicus . . . amicum: "The tale-bearing [old] Stoic slew his friend Barea" (my translation); Juvenal, *Satires,* III, 116.

A tragical catastrophe: A favorite Tuvillian phrase; see *Essays Moral and Theological,* p. 126, and *The Dove and the Serpent,* sigs. B4r, E2r.

There are some . . . defect of duty: An almost literal transcript of Bacon, *Advancement,* p. 24: "But to be speculative into another man, to the end to know how to work him or wind him or govern him, proceedeth from a heart that is double and cloven, and not entire and ingenuous; which as in friendship it is want of integrity, so toward princes or superiors is want of duty." A similar passage, also using the word *speculative,* occurs in the essay "Of Counsel"; see Bacon, *Essays,* ed. W. A. Wright (London, 1879), p. 86.

Scire volunt, etc.: Juvenal, *Satires,* III, 113.

Spurious and adulterate issue . . . fear: Compare the phrasing of *Asylum Veneris,* sig. C6v: "Jealousy that adulterate and spurious brat of love and fear." See also *Essays Moral and Theological,* p. 84.

Carus erit . . . potest: Juvenal, *Satires,* III, 53–54.

PAGE 52] *Hence was it that Tigellinus . . . accomplished:* A curious repetition of introductory formula; see p. 36. The passage is modified from Tacitus, *Annals,* XIV, lvii, and is repeated in *The Dove and the Serpent,* sig. D4r.

Like Agesilaus . . . or like Julius Drusus: These two illustrations, reversed, occur in Montaigne, *Essays,* p. 729. Both derive, ultimately, from Plutarch; the first from *Lives,* "Agesilaus," p. 720, the second from *Morals,* p. 351. For the second, see also Bodin, *Of a Commonweal,* p. 642.

The example of Philippides: Also in Montaigne, *Essays,* p. 717, where the Greek phrase is omitted. See Plutarch, *Morals,* pp. 199, 416.

I do but teach . . . deceived: In *The Dove and the Serpent,* sig. C4r, Tuvill gives (from Seneca) the Latin of this: *Multi fallere docuerunt, dum timent falli.*

This was it . . . deceived by him: Related in Guicciardini, *History* (1599), p. 872.

PAGE 53] *Hence was it that Otho,* etc.: Marginal reference to Tacitus, *Histories,* I [, lxxi].

Upon the good event of which, etc.: This witty and charitable reply of Louis XII is related by La Primaudaye, *French Academy,* p. 309.

Juno's jealousy or Argus' observation: See Ovid, *Metamorphoses,* I, 601 ff.

Charles V, etc.: Guicciardini, *History* (1599), p. 760.

PAGE 54] *A confounded dialect:* That is, confused and inharmonious doctrines, after the manner of the incomprehensible confusion of tongues at the tower of Babel, Gen. 11:1–9.

The Church of Sardis . . . naked: See Rev. 3.

But that I may not seem, etc.: One of the several intimations that Tuvill was aware of his habit of digressing.

Figulus figulo: Or, more fully, *Figulus figulo invidet, faber fabro:* "Potter envies potter, smith envies smith." Compare Plutarch, *Morals,* p. 649.

Page 55] *That microphily which Plato had:* This unequal, or "little" friendship, between Plato and the Syracusan ruler(s) is reflected in the so-called *Epistles* of Plato—of doubtful authenticity.

Quid . . . olla ad cacabum: Marginal reference to Ecclus. 13[:3], misquoting the Vulgate. See also *Essays Moral and Theological,* p. 126.

Which considered . . . his expectation: See the similar anecdote in Bacon's *Apothegms* (in *Resuscitatio,* ed. 1661), p. 303.

That comfortless reply: Luke 16:26. Tuvill's Latin does not correspond with that of the Vulgate.

Last of all . . . safety: The Latin of this final paragraph derives from Horace, *Satires,* I, iv, 81 ff.; "he carries hay in his horn" = *faenum habet in cornu* (I, iv, 34).

VII   Of Three Things Prejudicial to Secrecy

The very title of this essay determines its pattern of organization and helps restrain Tuvill from digressions or random observations. Such a tightness of structure suggests Bacon; and, indeed, from first to last the essay has some obligations pointing in that direction, especially to *The Advancement of Learning,* as the notes will show. On the other hand, it may just be possible that Bacon owes a touch to Tuvill. Consider, for instance, the statement in "Of Simulation and Dissimulation" (added to the *Essays* in 1625): "Therefore set it down, that a habit of secrecy is both *politic and moral"*—Tuvill's title.

Some echoes of the present essay, as well as further echoes of Bacon, may also be read in Tuvill's *The Dove and the Serpent,* chap. 2, "Of Wise Distrust and Slowness of Belief," sigs. C2v-C3r. It is perhaps relevant to observe that the first chapter of *The Dove and the Serpent* is entitled "Of Secrecy"; and it should also be noted that Tuvill here begins, almost by way of retraction of his second stricture, that defense of *good* women (*de claris mulieribus*) observable in his later writings.

Though no particular writer dominates the thought of the essay, the general draught upon the classics continues undiminished.

Page 56] *As for the first, Momus,* etc.: Lucian, *Works,* tr. H. W. Fowler and F. G. Fowler (Oxford, 1905), II, 52.

Will with Plutarch answer him: Marginal reference reads: *"In Sympos. lib.* 3"; see *Morals,* p. 681, where the Momus-window idea, above, may also be found.

That disguised and personated habit: Compare *The Dove and the Serpent,* sig. B4r: "The world affords us almost nothing now, which is not personated and disguised."

That verse of Horace: Marginal reference to *De arte poetica* [, ll. 434–36].

In oculis, loculis, or poculis: That is, "in his eyes, in his purse, or in his drinking." The witty author is not known. Thomas Grocer, "A Banquet of Sweetmeats" (1657), says: "The Hebrews have a saying that a man's mind is soonest seen, in oculis, in loculis, in poculis, in his eyes, expenses, cups" (Folger MS V.a.178, p. 298).

One of the chiefest . . . hasten his: See Tacitus, *Annals,* XII, lxiv; and compare *The Dove and the Serpent,* sig. B2r: "And Claudius, by venting forth a word in his distemperature, gave Agrippina warning to hasten his destruction."

PAGE 57] *And indeed il vino . . . from laying any:* Passage derived from Guazzo, *Civile Conversation,* "The Fourth Book"; see esp. II, 151–52, which include the proverb, the "cup of pleasure," the danger of shipwreck, and the illustration of Aesop's hen.

Quid non ebrietas, etc.: Horace, *Epistles,* I, v, 16. For Tuvill's *designat* Loeb reads *dissignat.*

And indeed . . . foolishly surmised: Both the proverb and the apothegm of Bias are in Plutarch, *Morals,* p. 194.

Envenomed cups of . . . Circe: = the *Circae pocula* of Horace, *Epistles,* I, ii, 23.

The second thing . . . the wisest: Compare *Asylum Veneris,* chap. 2, sig. B7r.

PAGE 58] *They are for . . . anything regard:* Compare *Asylum Veneris,* sigs. F2r-v.

'Αγγεῖα σάθρα, *leaking vessels:* Tuvill apparently has Plutarch in mind; see *Morals,* p. 199.

That comic servant, plenae rimarum, etc.: Terence, *Eunuchus,* I, ii; also cited in Montaigne, *Essays,* p. 590.

A Roman lady . . . thither himself: Plutarch, *Morals,* pp. 198–99.

Plus virtutis . . . armis: "More of virtue in the gown (women) than in arms (men)."

Nero, after the detection, etc.: The substance and the Latin quotations of this paragraph derive from Tacitus, *Annals,* XV, lvii. Tuvill again notices Epicharis and her constancy in *Asylum Veneris,* sigs. F2v-F3r.

PAGE 59]   *A Portia and a Leaena:* These are classic instances of woman's resolution under torture. In addition to the Tacitus reference of the preceding note, see, for Leaena and Epicharis, Battista Fregoso, *De dictis factisque memorabilibus collectanea* (Milan, 1509), bk. III, chap. iii; for Epicharis see also Plutarch, *Morals*, p. 196, and Montaigne, *Essays*, p. 649.

Sed non omne mare, etc.: Horace, *Satires*, II, iv, 31. For *generosae est* the Loeb text reads *est generosae.*

Quid deceat . . . amans: Ovid, *Heroides*, Epist. IV, "Phaedra Hippolyto," l. 154. "No lover perceives what is appropriate."

"Awake, Samson" . . . so eminent: See Judg. 16:6–21. Tuvill's *eminent,* as earlier (p. 57), seems to mean *imminent.* Samson's betrayal by Delilah is given similar treatment in *The Dove and the Serpent,* sig. B2r, and in *Essays Moral and Theological,* p. 130.

PAGE 60]   *Antony cannot choose . . . folly:* Plutarch, *Lives,* "Antony," *passim.*

Curius . . . in them as he: See Sallust, *Bellum Catilinae,* xxiii, 1–4; xxvi, 3.

The Prior of Capua . . . Senate: Bodin, *Of a Commonweal,* p. 523. The "Prior of Capua" (or Campania) was Leone Strozzi (1515–54), admiral for the French.

Their high-built purposes: A favorite construction with Tuvill; see p. 68 and *Essays Moral and Theological,* pp. 79, 93 ("low-built roof"), 117.

Wherefore, let us with David . . . eyes: See Ps. 25:14–15. But the "kingly shepherd's" eyes wandered a bit in the matter of Bath-sheba; see II Sam. 11:2 ff.

Like Alexander . . . their beauty: Plutarch, *Lives,* "Alexander," p. 816.

The Grecian courtesan: = Lais.

Qui curios simulant, etc.: Juvenal, *Satires,* II, 3. Tuvill translates the sense, not the words.

"I know not . . . any other": Tuvill's source is apparently Montaigne, *Essays,* p. 897.

They are angels . . . semipulchrae: Tuvill uses this same figure in *St. Paul's Threefold Cord,* sig. E2v. And, of course, he is punning on "whited sepulchers" and *semipulchrae.*

PAGE 61]   *The Creator . . . to deceive him:* Gen. 2:21–3:7, in essence. There is probably a more immediate source.

Their lips . . . hold on hell: Prov. 5:3–5.

Yea, God . . . alone intuitively knows: Compare *Christian Purposes and*

Resolutions, sig. M8v: "He [God] knoweth all things intuitively, and nothing can be hid from his discerning eye."

But when they once . . . bounty: Tuvill, as the Latin phrases indicate, is recalling Sallust's remarks about Quintus Curius and his Fulvia; see *Bellum Catilinae,* xxiii, 3.

Sweet words . . . sharp swords: Another touch of lingering euphuism.

It is not always . . . doth: A glance at Matt. 6:3.

Sejanus had . . . to his enemy: Tacitus, *Annals,* IV, iii; VII, lx.

Whose bosom . . . inmost purposes: Compare the opening sentence of the essay.

Page 62] *One who . . . a thousand times:* Seneca, *Epistulae morales,* CXIV, 6.

And Augustus . . . Sanus sis, Fulvi: Plutarch, *Morals,* p. 199.

But lest I seem an uncivil, etc.: The defense of women begun here is picked up and continued at length in Tuvill's *Asylum Veneris.*

That saying of Menander, etc.: See, among the doubtful fragments in the Loeb *Menander,* 1109K = ταμιεῖον αρετῆς ἐστιν ἡ σώφρων γυνή, "The woman who is discreet is a magazine of virtue."

Neither Cato nor Euripides: Both had reputations for misogyny.

Yet Rubius Celer . . . or jar: Compare *Asylum Veneris,* sigs. F1v-F2r.

Sejanus heartened Drusus, etc.: See Tacitus, *Annals,* IV, *passim.*

Page 63] *Fabius, therefore . . . subverted:* See Plutarch, *Lives,* "Fabius," esp. pp. 215–16. Quintus Fabius Maximus, "Cunctator," (d. 203 b.c.), Roman dictator and defender against Hannibal, was the son of Lucius Paulus Aemilius by his first wife, Papiria.

Si tantum . . . suadebat: Seneca, *Moral Essays,* "De ira," I, xi, 5. "If he had dared [to perform] all that anger prompted" (my translation).

(Like the wiser adder): On the "wiser" adder, see Ps. 58:4–5; Guazzo, *Civile Conversation,* II, 125; and P. Ansell Robin, *Animal Lore in English Literature* (London, 1932), pp. 147–48. The use of the comparative form of the adjective for the simple is common with Tuvill and not uncommon among his contemporaries.

Whereof the poet . . . et ira: Although Tuvill, in the margin, correctly identifies the Latin verse as from Horace, *Epistles,* I, xviii [, 38], the whole passage, including the verse, is lifted from Bacon, *Advancement,* p. 231.

Tiberius, who (as Tacitus reports) . . . regnaret: Marginal reference to

Annals, IV [, lii]. Tuvill nevertheless owes the entire passage to Bacon's *Advancement,* p. 231.

And Catiline . . . his bosom: See Sallust, *Bellum Catilinae,* xxxi, 7–9. Tuvill's readings show minor deviations from the Latin original.

PAGE 64] *Wherefore let every man . . . a truth:* Again adapted from Bacon, *Advancement,* p. 231.

VIII OF REPUTATION

Like the preceding essay, "Of Reputation" owes something to Bacon, being evidently written with an eye on the *Advancement of Learning,* bk. II, sec. xxiii. Tuvill's main draught, however, continues to be upon Plutarch and Tacitus, with Montaigne lurking in the background. Brief as it is, "Of Reputation" is rich in characteristic Tuvillian locutions.

PAGE 65] *That specious fig tree:* See Matt. 21:19–20 or Luke 13:6–9.

The silly sheep . . . desired: Plutarch, *Morals,* p. 455.

It hath been often seen, etc.: For the Galba-Vespasian contrast of this paragraph, compare Bacon, *Essays,* "Of Great Place."

Galba, major privato . . . imperasset: Tacitus, *Histories,* I, xlix.

Omnium ante se, etc.: Tacitus, *Histories,* I, l; also cited in Bacon, *Advancement,* p. 207, and again in Tuvill's *The Dove and the Serpent,* sig. I2r.

Which may be likewise instanced . . . England: The Prince Hal of Shakespeare's *Henry IV.* A contemporary work by Robert Fletcher, *The Nine English Worthies* (1606), drawn largely from Holinshed, records thus the change in Henry's manners: "No sooner was he invested king and had received the crown, but he did put upon him the shape of a new man, turning insolency and wildness into gravity and soberness. And whereas he had passed his youth with wanton and dissolute wild young gentlemen who had led him into all excess of riot . . . [now] he called these gallants before him, told them of his and their own faults, banished them from his presence—not unrewarded nor yet unpreferred—inhibiting them upon a great pain, not once to approach, lodge, or sojourn within ten miles of his court or mansions. And then he made choice of grave, wise, and politic counselors" (sig. E3v).

Entitled, after the decease, etc.: Compare the phrasing with that of *Essays Moral and Theological,* p. 82.

True valor . . . venturous: Compare idea and phraseology with those of *Essays Moral and Theological,* p. 125, "to be valorous is not always to be venturous."

Antigonus had a soldier, etc.: Plutarch, *Lives,* "Pelopidas," p. 347; retold in Montaigne, *Essays,* pp. 294–95.

Page 66]   *And hither may . . . at home:* Also from Plutarch, as in the preceding note. Plutarch (p. 347) calls the Sybarites "a soft and dissolute people."

Rebus in angustis, etc.: Martial, *Epigrams,* XI, lvi, 15. "In narrow means 'tis easy to despise life."

To die as Cato did: See Montaigne's essay, "Of Cato the Younger," bk. I, sec. xxxvi.

Hercules, in his travels, etc.: *Travels* ("trauailes" in the original text) may mean either "wanderings" or "labors." Hercules "visited" Hades twice, once in completing the twelfth of the labors (to bring back Cerberus from the underworld) imposed by King Eurystheus and again to return to earth the wife of King Admetus (see Euripides, *Alcestis*).

Page 67]   *And therefore Domitius Corbulo . . . available:* Tacitus, *Annals,* XIII, viii; Tuvill has substituted *inserviret* for the *instaret* of his original. The last clause translates Tacitus' *quae in novis coeptis validissima est.*

And Julius Agricola . . . the rest: Tacitus, *Agricola,* xviii, [17–18], modified.

It is requisite . . . nest: An adaptation of the proverb, *pennas habere majore nido,* "to have wings broader than the nest."

The wiser sort . . . bane of many: Compare Bacon, *Advancement,* pp. 237–38.

Alcibiades . . . possibly escape him: Plutarch, *Lives,* "Alcibiades," p. 259.

John Guicciardini was accused: Machiavelli, *Discourses,* bk. I, chap. 8. This anticipates the more extensive use of the *Discorsi* in the next essay, "Of Accusation."

Page 68]   *It is reported of Poppaeus Sabinus:* Marginal reference to Tacitus, *Annals,* VI [, xxxix].

Agricola, saith Tacitus . . . glory: *Agricola,* viii, [10–11]. Tuvill uses this same illustration again in *Essays Moral and Theological,* p. 91.

Germanicus likewise . . . the doing it: Tacitus, *Annals,* II, xxii. See also Sir William Cornwallis, *Essayes* (1946), p. 45.

Sail by the card and compass: The "card" was the sailor's chart, or map. On the general unreliability of these, see an interesting comparison in Samuel Daniel, *Defence of Ryme . . . 1603,* ed. G. B. Harrison (London, 1925), p. 24.

If the sea swell . . . with thee: An often-quoted apothegm. Among his usual sources Tuvill might have found it in Plutarch, *Lives,* "Caesar," p. 277, or in the *Morals,* p. 631; or in La Primaudaye, *French Academy,* p. 444; or in Bacon, *Advancement,* p. 227.

IX OF ACCUSATION

Throughout this brief essay the informing theme is that favorite position of satirists and moralists in all ages, an alleged falling away from the supposed virtues of an earlier time. Although several snatches from Horace are quoted, there is little satiric intention here. Tuvill is in dead earnest, and the preacher, long disguised under the cloak of classical allusion and quotation, here once again dons his proper garb. The ancient moralist Plutarch still attends at his elbow, and he makes a startling momentary incursion into a modern morality of a differing sort—Machiavelli's. But the temper throughout is akin to that of the Old Testament prophets, and at the end Tuvill-prophet pulls his mantle about him in a fine flurry of biblical allusions pointing in the direction of the more religiously oriented *Essays Moral and Theological.*

PAGE 69] *An age so corrupted and depraved:* Compare the phrasing in "Of Opinion," p. 10, and in *Essays Moral and Theological,* p. 102. There are close thematic connections between this essay and the essay "Of Respect and Reverence."

Iam pridem equidem, etc.: Marginal reference to Sallust, *Bellum Catilinae* [, lii, 11]. After *equidem* Tuvill has omitted *nos vera vocabula.*

Simplicity hath . . . airy apparition: These sentiments and some of the wording are repeated in *The Dove and the Serpent,* sig. B4r.

The silly dove . . . the serpent: Biblical types of innocence and worldly wisdom; the passage looks forward to the theme of Tuvill's *The Dove and the Serpent.*

The lion thinks . . . subtle fox: Also biblical (and Plutarchan) types, though in view of the other borrowings in this essay and in the preceding one, this may be a reflection of Machiavelli's lion-fox figure in *The Prince,* chap. 18.

Never seen upon the scene: The wordplay, the balanced sibilants, and the imagery of the theater combine to give this sentence an unwontedly precious air.

It is said of Catiline . . . reward: Sallust, *Bellum Catilinae,* xvi, 3.

PAGE 70] *Non sum moechus,* etc.: This and the following lines of Latin verse are from Horace, *Satires,* II, vii, 72–74.

So that . . . by law: This paragraph is merely a loose translation, or free adaptation, of Machiavelli, *Discourses,* bk. I, chap. 7, beginning.

Wherefore . . . that government: Again, practically a translation of Machiavelli, *Discourses,* bk. I, chap. 7.

By ostracism: See above, note to p. 8.

There should not an Aristides . . . banishment: The reference is to Plutarch, *Morals,* pp. 418–19: "When the Athenians were assembled together in the general counsel, and hotly set to proceed unto that banishment which they called *Ostracism,* there was a certain rude and rustical peasant, one that knew never a letter of the book and could neither write nor read, came with a shell in his hand (as the manner was) unto Aristides and desired him to write within it the name of Aristides. Why (quoth he) knowest thou Aristides? Nay in good faith (quoth the clownish sot) I ken him not, but I am grieved to hear him called Just. Aristides answered him never a word, but wrote his own name within the shell, and gave it him again."

The advertisement of Medius . . . remain: Plutarch, *Morals,* pp. 104–5. Compare Bacon, *Advancement,* p. 236: *Audacter calumniare, semper aliquid haeret* ["Slander boldly; something will always stick"].

PAGE 71] *Callisthenes, Parmenio, and Philotas:* For their falls, see Plutarch, *Morals,* p. 105; and, more fully, *Lives,* "Alexander," *passim.*

Wisdom, therefore . . . feigned: Compare Machiavelli, *Discourses,* bk. I, chap. 8, conclusion.

As Tacitus reports: Annals, I, lxxiv.

Inevitable crime: = *inevitabile crimen,* Tacitus' phrase.

Nam quia . . . credebantur: Tuvill's gloss in the following sentence renders the sense adequately.

King Richard's banishing of Mowbray: See Shakespeare's *Richard II,* I, iii, 148 ff.

The Emperor Valentinian II: Not Valentinian II (d. 392) but Valentinian III, emperor of the West (425–55).

Alexander had deprived . . . others: The faithful physician was Philip, the Acarnanian. See Plutarch, *Lives,* "Alexander," p. 814.

For otherwise . . . without law: See Aesop, *Fables* (1889), bk. I, fable 2, II, 5–6.

Let Haman hang: Esther 7:9–10.

PAGE 72] *Let those rank . . . chastity:* See the apocryphal History of Susanna, vv. 51–62; = (Vulgate) Daniel 13:51–62.

Finally . . . lions' den: Daniel 6:16–24.

Neque . . . perire sua: "Nor is there juster law than that the contriver of mischief perish by his own craft"; adapted from Ovid, *Ars amatoria,* I, 655–56. The reference is to Perillus and the brazen bull he made for Phalaris, tyrant of Agrigentum. See Pliny, *Natural History,* tr. Philemon Holland (1601), p. 504.

Dedicatory Epistle

Page 77] *James . . . Bishop of Bath and Wells:* James Montague (1568?–1618), later Bishop of Winchester. He was the Master of the newly founded Sidney Sussex College, Cambridge, when Tuvill was admitted sizar in 1598.

Πεπλασμένον, etc.: Marginal reference to Pindar. I have been unable to find this in Pindar.

By Euripides is thus expressed: Iphigeneia at Aulis, 977–80.

D. T.: In the Folger copy, inked in under these initials in what appears to be a late seventeenth-century hand, is the following identification: "(Supposed to be Daniel Torvil.)"

I Of Learning and Knowledge

After the initial allusion to the Song of Solomon, this opening essay quickly adopts a secular and largely classical tone for the first half; then, abruptly, it swings into the pulpit for the second half. The reader gets the impression that Tuvill is deliberately trying to maintain an even balance between the *moral* and the *theological* of his title for the new volume. In the process, he continues that loose, unmortared, commonplace-book association of ideas already observed in the previous collection; and, in the present essay, he develops no distinctions adequate to justify the two terms, *learning* and *knowledge,* of the title. The essay, indeed, might just as well be called "Of True Intellectual Virtue"—mixing elements of Baconian practicality and utility with a bona fide parson's distrust of the "unregenerate" mind. Tuvill was no blazing advocate of intellectualism. In the next generation he could have walked hand-in-hand with a Joseph Glanvill.

Notwithstanding the increased draught upon the Bible, Bacon and Montaigne—particularly Montaigne—are still obviously at work in Tuvill's ideas and phrasing. And it is possible that in thus giving at least nominal first place to knowledge, Tuvill was paying continued respect to the *Advancement.* But it is also just possible that the impulse came from a less reputable source, Edward Topsell's *The Householder, or Perfect Man* (ed. 1610), sig. I7r: "Thus, and this have I spoken of knowledge, as it is a virtue Moral and Theological." Or, since both Tuvill's and Topsell's works were first published in 1609, and I cannot determine priority, it may be that Topsell is making a topical allusion (if so, the first recorded) to Tuvill's essays. For once, we may be well advised to follow Tuvill's hint and leave "the voiding of these controversies" to some present-day Didymus.

The reader should be wary of taking in good faith the occasional occurrences of the personal pronoun "I." Here, and elsewhere throughout the two series of essays, the "I" of any given passage is likely to be borrowed along with the ideas.

PAGE 79] *Virtue delights not,* etc.: Compare *Asylum Veneris,* sigs. E3v–E4r, where, in discussing artificial aids to beauty, as here, Tuvill says: "Virtue delights not in them at all; they be things which cannot any way advantage her."

She is black . . . Solomon: Song of Sol. 1:5.

Ye shall see . . . the other: Adapted by Robert Chamberlain in his *Nocturnal Lucubrations, or Meditations Divine and Moral* (1638), pp. 72–73.

High-built purposes: Compare the phrase with similar constructions in *Essays Politic and Moral,* pp. 60, 68; and in the present series, pp. 93, 117.

Her thoughts . . . mother of Aeneas: With these compare the frivolous questions which Tiberius was accustomed to ask his grammarians; Suetonius, *History of Twelve Caesars,* sig. L6r. H. C. Agrippa, *Of the Vanity and Uncertainty of Arts and Sciences,* sig. E1r, levels a similar attack upon such "frivolous doubts and inquisitions" among poets and grammarians: "There are moreover most grievous contentions among poets . . . for the country of Homer and for his sepulture, and whether Homer and Hesiod were first, whether Patroclus were before Achilles, in what state of body Anacharsis Scytha did sleep, why Homer did not give honor to Palamedes in his verses, whether Lucan is to be reckoned in the number of poets or historiographers, of the rubbery of Virgil and in what month of the year he died." See also Owen Feltham, *Resolves,* "Of Curiosity in Knowledge," pp. 62–64; and with this whole first essay, compare Feltham's "Of Wisdom and Science," pp. 90–92.

To such as Didymus: Didymus (*ca.* 63 B.C.–A.D. 10), "the brazen-boweled," so-called for his indefatigable scribbling, a Greek scholar who is said to have written more than 3,500 "books." See Seneca, *Epistulae morales,* LXXXVIII, 37; H. C. Agrippa, *Of the Vanity and Uncertainty of Arts and Sciences,* sig. C3v; and Montaigne, *Essays,* p. 853.

PAGE 80] *In Rome . . . related by others:* Sallust, *Bellum Catilinae,* viii, 5.

A phoenix without a match: Only one phoenix, according to common lore, could be in existence at any given time; see Sir Thomas Browne, *Pseudodoxia epidemica,* III, xii.

It is easy for a philosopher, etc.: Perhaps the philosopher Tuvill has specifically in mind is Seneca; see Seneca's *Epistulae morales,* XXIV.

Phalaris and his bull: See the accounts in Pindar, *Pythian Odes,* I, 96; Pliny, *Natural History* (1601), p. 504; and compare the verse ending of *Essays Politic and Moral.*

Every common mountebank: Ital., *montimbanco* = "mount-on-a-bench," a huckster or hawker of questionable goods. The fetches of the wily quack who "only swalloweth down poison (or seemeth so to do) to utter his trade or antidote to the people at as dear a rate as he can," are amusingly exposed by the skeptical Henry Peacham in *The Truth of Our Times* (1638), sigs. I9r-I11r.

The stoic that, with Mutius: For Mutius (Caius Mucius Scaevola), see Seneca, *Epistulae morales,* XXIV, 5; Valerius Maximus, *Dict. fact. memorab.,* III, iii; Martial, *Epigrams,* I, xxi.

PAGE 81] *Dediscas vivere . . . mori:* Sense adequately translated in the following line. I have not found a classical origin for the statement, though one probably exists.

Cast but an eye . . . incorporates none: This is the drift, though not the language, of Montaigne's argument, *Essays,* "Of the Institution and Education of Children," pp. 113–14.

Like Icarus: Icarus, in ancient fable, escaping from the Cretan labyrinth with his father on artificial wings devised by the latter, flew too near the sun, melting the wax which held the feathers, and so plunged to his death. See Ovid, *Metamorphoses,* VIII, 195–235.

They labor . . . compose their own: Compare Montaigne, *Essays,* p. 122.

Their disputations . . . to no end: Perhaps with an eye to Aristotle's *Problems* or Plutarch's *Natural Questions;* but certainly these are such scholastic "cobwebs of learning" as Bacon decries in the *Advancement,* pp. 31–32.

Their sophistical elenchs: = defective refutatory syllogisms. On *elenchs,* see Bacon, *Advancement,* pp. 159–60. Compare *The Dove and the Serpent,* sig. I3r, "sophistical and deceitful elenchs."

Most of their learning . . . a beetle: This long passage derives, frequently in the very phrase, from Montaigne, *Essays,* pp. 837–38.

A general corruption . . . their manners: Adapted by Barnabe Rich, *The Honesty of This Age,* p. 17: "A general corruption hath overgrown the virtues of this latter times, and the world is become a brothel house of sin."

PAGE 82] *If she finds them . . . exinanition:* The technical language of alchemy.

Entitled after his decease, etc.: Compare the phrasing in *Essays Politic and Moral,* p. 65.

As Guicciardini reports: Marginal reference: "Guicciard. lib. 1" = Guicciardini, *History* (1599), p. 34. The Italian should read, more exactly, *appena gli furono cogniti le lettere.*

His father was content . . . to reign: A political aphorism of considerable currency; see Thomas Danett's translation of Philippe de Comines' *History* (1601), sig. F3v, margin; Sir Robert Dallington, *The View of France* (1604), sig. I3r; Henry Peacham, *Truth of Our Times* (1638), sig. B9v.

And that in a prince . . . than the other: Tuvill is following Bodin, *Of a Commonweal*, p. 255.

Like a dangerous knife, etc.: A manuscript marginal note (Evelyn's?) in the Huntington copy reads: *Armata nequitia.* The sentiment here and to the end of the paragraph is echoed in *Asylum Veneris,* sig. F7r, where it is applied not to princes but to women. "To put a sword (weapon) in a madman's hand" was proverbial; see *Oxford Dict. Eng. Prov.,* p. 236.

Never any emperor . . . more ignorant than Trajan: This needs the modification supplied by Bacon, *Advancement,* p. 54: "Trajan . . . was for his person not learned: but . . . there was not a greater admirer of learning or benefactor of learning; a founder of famous libraries, a perpetual advancer of learned men to office, and a familiar converser with learned professors and preceptors, who were noted to have then most credit in court."

More learned than Nero: Manuscript marginal note in HN copy: "Tacitus taxeth Nero for want of learning."

Hence was it . . . do it in them: Bacon, *Advancement,* p. 49, states this more succinctly.

To them he saith: Marginal reference to Matt. 4:18[i.e., 19]. Repeated in *Christian Purposes and Resolutions,* sig. G11r.

St. Paul, writing to the Corinthians: Marginal reference to I Cor. 1:26–27.

Page 83] *He chose (saith St. Augustine)*: Marginal reference to *De civitate Dei,* XVIII, xlix.

The Prophet Elisha, etc.: Marginal reference to II Kings 4:3.

Virtue cannot endure . . . at her command: Compare *Christian Purposes and Resolutions,* sig. F11: "He [God] will not brook a partner in His dignity, nor yet resign His glory to a third. Man's heart is that which He demands; and He will have it all, or none."

Such as will adorn . . . abide the touch: Compare *Asylum Veneris,* of women's beauty, sig. C1v.

Both Martha and Mary: See Luke 10:38–42; also p. 95.

Those Scribes and Pharisees . . . their hearts: See Matt. 23:2–5. For *Urim and Thummim,* see Exod. 28:30 and Lev. 8:8; also Gulielmus Bucanus, *Institutions of Christian Religion,* tr. Robert Hill (1606), sig. D6v.

They will not stick, like Balaam: Marginal reference to Num. 22[:1–21].

Page 84] *Adulterate and spurious generation:* Compare *Asylum Veneris,* sig. C6v, and *Essays Politic and Moral,* p. 51.

Those cherubim of Ezekiel: Marginal reference to [Ezek.] 10:21. Tuvill refers again to these in *The Dove and the Serpent,* sig. B1v, and in *Christian Purposes and Resolutions,* sig. B8r: "He is like those cherubim in Ezekiel."

As Aeschylus affirms: This is one of the fragments quoted by Stobaeus (*Anthology,* III, iii, 11); see *Fragments* in *Aeschylus,* no. 218 (390).

It is better . . . at all: Seneca, *Epistulae morales,* LXXXVIII, 45: *Satius est supervacua scire, quam nihil.* But Tuvill is probably drawing from Montaigne, *Essays,* p. 456.

II Of Policy and Religion

This, the briefest of Tuvill's essays, is one which an a priori judgment might well have expected to be his longest. That he was himself uneasily conscious of its brevity is witnessed by the considerable augmentation it received in subsequent editions. The bare title of the essay may have been suggested by the Catholic Thomas Fitzherbert's *First Part of a Treatise concerning Policy and Religion* (Douai, 1606), though Tuvill could have had little sympathy with Fitzherbert's ideas. The subject is given an explicit treatment nearer to Tuvill's in the two books of John Saltmarsh's *The Practice of Policy in a Christian Life* (1639).

Exclusive of religious padding, the *thought* of the essay is taken, with little modification even of wording (though with some juggling of sequence), from Bacon's *Advancement of Learning* (pp. 245–48). Nowhere does Tuvill's scissors-and-paste, commonplace-book method of composition more clearly reveal his essential unoriginality; for he has digested nothing. It is all very well for Montaigne to say of *his* reading-turned-to-writing that it is "no more according to Plato than according to Montaigne." Here, even a dull eye can see that it is considerably more "according to Bacon" than "according to Tuvill."

Page 85] *It is as hard . . . truly moral:* Verbatim from Bacon's *Advancement,* p. 228.

There are many . . . gross errors: Also from the *Advancement,* p. 245.

There are others . . . much about: Adapted from Bacon, *Advancement,* p. 246.

But it is in life . . . much about: Marginal reference: "Sir Fran. Bacon."

Such, therefore . . . is a curse: Again from Bacon, *Advancement,* pp. 246–47.

That all things are vanity, etc.: Eccles. 1:14 (and *passim*).

Non est vivere, etc.: Martial, *Epigrams,* VI, lxx, 15; compare Seneca, *Moral Essays,* "De beneficiis," III, xxxi, 4: *Non est bonum vivere, sed bene vivere.*

It is said of Saul . . . followed after: This passage is quoted without mention of Tuvill in John Spencer, Καινα και παλαια: *Things New and Old,* II, 27.

Duobus annis regnavit: Marginal reference to I Sam. 13:1 (Vulgate = I Regum 13:1). The scriptural reference is correct; but it seems likely that the whole passage, reference included, perhaps derives from Sir John Hayward's *The Sanctuary of a Troubled Soul* (1604, 1607): "Saul was a king twenty years, but the Scripture saith that he reigned two years because it made no reckoning of any years but of those wherein he reigned well" (ed. 1623, sig. G4v).

The words of our Saviour Christ: See Matt. 26:24.

Judas, that apostata: Tuvill's customary phrase; see pp. 87, 136.

Page 86] *Hic murus aheneus esto,* etc.: Horace, *Epistles,* I, i, 60–61: "Be this our wall of bronze, to have no guilt at heart, no wrongdoing to turn us pale." A marginal reference reads, simply, *"Hor."*

And so of the contrary: The phrase, though not the logical connection, comes from Bacon, *Advancement,* p. 247.

Thirdly . . . a vain thing: Slightly rephrased from Bacon, *Advancement,* p. 247.

I will not, etc.: Note here and on the following pages the use of this "resolves" formula. Such passages look forward to the *Christian Purposes and Resolutions* and demonstrate that Tuvill was among the first to write in the genre.

The Romans will come, etc.: Marginal reference to John 11:48.

I desire not . . . chariot of Elijah: That is, if he "climbs," heaven itself shall be the object of his ascent; see Gen. 28:12–15 and II Kings 2:11. Possibly Tuvill had in mind also the title of a sermon by the popular Puritan preacher, Henry Smith, "Jacob's Ladder, or The Way to Heaven." Barnabe Rich, *Honesty of This Age,* p. 14, quotes this passage.

I will not build . . . hurt thee: Modified from Bacon, *Advancement,* p. 248.

Primum quaerite regnum Dei: Matt. 6:33; Tuvill, however, has his eye on Bacon, *Advancement,* p. 248.

To say I will . . . purposed: Selected sentences from Bacon, *Advancement,* p. 247.

To take from Peter . . . observe the stars: A passage built upon the lingering pattern of euphuistic balance, antithesis, alliteration. "To rob Peter and pay Paul" was, of course, proverbial; see John Heywood, *Proverbs,* p. 31.

And as before . . . by the other: Based on Hooker, *Laws of Ecclesiastical Polity,* p. 76.

I will therefore lay . . . sands: Modified from Bacon, *Advancement,* p. 248.

PAGE 87]   *Hand on the helm . . . stars:* The same figure is used in Christopher Sutton's *Disce vivere. Learn to Live* (1602), sigs. F1v–F2r.

Good ends . . . evil means: The statement would have been recognized in Tuvill's day as anti-Machiavellian, anti-Jesuit. See William Penn, *Some Fruits of Solitude,* ed. Edmund Gosse (New York, 1903), pp. 170, 198.

Lay hold on him . . . warily: Mark 14:44.

Κρατήσατε *. . . the Lamb:* Mark 14, as above; and cf. Matt. 26:48–50.

III   OF CIVIL CARRIAGE AND CONVERSATION

"Of Civil Carriage and Conversation" is written in the tradition of the Renaissance courtesy book, to one of which books (Guazzo's) it is specifically indebted. It is remarkable among Tuvill's essays for the multiplicity of sources drawn upon and, paradoxically, for the coherence of its subject matter. It acts, so to speak, as something of a prelude to Tuvill's later conduct manual, *St. Paul's Threefold Cord,* a systematically developed model for a "Christian Economy."

Conversation, in the sense here employed, is equivalent to "polite conduct." The title of the essay reflects its relation to such other works as Thomas Wright's *Passions of the Mind,* especially bk. IV, chap. 2, sec. 7, "Discovery of Passion in Conversation"; Guazzo's *Civile Conversation;* Bacon's "Short Notes for Civil Conversation" (first published 1648, in *Remains*). In *Stefano Guazzo and the English Renaissance* (Chapel Hill, N.C., 1961), pp. 110–13, I have attempted to place the essay within this setting.

Here Tuvill exhibits an emphatic return to two of his favorite "authorities" in the *Essays Politic and Moral,* Tacitus and Montaigne. And here, too, he returns cautiously to quotation of the Latin poets, notably absent from the two preceding essays. Attention may also be drawn to the fact that whereas "Of Policy and Religion" was much expanded in subsequent editions, the present essay suffered several omissions—the satiric poetry among them. We witness the familiar palinodic withdrawal of the maturing writer who looks askance upon the productions of his greener years.

Page 88]   *Man is like . . . human society:* Opening patched together out of Guazzo, *Civile Conversation,* I, 35.

Such offices . . . avoideth conversation: This description squares exactly with Guazzo's definition (*Civile Conversation,* I, 56): "civil conversation is an honest, commendable, and virtuous kind of living in the world." Compare Henri Estienne, *A World of Wonders,* attrib. tr. Richard Carew (1607), sig. L2r, who, speaking of one's ordinary daily affairs among men, calls them "matters of common course or civil conversation."

Non est bonum, etc.: Gen. 2:18 (Vulgate, slightly misquoted).

Hence then . . . tombs: Tuvill could have read about "Athenian Timons" and "Diogenical cynics" in any of various classical and modern sources, but the juxtaposing of their names suggests that he is here following Montaigne, *Essays,* pp. 262–63. A similar passage occurs in Robert Greene's *Mourning Garment* (in *Works,* ed. Alexander Grosart [London and Aylesbury, 1881–86], IX, 129). The final idea seems to have been suggested by Seneca, *Epistulae morales,* LX, 4. Guazzo, *Civile Conversation,* I, 21, also mentions "the melancholic Athenian" (i.e., Timon), "who no less at his death, than in his lifetime, refusing the conversation of men, left these verses upon his tomb," etc.

He merits not . . . employ it: Compare Guazzo, *Civile Conversation,* I, 33. See also Matt. 5:15 and 25:24–28.

Or like the fox . . . wants withal: Guazzo again; see *Civile Conversation,* I, 36–37. See also Geoffrey Whitney, *Choice of Emblemes,* p. 142.

Our being . . . from abroad: Compare Guazzo, *Civile Conversation,* I, 35.

But by reason . . . be preserved: This is a neat summary statement of the theme of Guazzo's *Civile Conversation.*

Our Master hath taught us . . . dove: Directly from Wright, *Passions of the Mind,* sig. G8v. The biblical allusion is to Matt. 10:16.

Page 89]   *Alexander asked a pirate,* etc.: Adapted from Wright, *Passions of the Mind,* sig. H1r.

Likeness of manners . . . affection: "Likeness . . . likely . . . liking": the passage playfully descants upon the proverb, "Like will to like"; but the descant is not Tuvill's. He has quoted it from Sir Philip Sidney, *Arcadia,* I, 32.

Caius Caesar . . . possibly he could: Marginal reference to [Tacitus,] *Annals,* VI [, xx].

Pari habitu . . . verbis: Marginal reference to Tacitus, *Annals,* VI [, xx].
Tuvill quotes the same passage in *The Dove and the Serpent,* sig. F2v.

Obstinate and inflexible: Phrase borrowed from Bacon, *Advancement,* p. 15.

Fili, ne innitaris . . . mouth of Wisdom: Marginal reference to Prov. 3:5.
But the whole passage, including the reference to the source in Proverbs, is
copied from Wright, *Passions of the Mind,* sig. G8r.

Vaporous or imaginative . . . present world: Like the phrase above, these
two lines come almost verbatim from Bacon's *Advancement,* p. 15.

Antipodes: See Antonio de Torquemada, *The Spanish Mandevile of Miracles, or The Garden of Curious Flowers,* tr. attributed to Sir Lewis
Lewkenor (1600), sig. Gg3r: "Antipodes are they which are on the other
part of the world, contrary in opposite unto us, going with their feet
against ours; so that they which understand it not, think that they go with
their heads downward, whereas they go in the selfsame sort with their
heads as we do."

Ulteriora mirari . . . saith Tacitus: Marginal reference to *Histories,* III.
The correct reference is *Histories,* IV, viii.

Saturnus periit . . . sequare Jovis: Marginal reference to Ovid, [*Heroides,*
Epist. IV,] "Phaedra Hippolyto." Not found.

For frustra niti, etc.: Marginal reference to Sallust [, *Bellum Iugurthinum,*
iii, 3], adapted.

It is madness . . . stream: The translation is cast in proverbial form. Compare Heywood, *Proverbs,* p. 68:

> Folly it is to spurn against a prick;
> To strive against the stream, to winch or kick
> Against the hard wall.

For similar phrasing, see pp. 125, 126.

PAGE 90] *I often think . . . Antigonus again:* See Plutarch, *Lives,* "Phocion," p. 912.

The nature . . . least have tried: Verbatim from Hooker's *Laws of Ecclesiastical Polity,* p. 23.

I will not suffer, etc.: Note again the use of the "resolves" formula.

With Marcus Lepidus . . . vacuum: Marginal reference to Tacitus, *Annals,*
IV [, xx], adapted.

Adulatio perinde anceps, etc.: Tacitus, *Histories,* IV, xvii.

It is as dangerous . . . too much: Quoted by Rich, *Honesty of This Age,*
p. 31.

Emanuel, king of Portugal, etc.: A manuscript marginal note in HN copy (by Evelyn?) reads: "This fellow made an unseasonable use of his wit." I have not identified the source.

PAGE 91] *For when Charles . . . his son:* Sir John Harington, *Nugae antiquae,* ed. Thomas Park (London, 1804), I, 222–23, relates a similar anecdote of Philip II and a courtier or, alternatively, "of our worthy King Henry VIII and Domingo."

Gave up his hand: Marginal manuscript note in HN copy: "He lost to a good end."

Saul was mightily incensed: Marginal reference to I Sam. [18:]8. Tuvill's Latin does not follow the Vulgate (I Regum 18:8): *quid ei superest nisi solum regnum?*

It is said of Agricola . . . glory: Marginal reference to Tacitus, *Agricola* [, viii, (10–12)]. The whole passage, in much the same language, is used by Tuvill in *Essays Politic and Moral,* p. 68. Note especially the correspondence of final phrases.

Tacitus pasci si posset, etc.: Marginal reference reads: "*Hor. Ep.* 17. *lib.* 2." The correct reference is Horace, *Epistles,* I, xvii, 50–51.

Service is no longer respected . . . acknowledge: Idea drawn from Tacitus, *Histories,* bk. I; compare Grey Brydges (?), *Horae subsecivae. Observations and Discourses* (1620), p. 279. A similar idea, also from Tacitus (*Annals,* bk. IV), is quoted in Lorenzo Ducci, *Ars aulica* (1607), sig. L5r-v.

Antonius Primus . . . valiant deeds: See Tacitus, *Histories,* III, *passim,* esp. liii; also IV, lxxx.

And Caesar: I.e., Tiberius, the emperor. The quotation, *Destrui Caesar,* etc., is from Tacitus, *Annals,* IV, xviii, slightly misquoted.

PAGE 92] *Physicians may converse . . . kill themselves:* Modified from Wright, *Passions of the Mind,* sig. K6r.

It is good . . . brothelry: Very close to Wright, *Passions of the Mind,* sig. K6r.

The lustful satyr: On the lustfulness of the satyr, classed by Edward Topsell with the apes, see *The History of Four-Footed Beasts* (1607), sig. C1r.

He that walketh . . . defiled: Both statements are proverbial; for the second, see Ecclus. 13:1. Tuvill repeats the combination in *Christian Purposes and Resolutions,* sig. F7r, opening statement of sec. XXXI: "He that walketh in the sun shall be tanned; and he that meddleth with pitch shall be defiled. A man can hardly converse with such as are infected and yet rest free from all contagion."

Grex totus . . . ab uva: Marginal reference to Juvenal, *Satires,* II [, 79–81]. Trans.: "In the fields the scab of one sheep, or the mange of one pig, destroys an entire herd; just as one bunch of grapes takes on its sickly color from the aspect of its neighbor." Quoted again in *Asylum Veneris,* sig. K7v.

Augustus, being present . . . sympathize together: Marginal reference reads: "Sueton." I do not find this account in Suetonius. Apparently Tuvill has simply transferred the reference, along with the rest of the statement, from Wright, *Passions of the Mind,* sig. F7v.

He that talketh much . . . indiscretion: Wright, *Passions of the Mind,* sig. K6r.

Either a Phocion or a Pythagorean: For Phocion, see Plutarch, *Lives,* "Phocion," p. 898; Montaigne, *Essays,* pp. 644, 678, discusses both; and Tuvill elsewhere (*The Dove and the Serpent,* sig. A4r) praises the restraint of "the Pythagoreans, who after three years of silent contemplation, were permitted to intermeddle with public actions and to reduce their long-conceived speculations into practice." On the Pythagorean silence, see further Aulus Gellius, *Attic Nights,* I, ix, 1–7.

PAGE 93] *To converse much . . . capacity:* Modified from Wright, *Passions of the Mind,* sig. K6r.

Low-built roof: Compare p. 117. This favorite phrasal formula of Tuvill's recurs in *The Dove and the Serpent,* sig. D4r: "to raise the low-built roof of his estate"; and sig. H3v: "Their desires are lightly of a low-built roof."

For as Valerius said . . . inferior: Valerius Maximus, *Dict. fact. memorab.,* V, i.

The praetorship: See Sir William Segar, *Honor Military, and Civil* (1602), sig. A1r: "Justinianus, desiring to unite laws and arms, authorized one officer to command both martially and civilly, whom he called *praetor;* and so the Romans continued that name for their general of war. His office was mixed both of authority martial and civil."

To enter abruptly . . . contempt: Wright, *Passions of the Mind,* sig. K6v.

To laugh overprofusely, etc.: Compare Epictetus, *Manual,* tr. John Healey (ed. 1616), sig. D9v: "Let not thy laughter be profuse, nor be led by every light occasion." See also Ecclus. 19–21, *passim.* And with what Tuvill here says of jesting, compare Feltham, *Resolves,* "Of Truth, and Bitterness in Jests," pp. 81–83.

Facetiarum, si acerbae . . . saith Tacitus: Marginal reference to Tacitus, *Annals,* V [, ii]. See also *Annals,* XV, lxviii, and Lorenzo Ducci, *Ars aulica* (1607), sig. H12r.

He that would please . . . element: Idea and language indicate that this derives from Montaigne, *Essays,* p. 40.

PAGE 94] *I will never . . . ignorance:* This paragraph, like part of the preceding, would seem to derive from Montaigne, *Essays,* p. 40. It has some affinity, also, with Sir William Cornwallis, *Essayes* (1946), "Of Resolution," p. 8. Notice that Tuvill has slipped again into the "resolves" formula.

I will invite . . . storms: The original of this is Propertius, II, i, 43–45; but Tuvill could have found it nearer to hand in Guazzo, *Civile Conversation,* I, 149, or in Whitney, *Choice of Emblemes,* p. 145.

IV OF ALMS AND CHARITABLE DEEDS

As if alarmed at the almost exclusively secular tone of the preceding essay, in "Of Alms and Charitable Deeds" Tuvill swings to a distinctively religious matter and to a manner approximating that of the sermon. Indeed, without reorganization and expansion to meet the customary hour's span for delivery, what we have here would seem to be little more than the raw notes for a sermon upon what the age might have styled an Emergent Occasion. Although the initially misleading threefold division of the "text" quickly settles down to consideration of the second point only, the pulpit-pattern is clearly marked: text, division of text, exposition, hortatory conclusion (here cast in the "resolve" pattern). The temper of the essay, while fully as "practical" as that in any of Bacon's, is agreeable with the professed Christian dogma of Charity; and if one could *ever* feel quite certain that he had caught the authentic voice of the man himself—as he can with Tuvill's model, Montaigne—it would be pleasant to consider this essay a declaration of the author's preference of the practice of piety to the mere theory of it.

PAGE 95] *Sit with Mary:* See Luke 10:38–42; and, for another instance of the Mary-Martha, contemplation-action contrast, see p. 83.

He must with Lazarus: See John 11:1–44.

St. Paul confirms it: Marginal reference to Rom. 15:[26–]28.

Those that are courteous . . . gratify themselves: Marginal reference to Eph. 4:32.

Hence is it . . . own sakes: So stated in Montaigne, *Essays,* p. 807. The idea is repeated and slightly expanded, perhaps from Tuvill, in Ralph Venning's *Canaan's Flowings* (1658), p. 252: "The Italian beggars many times use this phrase, do good for your own sake; he gains most good who doth most good, he that gives to the poor for God's sake, gains more than he gives. The giver receives most."

The Lord that fed five thousand: Marginal reference to Matt. 14:1; the correct verse reference should be 14–21.

Relieved by the hands of women: Marginal reference to John 4:7.

It is as hard . . . needle: Matt. 19:24; Mark 10:25; Luke 18:24–25.

PAGE 96] *Let him follow . . . habitation:* Marginal reference to Luke 16:9. The editions of 1629, 1631, and 1638 correct the marginal reading, erroneously, to Luke 19:9.

If God have blessed . . . increase: Compare Christopher Sutton, *Disce vivere* (1602), sig. M3v: "The rich man in the Gospel cared for filling his barns, the Scripture calleth him fool: he never cared for filling the best barns, to wit, the bellies of the poor." See Luke 12:16–18.

Mane semina semen tuum, etc.: Eccles. 11:6 (Vulgate).

Afford a mite: In allusion to the widow's offering (Luke 21:2) of her *two* mites. The mite was anciently a copper coin (lepton) of small value.

He that sounds a trumpet: See Matt. 6:1–4. Whitney, *Choice of Emblemes,* p. 224, has an emblem illustrating the idea.

Concludamus eleemosynam, etc.: Marginal reference to Ecclus. 29:12 (= Vulgate, verse 15). Tuvill has adapted rather than quoted the passage.

"I wept," said Job: Marginal reference to [Job] 30:25.

Seneca saith, lachrimandum, etc.: Marginal reference to [Seneca, *Moral Essays,*] "De clementia," II, vi [, 4]. The phrase *lachrimandum, non plorandum* is borrowed not from the "De clementia" but from *Epistulae morales,* LXIII, 1; and Seneca's text for the rest of the Latin quotation runs: *Imbecillos oculos esse scias, qui ad alienam lippitudinem et ipsi subfunduntur . . . .*

To think that mercy . . . doctrine: It is not mercy (*clementia*) but pity (*misericordia*) which Seneca says (*Moral Essays,* "De clementia," II, vi, 4) is allied to misery: *Misericordia vicina est miseriae.*

"Be ye merciful": Marginal reference to Luke 6:36. Eds. 1629, 1631, and 1638 correct the marginal reading, erroneously, to Luke 16:6.

If we observe . . . compassion only: Contrast with Thomas Fitzherbert, *First Part of a Treatise Concerning Policy and Religion* (Douai, 1606), sig. C2r.

The Lord had . . . inheritance: Perhaps suggested by Bacon, *Advancement,* p. 215.

PAGE 97] *"Ask of me,"* etc.: Marginal reference to Ps. 2:8.

Invenisti patrem . . . imitare patrem: In the HN copy of 1609 the Latin of the text is underscored and a manuscript note in the margin reads: "be merciful as thy father is merciful." Compare the title (and theme) of Giovanni Papini's collection of essays on the Renaissance, *L'imitazione del padre* (Firenze, 1943).

The eagle . . . disinherit them: Compare the somewhat similar use of this "unnatural" natural history in Henry Smith's sermon "The Way to Walk In," *Works* (1866–67), I, 166: "As the eagle doth count them bastards that cannot abide to look upon the sun; so Christ doth account them bastards which will not take him to be an example of lowliness." See also William Averell, *A Marvelous Combat of Contrarieties* (1588), sig. E2v.

Interroga jumenta, saith holy Job: Marginal reference to [Job] 12:7–8. Gulielmus Bucanus, *Institutions of Christian Religion* (1606), sig. E6r, commenting on this passage in Job, explains that one "end and use of fishes and birds" is "for the example of virtues which we should follow, and of vices which we should shun, being set before our eyes in their natures. As namely, of humanity and love to man in the dolphin; of flattery in the fish polypus; of the resurrection in the phoenix; of piety and remuneration in the storks; of simplicity and matrimonial fidelity in the turtles [doves]; of unnatural affection in the ravens, and of crying unto God. And therefore it is well said: 'Ask the beast and he shall tell thee; and the bird of the air, and she will declare unto thee,' Job 12. 7. 8.''

The dolphin . . . to the shore: Tuvill tells only half the tale. John Carpenter, *Schelomonocham, or King Solomon His Solace* (1606), sig. H6v, gives a fuller account: "We find of the sea dolphins . . . that if perchance they find a dead man in the seas, they feel by the smell of him whether he hath ever eaten of dolphin fish; the which if at any time he hath, then they devour him, if not, then they defend him from the biting of all other fishes and bring him to the shore, as it were to his funerals in the earth."

Meats . . . defiled with: Comparison possibly suggested by one in Macrobius; see Thomas Pritchard, *The School of Honest and Virtuous Life* (*ca.* 1579), sig. B4v: "As the meat lodged in the mouth or clunged in the stomach, feedeth not the body, nor hath not concoction, for lack of natural heat, to digest the same into good blood and maintenance of the body; so doth not reading profit, except it be converted to the behoof of the weal public."

"Give . . . clean unto you": Marginal reference to Luke 11:41.

Daniel's counsel to Nebuchadnezzar: Marginal reference to [Dan.] 4:24. This is the numeration (and language) of the Vulgate; the King James Version numbers the verse 27.

PAGE 98] *Let us not turn our faces:* Compare Tob. 4:7 (Vulgate)—*Ex substantia tua fac eleemosynam, et noli avertere faciem tuam ab ullo paupere.*

Be always ready . . . unto them: Marginal reference to Gen. 18:2 and 19:1.

St. Paul so fervently exhorts: Marginal reference to Rom. 12:13.

Do good . . . and give him: Marginal reference to Ecclus. 14:13.

The alms . . . apple of the eye: Marginal references to Tob. 4:10 [i.e., 11] and Ecclus. 29:13. The more relevant reference to Ecclesiasticus would be 17:18—*Eleemosyna viri quasi signaculum cum ipso, et gratiam hominis quasi pupillam conservabit.*

Besides . . . before a sinner: Marginal reference to Luke 13:4. Tuvill's reference is in error; the editions of 1629 and 1631 omit it. What he perhaps has in mind is Ecclus. 12:1–5. But see Gal. 6:10; and compare also William Perkins, *An Exposition of the Symbol or Creed of the Apostles,* in *Works* (1605; *STC* 19648), sig. Hh5v.

Who would not . . . a hundred: Adapting Christ's familiar parable, Luke 8:5–15; Matt. 13:3–8.

Last of all . . . patient: Reproduced in Spencer, *Things New and Old,* I, 409.

As the proverb saith: G. L. Apperson, *English Proverbs and Proverbial Phrases* (London, 1929), pp. 49–50, cites as the first English instance "1638: D. Turvill [*sic*], *Vade Mecum."*

I will not, therefore: The introductory "resolve" formula, exactly repeated in *Christian Purposes and Resolutions,* sig. K11r.

Neglect to put my oil: Alluding to the parable of the wise and foolish virgins, Matt. 25:1–13.

The rich man in the Gospel: Marginal reference to Luke 12:17.

Stored with nothing . . . store: This recalls the troublesome "want that you have wanted" of *King Lear,* I, i, 282.

If my hand be withered: Marginal reference to Matt. 12:9. More exactly, the verse reference should read 10–13.

Page 99] *If my neighbor's sheep . . . out:* Marginal reference to Matt. 12:11. The "neighbor's" is Tuvill's own charitable addition. Compare also Luke 14:5.

Whatsoever is good . . . done: A loose version of Virgil, *Georgics,* I, 268–69. Compare William Perkins, *A Golden Chain,* in *Works* (1605), sig. D4v: "we are not forbidden to perform such works even on this day, as are both holy and of present necessity."

Rivos deducere, etc.: Marginal reference to Virgil, *Georgics,* I [, 269–72]. Tuvill provides an explanatory paraphrase in the following sentences.

And by the law . . . Holy One: Exod. 20:8–11, 31:14–16. Compare Perkins, *A Golden Chain,* in *Works* (1605), sig. D4v.

Festis quaedam, etc.: Virgil, *Georgics,* I, 268–69, translated above.

The Lord hath taught . . . offering: Hos. 6:6; Matt. 9:13. See also Prov. 21:3.

V Of Respect and Reverence

Biblical language and illustration, though not abandoned in this essay, are diminished. Once again, as in his earlier essays, and particularly in those of the 1608 series, Tuvill sounds a predominantly classical note. Livy, Tacitus, and Juvenal are much in evidence, especially Juvenal. The latter half of the essay, in fact, beginning with the statement (p. 102) that "These later ages are corrupted and depraved," is little more than a prose paraphrase of Juvenal, whose *Satires* XIII and XIV are laid under heavy draught. In this respect the essay is closely akin to Essay XII, "Of Poverty," below, and to "Cautions in Friendship" in the earlier series. It is perhaps some sort of measure of Tuvill's basic conservatism and tendency to laud "the good old times" that the similarly minded Barnabe Rich should find this particular essay so congenial (see "A Word about Barnaby Rich," *Journal of English and Germanic Philology,* LV [July, 1956], 381–92).

The real subject of the essay, the power of virtue to discipline society, might be better reflected in a different choice of title; and unity of theme might be more readily apparent if less emphasis were placed upon the conventional contrast between a vicious present and a virtuous past. In the original text, after the first half-dozen paragraphs, the structure quickly disintegrates into a loose agglomeration of illustrative notes: thirty-one scrappy "paragraphs" (here reduced to eleven), to be exact, further broken up by the interspersed quotations from Juvenal, all chosen in haphazard, nonsequential fashion. By regrouping in larger units, wherever possible without departure from Tuvill's order—if "order" it should be called—I have attempted to lessen the impression of jumble left by the original. But in theme, in structure, in abject dependence upon a single source, "Of Respect and Reverence" remains, I fear, one of the least impressive of Tuvill's efforts.

PAGE 100] *It is not with virtue . . . manger:* Compare sentiment and language with *Essays Politic and Moral,* "Of Praises," p. 26. Barnabe Rich, *Honesty of This Age,* p. 47, adapts the first three sentences.

Kings have adored . . . manger: Compare *The Dove and the Serpent,* sig. A3r: "The dove will teach us with the wise men how to honor an untainted merit, though it harbor in a manger."

She hath rid . . . on an ass: Matt. 21:5.

One word . . . greatest rage: See (1) Josh. 10:12–13; (2) Matt. 8:24–26.

The lion hath stood: The most likely reference would seem to be Dan. 6:16–22.

The Romans . . . to themselves: See Valerius Maximus, *Dict. fact. memorab.,* II, v. Compare Feltham, *Resolves,* "That Sin Is More Crafty Than Violent," p. 77: "Cato's presence stopped the practices of the Romans' brutish Floralia."

PAGE 101] *Scipio . . . hope for more:* Notwithstanding a marginal ascription in the editions of 1629, 1631, and 1638 to Livy, this whole paragraph, including the Latin quotation, derives from Valerius Maximus, *Dict. fact. memorab.*, II, v.

Virtue hath . . . few followers: Sentence copied by Rich, *Honesty of This Age,* p. 14.

Quis tam perditus, etc.: Marginal reference to Juvenal, *Satires,* VIII [, 211–12].

Hell . . . when she is by: A contrary sense seems to be called for.

Cerberus: The triple-headed watchdog of the classical underworld. See p. 136.

The serpent . . . thrust out his sting: Tuvill, a city man, evidently had little experience with serpents. Perhaps he thought the "sting" was in the tongue, "continually thrust out"; or, with his fellow preacher, Henry Smith, "A Glass for Drunkards," *Works* (1866–67), I, 305, that "the serpent's sting is in his tail."

'T is said of Tiberius . . . accessory: Tacitus, *Annals,* VI, li.

PAGE 102] *Qui scire . . . prohibebant:* Marginal reference to Terence, *Andria,* I, i [, 53–54]. Trans.: "one had no means of knowing the truth or telling his bent, while he was under the constraint of infancy, fear, and a master."

The disposition . . . from forced respect: A conclusion restating the idea drawn from Terence, above. Bacon, whom Tuvill elsewhere follows "at an inch," holds an opposite view. See *Advancement,* pp. 89–90: "a man's disposition is never well known till he be crossed, nor Proteus ever changed shapes till he was straitened and held fast."

Hence was it that Scipio . . . happiness: Cf. Livy, *Ab urbe condita* (Summaries), XLVIII, end; St. Augustine, *De civitate Dei,* I, xxx.

Without a harbinger: See note above, p. 168.

Improbity . . . a wonder: Translates Juvenal, *Satires,* XIII, 53.

Sed genus hoc, etc.: Juvenal, *Satires,* XV, 69. For *Sed,* Loeb reads *nam.* Trans.: "For even in Homer's day the race of man was on the wane."

Terra malos homines, etc.: Juvenal, *Satires,* XV, 70: "Earth now produces none but weak and wicked men."

The Cynic . . . his mind: Diogenes, the Cynic philosopher, was said to have carried a lantern in broad daylight in his quest for an honest man. A work contemporary with Tuvill's, Samuel Rowlands' *Diogenes Lanthorne* (1607), so depicts the Cynic on its title page. See also Diogenes Laertius, *Lives of Eminent Philosophers,* VI, 41.

Rari quippe boni, etc.: Marginal reference to Juvenal, *Satires,* XIII [, 26–27]. The passage is also quoted and translated in Montaigne, *Essays,* p. 188.

It was a capital offense . . . elder: A free version of Juvenal, *Satires,* XIII, 54–56. Thomas Pritchard, *The School of Honest and Virtuous Life (ca.* 1579), sig. E2v, comments with delightful quaintness upon this "Duty Toward Old Age": "The Romans, schooled in Cicero his trim tract of duties, made a law that whosoever passed by the elder sort of citizens without obeisance of bonnet and bowing of bones, should be punished by the head: which, as I construe, to be beheaded, or else to stand a shameful anathemate yoked in pillory, to the utter crack of their credit."

But now if . . . detained it: Translates Juvenal, *Satires,* XIII, 60–61.

Prodigiosa fides, etc.: Juvenal, *Satires,* XIII, 62–63. Compare Montaigne, *Essays,* p. 586.

Not to be poor . . . ominous: Tuvill never wearies of describing in hyperbolic terms the degeneracy of his time. Compare, for instance, *The Dove and the Serpent,* sig. B4r: "Simplicity lieth speechless, and upright dealing is ready to give up the ghost."

PAGE 103] *Serpente Ciconia pullos . . . their prey:* Quoting and translating Juvenal, *Satires,* XIV, 74–76; also quoted in Montaigne, *Essays,* p. 408.

Children can neither . . . unmeet: Quoted by Rich, *Honesty of This Age,* p. 32.

Besides the forwardness . . . encourage them: Condensed paraphrase of Juvenal, *Satires,* XIV, 31–37.

Catilinam . . . avunculus usquam: Juvenal, *Satires,* XIV, 41–43.

Men are curious . . . their child: Based on Juvenal, *Satires,* XIV, 59–69.

How is it possible . . . the least: Compare Juvenal, *Satires,* XIV, 25–28.

Many presume . . . reprove him: Based on Juvenal, *Satires,* XIV, 38–58.

PAGE 104] *Loripedem rectus,* etc.: Juvenal, *Satires,* II, 23.

I will therefore esteem: Note the recurrence here and in the following sentences of the "resolves" formula.

Tiberius could not endure . . . his own: See Tacitus, *Annals,* I, xiv; and compare *Essays Politic and Moral,* p. 30.

Additions . . . to her style: Compare Bacon, *Advancement,* p. 57: "In such renown and veneration was the name of these two princes [Augustus and Antoninus] in those days, that they would have had it as a perpetual addition in all the emperors' style."

If greatness . . . of Spain: This paragraph derives from Bodin, *Of a Commonweal,* pp. 505–6.

The King of Borneo . . . their ears: Also related in Montaigne, *Essays,* p. 77.

Majestati . . . reverentia: Proverbial; equivalent to "Distance lends enchantment."

There is in magistrates . . . deity: Compare *Hamlet,* IV, v, 123.

PAGE 105] *The censors branded . . . presence:* Aulus Gellius, *Attic Nights,* IV, xx, 7–9, relates the incident but says that the sentence was remitted.

The ass may clothe: Aesop's familiar fable.

VI OF GIFTS AND BENEFITS

"Of Gifts and Benefits" is not only the longest of the essays in Tuvill's second series, it is also the one which shows most signs of reworking in the subsequent editions. The changes are of various sorts: interesting but minor variations of wording, correction of a few misprints, additions of considerable length, and, most important, omission of most of the poetry. Inasmuch as the omitted parts were mainly drawn from Martial, the omission works an appreciable softening of satiric tone and effectively disguises a major source-obligation of the original version. What remains are the moralizings of Seneca and the relative respectability of Terence, Horace, and Tacitus.

As usual, Tuvill handles his Latin quotations with careless liberty, adapting or misquoting *ad libitum.* And if in "Of Respect and Reverence" we noted his retreat from biblical quotation, here, notwithstanding the sententious and "exemplary" mode of delivery (to say nothing of a theme that cries for Christian treatment), Tuvill seems even more definitely to have laid aside the cassock for the toga. Nevertheless, in characteristic phrasing and idea—even to the two-pronged title—"Of Gifts and Benefits" provides numerous links with other works of its author. These are duly indicated in the ensuing notes.

PAGE 106] *Hence was it . . . mine:* Derived from Seneca, *Moral Essays,* "De beneficiis," VI, iii, 1. Compare the last two lines of Martial's epigram quoted in the next paragraph.

Alfonso, king of Sicily, etc.: Compare Seneca, *Moral Essays,* "De vita beata," xx, 4: *Nihil magis possidere me credam quam bene donata;* "De beneficiis," VI, iii, 1.

The like hath Xenophon: Cf. *The Education of Cyrus,* III, iii, 6 (tr. H. G. Dakyns, Everyman's Library [London and New York, 1914], p. 98).

Curtius of his Alexander: The reference seems to be to Quintus Curtius

Rufus, *Historiarum libri X* (Amsterdam: Elzevir, 1630), bk. IV (p. 97).

And hence it was . . . thine own: Marginal reference to [Martial, *Epigrams,*] V, xlii. For *extrustas* read *extructas.*

Inhuman cannibals: The identical phrase is used in *Essays Politic and Moral,* p. 36.

Page 107] *Like an Italianated courtier:* The phrase recurs in *Christian Purposes and Resolutions,* sig. C4r: "God is not an Italianated courtier; nor doth he ever entertain us with lip courtesy."

Multi, saith Tacitus, etc.: A manuscript marginal note in the HN copy reads: "many had rather be poor than say so."

Sero dedit . . . call them: Modified from Seneca, *Moral Essays,* "De beneficiis," II, ii, 1. John Spencer quotes it, with slight changes, in *Things New and Old,* I, 409.

Arcesilaus had no sooner . . . to ask: See Plutarch, *Morals,* p. 102. Montaigne, *Essays,* p. 903, relates the same story. According to Plutarch the friend's name was Apelles; Montaigne calls him Ctesibius.

Sex sestertia . . . perdidisti: Marginal reference to Martial, *Epigrams,* VI, xxx—a correct reference!

Page 108] *Diligo praestantem . . . say me nay:* Tuvill marginally identifies the two Latin quotations as coming (1) from Martial, *Epigrams,* VI, xlii (correctly, VII, xliii), and (2) *ibid.,* VI, xx.

Ἀ χάρις . . . χάρις: "A slow-footed gift is a graceless gift." Quoted as *versiculus Graecus* in Andrea Alciati, *Emblemata* (Padua, 1621), p. 690. This paragraph on the Graces probably owes something to Seneca, *Moral Essays,* "De beneficiis," I, iii-iv.

Page 109] *Munera magna . . . potest:* Adapted from Martial, *Epigrams,* VI, lxiii. A manuscript marginal note in HN copy reads: "give a penny and look for a pound."

A surgeon: The unstable early orthography of the word is well illustrated in the successive editions: 1609, "Sirurgian"; 1629, "Chyrurgian"; 1631 and 1638, "Chirurgian."

Quod non argentum . . . pain: Marginal reference to Martial, *Epigrams,* V, lx (= Loeb lix).

Page 110] *Non est aptus . . . Ulysses:* Marginal reference to Horace, *Epistles,* I, vii [, 41–43].

Parvum parva decent: Continuing the quotation from Horace just above. Trans.: "Small things befit small folk."

They are like a glass . . . before it: The same figure and virtually identical language are used concerning women in Tuvill's *Asylum Veneris,* sig F3v:

"They be like looking glasses, say their adversaries, which represent no object longer than it stands before them."

PAGE 111] *Extet . . . et convivat:* Seneca, *Moral Essays,* "De beneficiis," I, xii, 2.

But he that . . . benevolence: Compare "Of Alms and Charitable Deeds," p. 96 and note.

Quae mihi praestiteris, etc.: Marginal reference to Martial, *Epigrams,* V, liii (= Loeb lii).

Triobolary empirics: See glossarial note; also the title of a contemporary work by Matthew Sutcliffe, *A Threefold Answer unto the Third Part of a Certain Triobolar Treatise* (1606). Edward Forsett's *Comparative Discourse* (1606), sig. M3v, sets the empiric in his proper light: "the profound and rational physician is, for certainty of cure and direction in the regiment of health, to be chosen and used before the rash unskillful empiric."

A friend of Caesar's . . . life: Marginally credited to Tacitus in 1629, 1631, and 1638 editions; but notwithstanding the ascription, both the illustration and the Latin quotation (together with the following one) derive from Seneca, *Moral Essays,* "De beneficiis," II, xi, 1.

Restore me back again: A redundancy common in Edmund Spenser, one of Tuvill's favorite poets. Compare *Faerie Queene,* I, i, 16; I, i, 55; etc. See also Anthony Munday, *The English Roman Life, 1582,* ed. G. B. Harrison (London and New York, 1925), p. 10: "wishing us to return back again into England."

Lacerat . . . commemoratio: Seneca, as above. A manuscript marginal note (edges somewhat closely trimmed) in HN copy reads: "the often repetit[ion] of courtesies is distasteful[l]."

A serpent without a dove: Christopher Marlowe provides a gloss in one of Barabas' speeches; see *Jew of Malta,* II, iii, 36–38. The combination was an obsession with Tuvill, as can be seen in his later work, *The Dove and the Serpent.* It is perhaps of this latter work that Ralph Venning is thinking when he writes, in *Canaan's Flowings* (1658), p. 152, under the heading "Policy": "The most (and the most commonly used) policy is little better than circumstantial dissimulation: be sure therefore not to act the serpent without the dove. 'T is better to act the dove without the serpent, than the serpent without the dove; 't is better to be pious without policy, than to be politic without piety." See also *Asylum Veneris,* sig. G6r.

PAGE 112] *Quel che ti fa . . . proverb:* Samuel Rowlands, *Diogenes Lanthorne* (1607), sig. F1v, thus translates the proverb:

> He that more kindness showeth thee
> Than thou art used unto,
> Either already hath deceived
> Or shortly means to do.

The siren's song . . . fish's bane: This has the air of being drawn from some euphuistic romance. I have not found a source.

The wolf . . . wether's skin: = "a wolf in sheep's clothing"; one of Tuvill's many proverbial adaptations.

Davus: A sly servant in the *Andria* of Terence.

Latet anguis in herba: The proverbial "serpent in the grass." See Whitney, *Choice of Emblemes,* p. 24.

Cuicunque nocere, etc.: Horace, *Epistles,* I, xviii, 31 ff.

Beatus enim iam . . . hire: Continues and translates the quotation from Horace begun just above.

PAGE 113] *The like hath . . . oppress them:* Possibly the capital instance of what Tuvill has in mind is the career of Sejanus under the Emperor Tiberius; see Ben Jonson's *Sejanus* and the life of Tiberius in Suetonius, *History of Twelve Caesars, passim.*

It is reported of Domitian, etc.: Suetonius, *History of Twelve Caesars,* sig. Aa1v.

Nero dismissed Seneca . . . death: Suetonius, *History of Twelve Caesars,* sig. S3v.

The praetorship: See note to p. 93.

Ira quae tegitur nocet: Marginal reference to Seneca, *Medea,* Act 2 [, l. 153].

Gravia quisquis vulnera, etc.: Seneca, *Medea,* ll. 151–53. For Tuvill's *motus* read *mutus.* A marginal note quotes and translates the next line of Seneca's play: *"professa perdunt odia vindictae locum;* hatred once known can hardly work revenge."

PAGE 114] *Who would imagine . . . least suspected:* Compare the passage on deceitful appearances, p. 129.

To veil a wrinkled heart: Tuvill uses the identical phrase in *Essays Politic and Moral,* p. 48.

In animo revolvente: Marginal reference to Tacitus, *Annals,* IV [, xxi]. A manuscript marginal note in the HN copy reads: "it is a passio[n] not soon forgotten thoug[h] the heat of it be quenched."

VII OF REPULSES AND DENIALS

In its brevity, this essay offers Tuvill small opportunity to wander from his theme, a theme pretty much the reverse of the coin offered in "Of Gifts and Benefits" The two thus stand as somewhat unequal companion pieces.

It is not surprising, therefore, to find in "Of Repulses and Denials" a continued levying upon Seneca's "De beneficiis." Other classical sources are also drawn upon, though with a notable soft-pedaling of the satirists. Something of an increased sobriety of tone may be reflected in the return to scriptural quotations and allusions; and the heavy incidence of "resolves" produces something of a kindred effect. The essay is developed throughout by a combination of aphoristic generalizations and supporting *exempla*.

PAGE 115] *I will strive:* The first of the "resolves" prominently stressed throughout the essay.

Offer him a serpent . . . bread: Tuvill here conflates two verses from the Sermon on the Mount; see Matt. 7:9–10 and Luke 11:11.

I will not, like Dionysius: Cf. Seneca, *Moral Essays,* "De beneficiis," II, xvi, 1 (of *Alexander,* however).

Churlish Nabal: See I Sam. 25:3–10. For a contemporary discussion of the uncharitable denial of Nabal, see the heated (and not wholly disinterested) commentary of Edward Topsell, *The Householder, or Perfect Man* (1610), sigs. C8r–D2r.

Durum est . . . rogeris: Martial, *Epigrams,* II, xliv, 11–12.

PAGE 116] *I would not . . . the shell:* Tuvill says just the reverse in *Christian Purposes and Resolutions,* sig. I2r: "I will bruise the serpent in the head, I will break it in the shell." And in *St. Paul's Threefold Cord,* sig. F11r, he advises: "Destroy therefore the cockatrice in the shell." See also p. 131.

Answer him, with Pericles: The answer of Pericles was *usque ad aras,* "as far as to the altar"; see Plutarch, *Morals,* p. 419; Aulus Gellius, *Attic Nights,* I, iii, 20.

Agesilaus, when his father, etc.: The three *exempla* of this paragraph apparently derive from Johann Gast's *Convivalium liber* (Basel, 1566), tom. II, sig. a6v, where, however, the order of the three anecdotes is reversed.

Est inter Tanaim, etc.: Horace, *Satires,* I, i, 105: "There is some mean between a Tanais and the father-in-law of Visellius."

Exorari in perniciem, etc.: A manuscript marginal note in the HN copy reads: "let not thy facili[ty] harbor and nourish thy friends vice."

Ille amando me occidit: Seneca, *Moral Essays,* "De beneficiis," II, xiv, 5.

PAGE 117] *I will not offer . . . fortune:* Seneca, *Moral Essays,* "De beneficiis," II, xvi, 1; and compare p. 110.

A low-built spirit: See note to p. 93.

The glory of humility . . . head also: See John 13:4–9.

Antigonus hath an evasion, etc.: See Plutarch, *Morals,* p. 415. The apothegm (without the Greek) is also related in Seneca, *Moral Essays,* "De beneficiis," II, xvii, 1.

Histories report of Titus: See Suetonius, *History of Twelve Caesars,* sig. Z2v.

VIII OF REPREHENSIONS AND REPROOFS

In treating this topic Tuvill shows himself a conservative psychologist and an adept follower of conventional patterns rather than an original thinker or innovator. The topic had been much handled, and certain commonplaces were expected features of its topography. Tuvill meets the expectation.

Interestingly, the essay returns to a balance between the biblical and the "pagan" elements. Greek ethical thought, the "wisdom" literature of the Old Testament, and the Sermon on the Mount are agreeably harmonized; and their cumulative authority lends to "Of Reprehensions and Reproofs" an impression of substantiality shared by few others of Tuvill's essays. As with the two preceding essays, revisions of the subsequent editions show a similar tendency to eliminate the original quotations from the Roman satirists. In idea and phraseology the essay offers many parallels with Tuvill's other writings, as the notes will exemplify. And, curiously (since the topics of the two works hardly suggest inevitable comparison), the essayist here returns to some degree of dependence upon Thomas Wright's *Passions of the Mind.* More closely akin is chapter XIV of La Primaudaye's *The French Academy,* entitled "Of Reprehension and Admonition."

PAGE 118] *It is casa d'Iddio . . . sound:* This is the theme of a popular contemporary work by Tommaso Garzoni, translated into English in 1600 as *The Hospital of Incurable Fools.*

"I prithee," said Plato, etc.: Plato here; but see Wright, *Passions of the Mind,* sig. G5v, where it is related of Architas. See also Montaigne, *Essays,* p. 643; Wright was probably following Montaigne, for the allusion to Architas precedes the Plato-Speusippus passage in the *Essays.* The anecdote appears in Seneca, *Moral Essays,* "De ira," III, xii, 7, and in Diogenes Laertius, *Lives of Eminent Philosophers,* III, 38. See also La Primaudaye, *French Academy,* p. 299, who follows Diogenes Laertius. Both the anecdote and the sentence following it are repeated in *St. Paul's Threefold Cord,* sigs. K10v-K11r.

It is hard . . . another's: Appropriated in Barnabe Rich's *Honesty of This Age,* p. 45.

It is impossible . . . his own: See Matt. 7:3–5.

PAGE 119] *The hand . . . be clean:* See *Essays Politic and Moral,* p. 13, where the saying is attributed to St. Gregory.

Physician cure thine own, etc.: See Luke 4:23.

Castigas turpia . . . cynaedos: Marginal reference reads, confusedly: *"Juven. lib.* 1. *Scen. [sic]* 2" (= *Satires,* II, 9–10).

His furor . . . veniam: Juvenal, *Satires,* II, 18–19.

Sed peiores . . . agitant: Juvenal, *Satires,* II, 19–21. Tuvill also quotes the last part of the Latin in *Essays Politic and Moral,* p. 12.

Ulcerous inflammations: The same phrase recurs in *Christian Purposes and Resolutions,* sig. C11v.

Cuivis accidere, etc.: The saying of Publilius Syrus, quoted admiringly (in reversed order, *potest accidere*) by Seneca, *Moral Essays,* "De consolatione ad Marciam," ix, 5, and again in "De tranquillitate," xi, 8. Seneca, rather than Publilius, is probably Tuvill's source. Compare *St. Paul's Threefold Cord,* sig. V2r: *"Cuivis accidere potest, quod cuipiam [cuiquam] potest,* saith the Mimic. Whatsoever we see happen to any man, may happen unto us."

Security is not . . . do not fall: The substance of these two paragraphs, as well as some of the phrasing, is reproduced at the opening of sec. 30 in *Christian Purposes and Resolutions,* sigs. F5v-F6r: "It is not good for a man to be confident in his own strength; it is a broken staff and will deceive his trust. He that is in heart a Christian, must work out his salvation with fear and trembling. Who beforehand so bold in vaunts and protestations to follow Christ as Peter, and yet (alas!) who at the point more timorous? . . . Let him that standeth, therefore, look well unto his footing that he do not fall. Let him not think upon security while he is here; it is not a creature of this world."

Our life . . . a temptation: Compare the quotation from St. Augustine, p. 130.

PAGE 120] *It is said of Saul,* etc.: Marginal reference to I Sam. 9 [i.e., 10]:24. Tuvill has improvised his Latin; the Vulgate reading (I Regum 10:24) is, *non sit similis illi in omni populo.*

David was a man . . . adultery: For the description "after His own heart," see I Sam. 13:14; for the sins of David, see II Sam. 11.

Peter . . . do not fall: The juxtaposing of the illustration (Peter's threefold denial) and the final scriptural citation suggests that Tuvill may have had in mind Henry Smith's "A Caveat for Christians," *Works* (1866–67), II, 36. For the final sentence, see I Cor. 10:12.

Peter was a disciple . . . detests Him: See Matt. 26:31–35, 69–75.

Ne glorietur accinctus, etc.: Marginal reference to I Kings 20:11 (= Vulgate III Regum 20:11).

Tu tot . . . aucta: Marginal reference to Tacitus, *Annals,* I [, xlii]. Trans.: "you who have shared his many fields and thriven on his many bounties."

Nimia pietas vestra, etc.: Marginal reference to Tacitus, *Histories,* I [, lxxxiii], adapted.

Yea, God himself . . . likewise hate: Marginal reference to Apoc. 2:6.

Ad reprehendenda . . . evolvat: Tuvill quotes this again in *The Dove and the Serpent,* sig. L3r, where it is marginally identified as coming from "Sallust de Rep. ordin. I," i.e., from the first of the pseudo-Sallustian *Duae epistolae de republica ordinanda.*

PAGE 121] *But if we did descend . . . intemperancy:* The reference, if not to some emblem or other pictorial representation, is apparently either to Seneca, *Moral Essays,* "De ira," II, xxviii, 8, *Aliena vitia in oculis habemus, a tergo nostra sunt;* or to Catullus in *Corpus poetarum latinorum,* ed. William Sidney Walker (London, 1889), XXII, 20–21,

> *suus [cuique] attributus est error;*
> *sed non videmus manticae quod in tergo est.*

Let us observe . . . thy husband: Marginal reference to John 4:18.

And with what art . . . the prophets: Marginal reference to Luke 24:21, 25, 27.

Lastly . . . flesh is weak: Matt. 26:40–41.

An open admonition . . . disgrace: But contrast Prov. 27:5, "Open rebuke is better than secret love."

There was placed . . . for all: The marginal reference ("1. King 7. 29"), misplaced, refers to the second half of Tuvill's paragraph; this first half is more properly reflected in Heb. 9:4.

Indeed, [if] rightly called: All eds. read "is"; but the context calls for "if."

Solomon . . . of the temple: I Kings 7:29.

PAGE 122] *To a heart . . . loathsome:* Sidney, *Arcadia,* I, 86.

There can be . . . must vail: This is the theme of Lucan's *Pharsalia.*

If a house . . . flame: Compare Wright, *Passions of the Mind,* sig. H2v.

But if a superior . . . another: Wright, *Passions of the Mind,* sig. H2v.

It is in sins . . . overawe them: Note the euphuistic balance and play on sound.

Argue sapientem, etc.: Prov. 9:8 (Vulgate); the clauses of Tuvill's translation (or paraphrase) reverse the order of the Latin statement.

To reprehend a fool . . . thereafter: In allusion to Matt. 7:6.

Adam and Eve . . . should have been: See Gen. 3:9 ff.

He cursed Cain . . . keeper: See Gen. 4:9–15.

He chased Saul . . . Samuel: See I Sam. chap. 15.

But pardoned David . . . Nathan: II Sam. 12:1–25.

And Christ . . . take your rest: Matt. 26:45.

Page 123]   *The rod of Aaron:* Exod. 7:9–10.

Better, with Tiberius, etc.: Marginal reference to Tacitus, *Annals,* III [, liii], Latin adapted.

IX Of Injuries and Indignities

The matter of this essay is well unified and coherently expressed, the combination of aphorism and example being here successfully ordered. Very little of that matter, however, is either novel or even strikingly expressed; rather more than most of Tuvill's essays, "Of Injuries and Indignities" employs the proverbial mode. Cliché and commonplace contribute their part to an impression of easy familiarity. Such "philosophy" or religion as is in the essay, when it is not simply the philosophy of expediency, leans toward a generalized Stoicism rather than the expected Christianity. Biblical allusion or quotation is conspicuously absent; but a few belated flickers of euphuism may be detected. Quotation of the classical poets, prominent up to this point, virtually disappears.

The conclusion of *The Dove and the Serpent,* chapter 5, also treats of this subject, introducing (as here) some of Tuvill's stock illustrations.

Page 124]   *She will not . . . substance:* One of the numerous Aesopic fables receiving illustration in Whitney's *Choice of Emblemes;* see p. 39.

The beaver . . . his stones: A "vulgar error" of some antiquity. Juvenal, whom Tuvill has elsewhere drawn upon heavily, may have suggested the idea to him; see *Satires,* XII, 34–36. But the notion was widely disseminated and was already exploded in Tuvill's own day. See Edward Topsell, *History of Four-Footed Beasts* (1607), sigs. E4v–E6r. It also appears as an emblem in Whitney, *Choice of Emblemes,* p. 35 — suggestively near to the Aesopic theme above.

To make a virtue of necessity: Proverbial phrase — as is the "rather bow than break," above.

Augustus . . . his imperial majesty: Bacon uses the same illustration, in much the same language, in "Of Friendship"; see *Essays,* ed. M. A. Scott

(New York, 1908), p. 121. Both Tuvill and Bacon are probably following Cassius Dio, *Roman History,* LIV, vi, 5.

Put himself upon the dice: = submit to chance.

His beginnings . . . his grandchild: See Suetonius, *History of Twelve Caesars,* sig. M6v.

To free his crown from check: A figure from the game of chess.

Led with . . . mar himself: See Guicciardini, *History* (1599), pp. 201–2.

Her brother Valentine: = Cesare Borgia, duke of Valentino.

PAGE 125] *Marry . . . or mar:* A pun so frequent as to have grown into a proverb. See Heywood, *Proverbs,* p. 18: "our one *marrying,* or *marring* day."

To be valorous . . . venturous: See *Essays Politic and Moral,* p. 65.

To swim against . . . wind: Modified proverbial phrases; for a more regular form, see p. 89.

Non sumit . . . aurae: Horace, *Odes,* III, ii, 19–20, slightly modified; also quoted (of Virtue) in *Asylum Veneris,* sig. B1v.

King Charles VII . . . his estate: See Bodin, *Of a Commonweal,* p. 606.

Who thereupon pronounced: The antecedent of the pronoun is *Philip.*

A blot . . . played upon: Compare *Asylum Veneris,* sig. H1v.

Eversio rei . . . praeceps dat: Marginal reference to [Tacitus,] *Annals,* VI [, xvii].

The reputation . . . his credit: A passage of mildly euphuistic pattern.

PAGE 126] *If an injury . . . saith Seneca:* Moral Essays, "De ira," II, xxxiii, 1.

And what avails . . . stronger teeth: Another Aesopic *motif;* see *Fables* (1889), bk. I, fable 2, II, 5–6.

'T is madness to kick . . . stone: Further modified proverbial phrases; see also Acts 9:5, 26:14.

He that shoots . . . endanger them: Compare *Asylum Veneris,* sig. B2r: "they that shoot against the stars may peradventure hurt themselves, but never endanger them."

One part of security, etc.: See the note (this essay) on Lucan, below. See also Montaigne, *Essays,* p. 811.

The earthen pipkin . . . tragical catastrophe: See *Essays Politic and Moral,*

"Cautions in Friendship," p. 55 and note. See also Guazzo, *Civile Conversation*, I, 210; Whitney, *Choice of Emblemes*, p. 164.

Veterem ferendo . . . novam: Publilius Syrus, *Sententiae*, l. 705; repeated by Aulus Gellius, *Attic Nights*, XVII, xiv, 4.

Alcibiades reports . . . saved himself: In Plato, *Symposium*, 221; but the likelier source is Montaigne, *Essays*, p. 811.

Page 127] *There is nothing . . . avoid it:* Compare Lucan, *Pharsalia* (*Belli civilis*, ed. A. E. Housman [Oxford, 1950], VII, 104–5).

There are many . . . hurtful quality: A favorite theme for euphuistic moralizing.

Like the noble sort . . . my pace: Perhaps influenced by Seneca, *Moral Essays*, "De ira," II, xxxii, 3, or III, xxv, 3.

Had the worst . . . the weakest: Modern usage would call for comparatives.

That common proverb . . . the wall: See *Oxford Dict. Eng. Prov.*, p. 469, "The weakest goes to the wall." An anonymous contemporary play (1600) is entitled *The Weakest Goeth to the Wall*. See also *Romeo and Juliet*, I, i, 17.

Marcus Cato . . . than [to] forgive: Seneca, *Moral Essays*, "De ira," II, xxxii, 2. For *ignoscere* Seneca reads *vindicare*. The anecdote is also told in Feltham, *Resolves*, "Of Apprehension of Wrong," p. 84. Tuvill himself uses it again in *The Dove and the Serpent*, sig. F1v; see the note on Lentulus, just below.

And when Lentulus . . . mouth: Seneca, *Moral Essays*, "De ira," III, xxxviii, 2. Lucio Domitio Brusoni, *Facetiarum exemplorumque libri VII* (Rome, 1518), sigs. b3v-b4r, makes Diogenes the speaker. An allusion to Cato in *The Dove and the Serpent*, sig. F1v, seems to confuse these two anecdotes.

Socrates received . . . helmet: Seneca, *Moral Essays*, "De ira," III, xi, 2; alluded to also in *The Dove and the Serpent*, sig. F1v. Diogenes Laertius, *Lives of Eminent Philosophers*, VI, 41, relates this of Diogenes the Cynic.

X   Of Temptations

This essay—not unnaturally, considering its topic—is again among those belonging almost wholly to the "Theological" category of *Essays Moral and Theological*. The opening paragraph steps at once into the well-worn medieval theme: the pilgrimage of the life of man; and the rest of the essay exploits the kindred formulas of the Christian warfare, the trial of the

Saints, the besieging of the castle of man's soul by that wicked triple alliance, the World, the Flesh, the Devil. Such rubrics were (and are still) part of the standard preacherly gear, inherited from the times of the Apostles and the early Fathers—upon whom Tuvill does not hesitate to call for inspiration and confirmation.

The general sense and some of the phrasing in "Of Temptations" are repeated in *Christian Purposes and Resolutions,* sec. XXII. Among so much that is commonplace and traditional, it is hazardous to attempt identifying sources other than those indicated by Tuvill himself, and he is not always either specific or accurate. Nevertheless, it seems not unlikely that the opening paragraph and some other touches in the essay *may* have been suggested to Tuvill by the following bit from William Perkins' *Combat between Christ and the Devil,* sig. C6v: "our life in this vale of tears is a continual warfare against the enemies of our souls; we must not therefore here look for rest and ease, but ever keep watch and ward against their assaults."

That, in any event, forms an adequate text for the sermon Tuvill preaches.

PAGE 128] *Man's life . . . warfare:* Repeated in *Christian Purposes and Resolutions,* sig. I1v.

A Pharaoh to destroy him: See Exod. 1:8–22.

A Herod to pursue him: See Matt. 2:13 ff.

Nascitur ad laborem, etc.: Marginal reference to Job 5:7. Tuvill is quoting the Vulgate—not quite accurately: *Homo nascitur ad laborem, et avis ad volatum,* "Man is born to labor, and the bird to flight." The King James Version uses a different figure: "Yet man is born unto trouble, as the sparks fly upward."

He must never, therefore . . . the other: See Eph. 6:13–17.

For it is not . . . disobedience: See Eph. 6:12.

Nor is the reward . . . ought to do: II Tim. 4:1–8. But for Tuvill's "crown of immortal glory" St. Paul has "crown of righteousness."

The skill . . . in temptation: Compare Anthony Stafford (?), *The Golden Mean* (2d ed., 1614), sig. B6r: "A sure pilot is proved in a doubtful storm; and a wise noble mind is truly tried in the storm of adversity, not in the calm of felicity."

We press the grape . . . the sound: The pattern of euphuistic balance and wordplay.

This earthly globe . . . theater: There is perhaps here a punning allusion to the famous Bankside "Globe"; see also *Essays Politic and Moral,* p. 35.

PAGE 129] *He hath marched . . . victories:* Compare *Essays Politic and Moral,* p. 26.

He hath plucked the sting, etc.: See I Cor. 15:54–55.

Job wooed her . . . win her: See Job 3:11–21.

The rich man in the Gospel . . . presently: See Luke 12:16–20.

A man may easily . . . sanctuary: This adapts the saying of Antigonus, p. 48 and note.

Who would imagine . . . mischief: Compare "Of Gifts and Benefits," p. 114.

She is like Absalom's mule: See II Sam. 18:9.

Impii quasi mare, etc.: Not "the Psalmist," but Isaiah 57:20. The threefold comparison may have been suggested by that in Sir John Hayward's *The Sanctuary of a Troubled Soul* (ed. 1623, sigs. B2v-B3r).

The waters of Siloam: See John 9:7.

All rivers . . . riseth not: Eccles. 1:7.

Page 130] *He goes about . . . devour:* Marginal reference to I Peter 5:8.

This little commonwealth: Alluding to man as microcosm; see E. M. W. Tillyard, *The Elizabethan World Picture* (New York, 1944), esp. pp. 84–87.

Being severed and divided . . . stand: Marginal reference to Luke 11:17.

She lulls our Samson . . . Philistine: See Judg. 16:19–20; and compare *Essays Politic and Moral,* p. 59.

He that trusteth . . . forever: Marginal reference to Ps. 125:1.

Vita ista, etc.: See also "Of Reprehensions and Reproofs," p. 119.

Patience and . . . heroic virtues: Compare Milton, *Paradise Lost,* IX, 25–33. Each of Milton's major poems is, in fact, something of a case history in which, through meeting temptation, these "heroic virtues" are permitted to shine.

Quae versantur circa difficilia: "Which address themselves toward difficult things."

Marcescunt sine adversario: Margin reads: Κίνησις κρατύνει ἀργίη δὲ Τήκει. Trans.: "Movement (activity) strengthens, idleness weakens (wastes)." Tuvill's text echoes Seneca's statement, *Moral Essays,* "De providentia," ii, 4: *Marcet sine adversario virtus.* Without exactly translating, the next few lines of Tuvill's essay also follow the line of Seneca's argument.

Page 131] *He loves . . . righteous man:* Compare *Christian Purposes and Resolutions,* sig. D1or: "He loves not to make a wanton of the least."

Some accident . . . the combat: Compare *Christian Purposes and Resolutions,* sig. D11r: "One accident or other shall provoke their valor and keep it from growing sluggish through want of exercise." See also *Essays Politic and Moral,* p. 44 and note.

The captain selects . . . general: Both the illustration and the comparison derive from Seneca, *Moral Essays,* "De providentia," iv, 8.

He will not dally . . . first: The method recommended by William Perkins, *The Combat between Christ and the Devil,* sig. F1r: "the best way to vanquish Satan is to give him no ground, but to withstand him manfully at the first."

Οἱ τεθνηκότες, etc.: Marginal reading: "Dead men cannot bite."

It is not amiss . . . hand: The story of the "kingly shepherd," David, and the Philistine giant, Goliath, is found in I Sam. chap. 17.

Temptations could . . . destroyed them: See p. 116 and note.

Satan could . . . so must we: Matt. 4:4, 7, 10. See also Perkins, *Combat between Christ and the Devil,* sig. D4v.

Sin is a slippery serpent, etc.: Compare the figure with that in Thomas Whetenhall's *A Discourse of the Abuses Now in Question in the Churches of Christ* (1606), sig. B2r-v: "But Satan so subtly often creepeth in the dark that men of most clear and excellent sight can hardly perceive him; and when he hath wrung in but only his toe, he applieth himself with such diligence that by little and little he getteth in his foot, leg, body, yea head, horns and all." William Perkins, *An Exposition of the Symbol or Creed of the Apostles,* in *Works* (1605), sig. V4v, uses a similar figure: "if the Devil may be suffered but to put one talent [claw] into thy heart, he will presently wind himself into thee, his head, his body, and all." And in a commentary on the temptations of Christ, *The Combat between Christ and the Devil,* sig. B6r-v, he repeats the figure in language even closer to that of Tuvill: "This is the subtilty of the old serpent: first he conveys one claw or talent into a man's heart, and then another; after that he gets in his head, and so at length winds in all his body."

Page 132] *Their thoughts are . . . vain:* Tuvill's language appears to be adapted from Ps. 2:1.

He that would vanquish . . . there: Marginal reference to Gen. 3:15.

Our Saviour, when . . . denied Him: See Matt. 26:36–45, 69–75.

Vere galeati lepores: "Proper helmeted hares."

Such as are strong . . . against them: See Matt. 16:18.

Daughter of the Canaanite: Marginal reference to Matt. 15:22. Also cited by Perkins, *The Combat between Christ and the Devil,* sig. C6v.

That same dumb demoniac: Marginal reference to Luke 11:14.

Last of all . . . detain him: See Luke 11:26.

PAGE 133] *Adam stood fast . . . his maw:* The pattern of wordplay distinctly echoes *Euphues.*

XI OF RECONCILIATION AND PEACE

Some traces of Tuvill's pillaging of classical sources remain in the present essay and survive into the later editions. Nevertheless, it is quite obvious that the preponderant influence upon the thought is biblical. The essay, in fact, may be said to take its inspiration from the Sermon on the Mount. Like "Of Alms and Charitable Deeds" and "Of Temptations," "Of Reconciliation and Peace" demonstrates, for Tuvill, the close relation between sermon and essay. All that would be needed to make it an acceptable pulpit-piece would be a slight augmentation in accordance with the rhetorical principles examined in the opening trio of essays in *Essays Politic and Moral.*

Although there is in Tuvill's later books less of wholesale repetition from this essay than from some others, there are still numerous small correspondences in phraseology as well as some family resemblances arising from similar modes of procedure. The combination of aphorism—the traditional form for dogmatic or prophetic utterance—and exemplary illustration continues to afford the principal means of ordering the thought, perhaps here best integrated. The sermon pattern appears markedly in the movement of thought from opening generalizations to reasoned discussion to personal application of the clustered "resolves" at the end. Tuvill, a university man trained in the rhetorical inheritance of his time, was no doubt here consciously attempting to fulfill "the duty and office of rhetoric" by applying "reason to imagination for the better moving of the will" (Bacon, *Advancement,* p. 177). But for the modern ear he sounds at least one false note: "Of Reconciliation and Peace" contains several instances of the most egregiously euphuistic wordplay to be found in either series of his essays.

PAGE 134] *To wrong another . . . thy wants:* Note the marked euphuistic pattern.

The law of retribution . . . tooth: See Matt. 5:21–38.

That impious exclamation . . . minstrels: Margin reads: "Either kill me, or I'll kill thee, 't was uttered by Caius Caesar [Caligula], when he provoked Jupiter to fight for thundering whilst he heard his minstrels." Both the Greek exclamation and its marginal explanation derive from Seneca, *Moral Essays,* "De ira," I, xx, 8. But see also Suetonius, *Lives of the Caesars,* tr. J. C. Rolfe; Loeb Classical Library (Cambridge, Mass.: Harvard University Press, 1951), IV, xxii, 4.

The Sun of Righteousness, etc.: See Mal. 4:2. In the Geneva, or "Breeches," Bible (ed. 1611) the verse is marginally glossed thus: "Meaning Christ, who with his wings or beams of his grace should lighten and comfort his Church, Eph. 5:14. And he is called the Sun of Righteousness, because in himself he hath all perfection and also the justice of the Father dwelleth in him: whereby he regenerateth us into righteousness, cleanseth us from the filth of this world, and reformeth us to the image of God."

He that smiteth . . . cloak: See Matt. 5:39–40.

The doctrine . . . enter into heaven: See Matt. 5:20.

Their anger . . . their fury: See Eph. 4:26. Whitney, *Choice of Emblemes,* p. 216, has an emblem on the theme.

They know that vengeance . . . repay it: See Rom. 12:19; also Deut. 32:35.

There are many sheep . . . fold: See Matt. 20:16, 22:14.

The saying of the satirist: Margin reads *"Iuven. lib 5. Sat. 13"* (= *Satires,* XIII, 189–91).

PAGE 135] *Hence is it . . . women:* Translates Juvenal, *Satires,* XIII, 191–92.

James and John . . . they were: Marginal reference to Luke 9:54. The complete reference should embrace verses 52–55.

When He himself . . . what they do: Marginal reference to Luke 22 [i.e., 23]:34.

Those Jewish cannibals: Modern Catholic dogma repudiates the implication. For similar phrasing, see pp. 36, 106.

Under the Law . . . kissed each other: The best modern comment on this paragraph is S. C. Chew's *The Virtues Reconciled* (Toronto, 1947).

Saying of the Psalmist: Marginal reference to Ps. 85:10.

"He will speak peace": Marginal reference to Ps. 85:8.

And to His Saints: "His" supplied from catchword on preceding page.

In a word . . . be reconciled: Marginal reference to Matt. 5:[23-]24.

If thou deny . . . the Gospel: Marginal reference to Matt. 18:[23-]34.

The promise . . . and an "as": See Matt. 6:12, 14–15.

PAGE 136] *Inflexible and obstinate:* Compare p. 89.

David in I Samuel . . . a flea: Marginal reference to I Sam. 24:15 [i.e., 14]. The preceding verses are also relevant. William Lightfoot, *The Com-*

plaint of England (1587), sig. B3v, uses this same illustration as an argument for the sacred untouchableness of the king's person.

Jacob, in his return . . . face: See Gen. 32:13–20.

Aurea sunt . . . amor: Margin reads: τὰ χρήματ' ἀνθρώποισιν εὑρίσκει φίλους. Trans.: "Money finds friends for men." Marginal reference to Ovid, *Ars amatoria,* II [, 277–78].

Melle . . . frugibus offam: Marginal reference to Virgil, *Aeneid,* VI [, 420]. Virgil's verse, misquoted here *and* in the corrigendum on p. 142*n.,* below, reads, *melle soporatam et medicatis frugibus offam.*

And then . . . forgoes his rage: Margin reads: χρυσὸς δ' ἄνοιγε πάντα, καὶ ἰδοῦ πύλας. Trans.: "Gold opens everything, and behold (?) the gates." Both this and the preceding Greek marginal passage disappear from all subsequent editions.

His courage . . . with a Joshua: Marginal reference to Josh. 9:24. The entire chapter is relevant.

Goes against the hair: Proverbial for something unnaturally difficult or distasteful in the doing (Lat., *contra pellem*). A modern writer or speaker would be more likely to say "against the grain."

But the practice . . . ne'er been born: See John 13:2–16 and Matt. 26:21–25.

A devil . . . Judas, that apostate: See John 6:70; compare *Christian Purposes and Resolutions,* sig. B11v, and also in the present text, pp. 85, 87.

PAGE 137]   *Vae homini,* etc.: Matt. (Vulgate) 26:24.

For he was a devil: See John 13:27.

As Augustus did . . . Captain General: Both of these illustrations (including the Latin quotation) occur in Bodin, *Of a Commonweal,* pp. 431–32. The first one is cited also (*sans* Latin, however) in Montaigne, *Essays,* p. 90. The ultimate source appears to be Seneca, *Moral Essays,* "De clementia," I, ix, 11. As Tuvill is known to have used all three upon other occasions, only the juxtaposing of the second illustration enables us to say confidently that he is here following Bodin.

I will shoot as Jonathan did: See I Sam. 20:20–22, 35–38.

XII OF POVERTY

Although poverty is sometimes regarded as almost a necessary Christian virtue, and Christ himself commented upon its enduring ubiquity, Tuvill's essay on the topic takes him from the Bible back to the classics, to Juvenal, and once again to a favorite refrain: The World is going to the dogs; the Good Old Days are gone forever; the glorious outside of villainy or incapacity takes precedence over the sobriety of inner worth. All such whimperings, of course, disregard the patent fact that every previous age has had its own prophets of doom. The present is decried in the voice of the past. Tuvill's excessive reliance upon Juvenal underscores the traditional nature of the lament; and it is doubly underscored when that pitiful scribbler, Barnabe Rich, in *The Honesty of This Age*, draws upon *Tuvill* to express "his" frustration with the maladjustments and inequities—as well as iniquities—of the social order. Even the "judicious" Hooker (*Laws of Ecclesiastical Polity,* p. 31) murmurs against "these last times, which for insolence, pride, and egregious contempt of all good order are the worst." The curious fact is that none of the loudest complainants really condemn riches or greatly admire poverty. Their anguish, real or assumed, arises simply from their own *always* unmerited disesteem. Raise one of them to eminence or wealth and tomorrow he would sing from the other side of his mouth. On this theme Tuvill's pathetic warblings of self-pity lack the note of conviction.

The great weakness of the essay, if the thought in "Of Poverty" is to be taken seriously, is that it offers complaint without proposing any effective means of self-discipline or public reform. Tuvill is here content to be a spectator-commentator dealing with a situation in which the reader might welcome some of the evangelical "resolves" so overliberally sprinkled throughout other essays. Perhaps, recognizing as he does at the end that "the humor of essays is rather to glance at all things with a running conceit than to insist on any with a slow discourse," Tuvill was reminded to forbear the "resolves" as smacking too much of sermonizing and pulpit propaganda. Recourse to Martial, happily, puts a final touch of lightness to an overheavy tirade.

In temper, in principal source (Juvenal), and in its effect upon Barnabe Rich's *Honesty of This Age,* "Of Poverty" shows close kinship with "Of Respect and Reverence."

PAGE 138] *The world . . . her youth:* With this theme of decay, compare "Of Respect and Reverence," pp. 102–3.

The time hath been . . . offense: Copied in Rich, *Honesty of This Age,* p. 31.

Et levis argenti . . . censorial crime: Compare Seneca, *Moral Essays,* "De vita beata," xxi, 3: *illud saeculum, in quo censorium crimen erat paucae argenti lamellae.*

Cornelius Rufinus . . . bad example: See Valerius Maximus, *Dict. fact. memorab.,* II, iv. See also Aulus Gellius, *Attic Nights,* IV, viii, 7.

Virtue at the plow: Referring to Lucius Quinctius Cincinnatus (fifth century B.C.), who was summoned from his plow to save his country.

A change of all things: The idea is, of course, an ancient commonplace. But Tuvill may have had in mind one (or both) of two contemporary works, (1) Louis Le Roy's *De la vicissitude ou variété des choses en l'univers,* translated by Robert Ashley as *Of the Interchangeable Course, or Variety of Things in the Whole World* (1594); or (2) John Norden's *Vicissitudo rerum* (1600), the running title of which is "The interchangeable courses and variety of things in this world," a title no doubt suggested by Ashley's translation.

Procedat vel Numa . . . ad censum: Marginal reading: *"Juven. lib.* 1. *Sat.* 3" (= *Satires,* III, 138–40). Trans.: "Numa himself might present himself, or he who rescued the trembling Minerva from the blazing shrine—the first question asked will be as to his wealth."

What need . . . no wealth: Tuvill varies the language, but not the sense or temper, of Juvenal, *Satires,* III, 141 ff.

Can any good . . . bringing up: See John 1:46; Mark 6:3.

Wisdom . . . ne'er respected: Juvenal still, with perhaps a suggestion of the saying of Christ in Mark 6:4, which Tuvill has just had under his eye.

The client . . . better clothes: Suggested by Juvenal, *Satires,* VII, 134–36.

PAGE 139] *Ciceroni nemo ducentos,* etc.: Juvenal, *Satires,* VII, 139–40. Tuvill's translation is somewhat free.

Conducta Paulus agebat . . . before: Margin reads: *"Juven. lib.* 3. *Sat.* 7" (= *Satires,* VII, 143–45). For "Cossus" Loeb reads "Gallus."

Desert . . . gates of greatness: Adapted by Rich, *Honesty of This Age,* p. 52.

Crates the Theban . . . man of merit: See Diogenes Laertius, *Lives of Eminent Philosophers,* VI, 86.

Lenonum pueri, etc.: Juvenal, *Satires,* III, 156.

The coast is clear: Already proverbial in Tuvill's day; see *Oxford Dict. Eng. Prov.,* p. 424.

But, with the poet . . . British clime: See Juvenal, *Satires,* VI, 634–37. Tuvill has cleverly adapted the original to his British scene and theme.

PAGE 140] *The princes . . . pastime:* See Judg. 16:25.

Men's ears . . . be heard: The reference is to the remark of Aristippus concerning Dionysius; see Diogenes Laertius, *Lives of Eminent Philosophers,* II, 79. See also Bacon, *Advancement,* pp. 26–27. The anecdote had wide circulation in the Renaissance.

All men do cherish . . . dialect: Repeated by Rich, *Honesty of This Age,* p. 52.

She is poor . . . importance: Also in Rich, *loc. cit.*

Let her protest . . . be taken: Adapted by Rich, *loc. cit.*

Contemnere fulmina pauper, etc.: Juvenal, *Satires,* III, 145–46.

PAGE 141] *A lie . . . poverty:* Adapted by Rich, *Honesty of This Age,* p. 52.

Speak in her defense: This is the correct reading of the text, but the catchword of the preceding page reads "the" for "her."

Libertas pauperis, etc.: Juvenal, *Satires,* III, 299–301.

Flectere si nequeat, etc.: Virgil, *Aeneid,* VII, 312.

That Spanish proverb: The equivalent of *"My* country, right or wrong." A somewhat literal translation might read: "By right or by wrong, *our* house [i.e., concerns] to the very roof-top."

Aestuat infoelix, etc.: Juvenal, *Satires,* X, 169–70. All editions read *parvaque scripso;* the original reads *parvaque Seripho.*

PAGE 142] *Qua fornace graves,* etc.: Juvenal, *Satires,* III, 309.

Whereas, before . . . kingdom: Translating Juvenal, *Satires,* III, 313–14.

The humor of essays: That is, the *nature* or characteristic feature.

Iam lector . . . libelle: Part (ll. 7–9) of the final epigram (no. lxxxix) in Martial, *Epigrams,* bk. IV. For *tam* in the final line, subsequent editions read, correctly, *jam.* Trans.: "Now the reader complains and falls away, now the scribe himself says, Little book, hold—enough!"

FINIS: Below this on the page Tuvill adds the following corrigendum: "Reader there are many things through negligence depraved in this book, especially a verse of Virgil's, p. [136], where read, *melle saporatam et medicatis frugibus offam."* This is the sibyl's "sop to Cerberus" in the *Aeneid,* bk. VI. Since the line is corrected in subsequent editions, the corrigendum disappears in them.